Poe in His Own Time

Edgar Allan Poe. Painting by Ezekiel Addison, 2009.

WRITERS IN THEIR OWN TIME BOOKS

Joel Myerson, *series editor*

Alcott in Her Own Time
Edited by Daniel Shealy

Emerson in His Own Time
Edited by Ronald A. Bosco
and Joel Myerson

Fuller in Her Own Time
Edited by Joel Myerson

Hawthorne in His Own Time
Edited by Ronald A. Bosco
and Jillmarie Murphy

Poe in His Own Time
Edited by Benjamin F. Fisher

Stowe in Her Own Time
Edited by Susan Belasco

Whitman in His Own Time
Edited by Joel Myerson

POE

in His Own Time

A Biographical
Chronicle of His Life,
Drawn from Recollections,
Interviews, and
Memoirs by Family,
Friends, and
Associates

EDITED BY

Benjamin F. Fisher

University of Iowa Press,
Iowa City

University of Iowa Press, Iowa City 52242
Copyright © 2010 by the University of Iowa Press
www.uiowapress.org
Printed in the United States of America

The University of Iowa Press is a member of Green Press Initiative
and is committed to preserving natural resources.

Printed on acid-free paper

Library of Congress Cataloging-in-Publication Data

Poe in his own time: a biographical chronicle of his life,
drawn from recollections, interviews, and memoirs by family,
friends, and associates / edited by Benjamin F. Fisher.
p.   cm.—(Writers in their own time)
Includes bibliographical references and index.
ISBN-13: 978-1-58729-863-9 (pbk.)
ISBN-10: 1-58729-863-5 (pbk.)
1. Poe, Edgar Allan, 1809–1849.   2. Authors, American—
19th century—Biography.   3. Poe, Edgar Allan,
1809–1849—Correspondence.   4. Poe, Edgar Allan,
1809–1849—Friends and associates.
I. Fisher, Benjamin Franklin.
PS2633.P64 2010
818´.309—dc22
[B]   2009046712

IN MEMORY OF
Thomas Ollive Mabbott,
Maureen Cobb Mabbott,
Jay B. Hubbell,
David K. Jackson

Contents

Contents

Contents

Contents

Introduction

LATE IN HIS CAREER Poe published "The Literary Life of Thingum Bob,
Esq. Late Editor of the 'Goosetherum Foodle'" (*Southern Literary Messenger*, December 1844), a tale that might well characterize the status of his
own life and career then and now. Although the piece is a satire aimed at
the literary periodical milieu of Poe's day, we should remember that many
a truth is told, in part, in jest, perhaps to avoid a direct confrontation with
grim reality. After a lengthy unfolding of the highs and lows in being a literary magazine editor and contributor, Thingum concludes:

> Yes, I have made history. My fame is universal. It extends to the uttermost
> ends of the earth. But I am meek and expire with an humble heart. After all,
> what is it?—this indescribable something which men will persist in terming
> "genius?" I agree with Buffon—with Hogarth—it is but *diligence* after all.
>
> Look at *me*!—how I labored—how I toiled—how I wrote! Ye Gods, did I *not*
> write? I knew not the word "ease." By day I adhered to my desk, and at night,
> a pale student, I consumed the midnight oil. You should have seen me—you
> *should*. I leaned to right. I leaned to the left. I sat forward. I sat backward. I sat
> upon end. . . . And, through it all, I—wrote. Through joy and through sorrow,
> I—*wrote*. Through hunger and through thirst, I—*wrote*. Through good report
> and through ill report, I—*wrote*. Through sunshine and through moonshine,
> I—*wrote*. *What* I wrote is unnecessary to say. The *style*!—that was the thing.
> I caught it from Fatquack—whizz!—fizz!—and I am giving you a specimen of
> it now.[1]

This passage of fiction is wholly fitting in the context of Poe biography because Poe himself became creative when he passed along information about his life and literary career to others. Those early biographical
accounts that Poe supplied have sustained considerable lasting power in
several respects because parts of them figure into many subsequent biographical and critical works, occasioning confusion over what may be fact
and what may be the embroiderings in Poe's own imagination. That Poe's

renown, like Thingum's, has become "universal" is indisputably attested by numerous biographical and critical-analytical publications that focus on him and his writings, as well as legion numbers of allusions in the popular sphere to the man and/or his writings. To give just one example of this latter variety of renown, I cite a recent issue of *Ellery Queen Mystery Magazine* (132.2 [August 2008], pp. 15, 89). Allusions to the French sleuth, Dupin, on the first page cited and to "The Purloined Letter" on the second, refer to Poe as the creator of modern detective fiction, understandably in context, but they likewise testify to his farther-reaching enduring fame.

Another fact worth remembering: like Thingum, Poe continued to write during the 1840s, and much of his writing in those years (but not exclusively in those late years) was done in what was for him the face of great adversity. His many caustic reviews of others' egregious publications had won him many enemies, and when he no longer controlled a forum for replying to those who disliked him, he became a target for facile slurs. Poe the writer and Poe the person were often one in the minds of many, so the situation of a helpless antagonist seemed to be absolutely relished by many who wished to retaliate. Consequently, many early publications feature Poe in what blandly may be called obscure portraiture—obscure as to the facts of his life, though not at all obscure in pillorying him.

To move forward far in time is in order here, to spotlight how confusion has maintained a strong hold as regards Poe and his place in the literary world. In the first edition of *Eight American Authors: A Review of Research and Criticism* (Stovall, 1956), Jay B. Hubbell commented on the long-standing legendry that had crept into and continued to influence biographies of Poe (5–7). He added this signal remark: "Poe's critics, like those of Whitman, have always been too ready to read into his poems and tales their own facile interpretations of his character and personality" (7)—creating a very unsatisfactory image of Poe. In a later edition (Woodress, 1971), Hubbell was more direct in beginning the section on biography: "Of all major American writers P[oe] is the most misunderstood, and the misunderstanding extends to both the man and his writings" (8). Hubbell assessed the strengths and weaknesses of significant biographies, concluding that the best factual biography was that by Arthur Hobson Quinn (1941, rpt. 1969, 1985). More recent overviews of Poe biography tend to concur with Hubbell's opinions.[2]

A volume on Poe in his time may cast much more oblique light than lime-

Poe amidst his works. Engraving by A. Bobbett, appearing in *Laurel Leaves*, edited by William F. Gill, published in 1876.

light. Of course, an image of Poe as a man of gloom and mystery has long circulated and continues to hold great popular appeal. In many respects, it would seem that his cradle was surrounded by shadows (or flames that cast a lurid glow) which continued to hover around him throughout his short life and which have secured lasting holds on many minds, past and present. Such obscurities and illuminations constitute what some would claim as knowledge in regard to the life and literary career of this writer, who has long been recognized as one of the greats in the literary canons of America and, indeed, of the world.

Advocates of Poe the man and Poe the writer have promoted him as a figure who ranges from the near-angelic to the near-demonic. Indisputably, Poe has usually elicited either highly commendatory or absolutely hostile reactions from many who knew him, from others who claim to comprehend him as person and writer, and from still others whose responses bypass any biographical accounts proper. This last group focus wholly or in part upon what Poe wrote and published, claiming much in the way of Poe the man from what they perceive as autobiographical substance in his creative writings.

Among the better known defenses, we find, for example, Sarah Helen Whitman's *Edgar Poe and His Critics* (1860), which casts Poe in a well-nigh angelic light, in an attempt to refute Rufus Wilmot Griswold's calumnies. This little book has been reprinted in recent times, in an edition prepared by Oral S. Coad (1949, 1981), as have the recollections of Lambert A. Wilmer, Poe's early friend in Baltimore, edited by that late doyen among Poe scholars, Thomas Ollive Mabbott (1941, 1973). Because of their ready availability, excerpts from these documents need not reappear in the present volume. Some that have appeared elsewhere, but that may nevertheless not be easily accessible, plus others that have never been reprinted, are included here either because they stem fairly directly from information provided by Poe or because they shed light on popular conceptions of him during his own era. Those items which report on Poe's performance in reading or reciting poetry and his abilities as a lecturer are important. They shed light on an aspect of Poe's literary career that too often has been ignored, though Sidney P. Moss and Kent P. Ljungquist have endeavored to emphasize their value.

The phrase, which umbrellas all volumes in this series, "in *his* own time" (italics mine) in reference to Poe is employed here with justifiable latitude. Despite the average brief life spans of nineteenth-century Americans, many lived on to far greater ages. Conceivably, Poe's own life might have extended well through that century. Moreover, some of the reminiscences by individuals who knew him in person and who lived far longer lives than he, did not appear until long after his death. Therefore I have not scrupled to include such materials, which, whatever time's passages between the actual events and the recording or publication of them, contain important viewpoints, whether or not those viewpoints may change already solidified opinions about Poe.

Of course there are other opinions, set forth by persons who had not known Poe in person but who nevertheless circulated in print their opinions as if those were informed by inside information regarding him and his literary creativity. Such are of equal interest, for example, the pieces by George Gilfillan or Bryan W. Proctor, who did not hesitate to publish accounts almost as scurrilous as the far more widely known slanders by Rufus W. Griswold. That by Joseph E. Snodgrass is also no paen on Poe's behalf, and the artist John Frankenstein's pique (in verse) because of Poe's failing to praise him is also far from complimentary. On this side of the Atlantic we find, however, balanced and more favorable accounts by Elizabeth Oakes Smith, who knew well the American literary milieu of Poe's own day, even if she hadn't known Poe himself. In England, William Moy

Poe's nemesis-biographer, Rufus Wilmot Griswold. Engraving, based on a portrait painted by Miner Kilbourne Kellogg, by the New York engraving firm Capewell and Kimmel. Appeared in *The Knickerbocker Gallery*, 1855.

Thomas and John Henry Ingram, Poe's devoted English biographer, also published opinions that present Poe in a sympathetic light. Ingram came to err in presenting laudatory accounts of Poe that often matched in their dare-to-disagree tone the apparently plausible portrayals by Griswold and other hostile persons.

Poe himself had set in motion ambiguities, as I remarked above, which were to enjoy circulation that still colors many writings about him and his accomplishments. In these publications, usually from persons who had not known Poe, the treatment is often fast and loose with "facts" about his personal life and his writings, on occasion adapting situations from the life of his brother, William Henry Leonard Poe, as parts of Edgar's own biographical record. Because much remains obscure about this older brother, also a writer who died at an early age, separating fact from fiction regarding either brother has remained difficult. The only extended biography, *Poe's Brother*, by Hervey Allen and Thomas Ollive Mabbott (1926), is brief, and it raises as many or more questions about both brothers, whatever answers it offers about either. Kenneth Silverman's more recent biography, *Edgar A. Poe: Mournful and Never Ending Remembrance* (1991), raises another type of question, namely: Did Poe's writings spring mainly from his memories of dying and dead women in his life? Silverman's Freudian approach, recalling that of Marie Bonaparte, may not present wholly satisfying interpretations of connections between the man and his writings.

To pursue how such approaches may not strongly grasp the magnitude of inspirations for Poe's creative writings and his literary principles, let us turn momentarily to one of his own pronouncements that has often been repeated as straightforward thought, that is, that the death of a beautiful woman constitutes the most poetic of all themes. Read at face value, this remark has been interpreted as revealing Poe's own antipathies toward women, with confirmation for this viewpoint being attested in works such as "The Raven," "Ulalume," "Berenice," "Morella," "Ligeia," or "The Fall of the House of Usher." Critiques of these works about dead or dying women typically fail to include "The Assignation" or "Eleonora." In these two tales the deaths respectively of the Marchesa Aphrodite and of Eleonora admit of more positive implications—despite the sensationalism that attaches to the suicide of the former—than those generally associated with the deaths of females in the other works. Moreover, knowing about Poe's love of wordplay and his tendencies to perpetrate hoaxes, we may read his oft-repeated dictum not as testimony to his personal ideas about women but as a bit of mirth involving his own name in literary contexts. In other words, the death of a beautiful woman is the most "*Po[e]*-etic" of all themes (italics mine). Viewed from this angle, the seriousness in "The Philosophy of Composition" (1846), an essay Poe published in *Graham's Magazine* (April 1846) to capitalize on the success of "The Raven" and wherein he put forth the death of a beautiful woman as a cardinal theme in that poem, may be reasonably questioned, though generations have been encouraged to consider the essay as a blueprint for Poe's methods of writing somber poems and tales according to rational principles of near mathematical exactness.[3]

Information provided by Poe for several early biographical accounts was substantially inaccurate and self-promoting. See, for example, the introductory essay (which was invited, according to Griswold's practice) published in Rufus W. Griswold's *The Poets and Poetry of America* (1842, with several reprintings during the nineteenth century), or the lengthy biographical article published in the *Philadelphia Saturday Museum* (originally 26 February 1843, reprinted in the 4 March issue, which version seems to be the only one extant), or James Russell Lowell's portrayal of Poe published in *Graham's Magazine* (February 1845). Poe enjoyed glamorizing his life, as is evident in these pieces, though when they originally appeared, the presumed veracity in the contents long went unchallenged. Nevertheless, such romanticizing persisted, as is evident in many of the items gathered here.

Along with these articles, what has proved to have more influential—and harmful—extended currency have been the malicious obituary by Griswold, using the pseudonym "Ludwig," in the *New York Tribune* (9 October 1849), followed by his extended "Memoir" in the four-volume *The Works of the Late Edgar Allan Poe*, which Griswold edited and published after the author's death (1850–1856). The Griswold accounts were looked to as presumably accurate sources by many who wrote about Poe's life and art (or lack thereof), but who wrote in equally skewed fashion. To cite but a few examples, one might turn to George Gilfillan or Bryan W. Proctor's hostile responses or to Francis Gerry Fairfield's hypothesis that Poe was epileptic and that this condition had strong impacts upon his creativity, especially in the poems. Rebuttals followed, directly toward Fairfield—probably because his hypothesis was so bizarre, even in an age when biographies tended to be less than factually sound. That from Sarah Helen Whitman is especially pertinent because, unlike Fairfield, she knew Poe in person. Less directly, responses that implicitly questioned the apparent hostility behind other publications were not long in appearing. These hostile or otherwise questionable viewpoints may suggest more about their authors than about Poe, no doubt, but they did attract attention in their day, and that kind of attention has continued to have fallout when Poe has been the subject. The cultural milieu of the nineteenth century was rife with egotism and jealousies, added to which are related attempts to vent spleen, in print and otherwise, upon anyone who may have questioned the status of self-important artists and writers. Thus the negative reaction to Poe, mainly Poe the critic, should not be surprising, nor should those that offer to illuminate his life or works with otherwise oblique lights.

If the first three items mentioned in the previous paragraph present essentially favorable impressions of Poe the man and writer, the figure depicted by Griswold after Poe's death is wholly negative. Reading Griswold's commentaries in the *Tribune* and the *Works*, one is reminded of Oscar Wilde's remark that "it is usually Judas who writes the biography."[4] Assuredly, Griswold proved to be just such a Judas, and, as with the results of the biblical Judas's treachery, Griswold's have had lasting consequences. Because of his eminence and reliability as an editor of widely respected anthologies, Griswold's biographical portraiture of Poe seemed, to many, to be factually paramount, although the testimonies of Lowell and Nathaniel P. Willis provide counters to his vilification, as did those of several writers later in the nineteenth century. Nonetheless, what I will designate the "Griswold Poe" has enjoyed widespread currency, with many subsequent writers either unquestioningly following in Griswold's footsteps when they prepared their own biographies of Poe or even intensifying the sensational, as they imagined it, in Poe's life (and in the writings, which, they assumed, closely reflected that life).

Griswold and Poe became acquainted because their literary careers intersected now and again, whether in regard to Griswold's anthologies or his succeeding Poe as editor of *Graham's Magazine* in mid-1842. Both men were, of course, well known in American literary circles during the early 1840s. By the time of Poe's death, Griswold's outlook concerning his former friend had shifted, however, to an increasing antipathy. Believing that Poe had attacked *The Poets and Poetry of America* in a review and in his lecturing on poetry, Griswold became unforgiving (to understate), albeit

Office of the *Southern Literary Messenger* in Richmond, Virginia. This engraving appeared in 1904 in *Century Magazine*.

he displayed none of his displeasure directly to Poe. Only after Poe's death did he take revenge—and that of a most damaging type. The image of Poe wrought by Griswold is a well-nigh Satanic creature: evil, half deranged, and grim, much like one of the protagonists in fiction or poems by Poe himself or those in more widespread Gothic tradition.

Somewhat more balanced, but not wholly admiring, is Charles Frederick Briggs's posthumous sketch of Poe, which appears last in this book. Briggs also knew Poe during the 1840s, worked briefly with him, realized that his writings were valuable, but came to dislike the man because of what Briggs thought were Poe's treacheries to persons who were supposedly his friends. The Briggs view of Poe as a split personality is well worth having in convenient form because it went on record long before some of the psychoanalytic biographies of the twentieth century were published.

From the era of Byron, who a generation before Poe had created uncertainties as to whether his life affected his poetry or whether he attempted to enact in his everyday conditions the characteristics of the enticingly enigmatic protagonists in his verse, such interchangings of an author with his or her character(s) have become commonplaces in regard to many writers. Just so, that type of representation quickly occurred, and often continues, as regards Poe, and even his sympathizers have often blurred distinctions between the man and his writings. Griswold's likening Poe to Francis Vivian, an erratic character in Edward Bulwer-Lytton's novel, *The Caxtons* (serialized in *Blackwood's Edinburgh Magazine* 1845–1849), long went overlooked. Poe might, however, have relished the comparison, had he known about it, no matter Griswold's unflattering employment of the material, because of his familiarity with and high regard for much that appeared in that renowned Scottish literary periodical. One who did not blur the borders between Poe's everyday life and his writings was Briggs. In this respect Briggs (unintentionally) anticipated formalist critics of the twentieth century who argued that the reading of literary works should be undertaken with no reference to a writer's life but only to what appeared in the text of a creative work itself.

As some of the selections that appear in this volume attest, Griswold's vilifying portrayals influenced many others who wrote about Poe, and contending opinions were also offered. Probably the most significant among these were the full-scale biographies published by an American, William Fearing Gill (1877), and by John Henry Ingram (1880), in England. Both books exude strong pro-Poe opinions. Although it is the first book-length biography of Poe authored by an American, Gill's is not nearly so well written as Ingram's, and Ingram subsequently took umbrage at Gill's managing to publish a book-length biography of Poe before he did, although he had accepted whatever help Gill tendered him for his own biographical volumes. Ingram's jealousies toward any other biographer of Poe mounted to near paranoia, and he proved to be especially ungrateful to Sarah Helen Whitman, who had worked tirelessly to supply him with useful materials for his project. Ingram's labors on behalf of Poe are deftly chronicled by the late John Carl Miller in *Building Poe Biography* (1977) and *Poe's Helen Remembers* (1979). Drawing substantially on the Ingram Collection at the University of Virginia, Miller made readily available many documents that had previously been difficult to access pertaining to Poe's life and writings, thereby expanding our knowledge of both. Miller's volumes reveal Ingram's repeated opinions about difficulties in producing an accurate biography of Poe. Such inaccuracies, whether they were recognized as difficulties or not, certainly pepper the record in many more brief accounts of Poe's life, as will be evident in the selections marshaled later in this book.

Two more biographical works from the late nineteenth century should be mentioned. Richard Henry Stoddard published several articles, as well as an introduction to an edition of Poe's writings (1880), in which the biographical portraiture was anything but flattering. Far more significant was George E. Woodberry's *Edgar Allan Poe* (1885), in the American Men of Letters series. In Woodberry's book, which is based on sound documentation, we find greater reliability than is to be encountered in earlier biographies, though Woodberry was not the warmest admirer of his subject. An expanded, revised biography by Woodberry, *The Life of Edgar Allan Poe, Personal and Literary*, appeared in 1909. This expansion and revision provides a far more persuasive biographical approach with more ample—and more positive—critical commentary than the earlier volume contains.

In the early twentieth century, James Southall Wilson—one of the best informed Poe specialists of his era, which extended into mid-century—stated that Hervey Allen (1926) was Poe's first really informed and sympathetic biographer, adding that

> Poe has been the victim of many biographers. Of those who have written his life few have been either trained or gifted in the methods of investigation or pleasing literary expression. And the writing of nearly all has been qualified either by an outspoken distaste for their subject or by a conscious determination to select or suppress material unfavorable to Poe or to some of those who came in contact with him.[5]

A revision of Allen's biography appeared in 1934, and it has been far more critically acclaimed than the first version, though many readers believed that Allen the novelist, more so than Allen a factual biographer, remained uppermost in these books. Significantly, in *American Fiction: An Historical and Critical Survey* (1936), Arthur Hobson Quinn, perhaps with a nod

The Poe House, Amity Street, Baltimore. This ink drawing is by Howard Frech. Courtesy of the Edgar Allan Poe Society of Baltimore.

to Wilson's opinion, stated that Poe's critics often revealed more about themselves than about Poe.[6] Although this particular remark by Quinn preceded by some years his monumental account, *Edgar Allan Poe: A Critical Biography* (1941), which, like Allen's, is the work of one who was informed about and sympathetic toward his subject, we might even now find that Quinn's biography remains viable after nearly three-quarters of a century, whether or not his critical assessments of Poe's writings have been, for the most part, superseded. Very little factual material connected with the biography of Poe has been discovered since Quinn's book appeared.

Many of the following pages present Poe in a less than wholly sympathetic light, but they are nevertheless testimony to an image of the man and writer that has prevailed for over a century. Furthermore, if the writings in this book seem weighted toward unsympathetic portrayals of Poe, we should keep in mind that even some of the most overall grudging viewpoints do not lack awareness that his writings contain great literary art. For example, Griswold's remarks concerning Poe's abilities as a comic writer, published after he vilified Poe, reveal that amidst overall repulsion, those who wrote about Poe's personal faults often could not refrain from complimenting his literary achievements. Several items suggest that their authors might as easily be characters in one of Poe's tales as journalists or critics, especially the odd theories of Francis Gerry Fairfield.

Although Griswold's treachery toward Poe has long been known, his obituary notice from the *New York Tribune* and the expanded "Memoir" in the edition of Poe's *Works*—like the other Griswold writings herein—have not in their complete forms been easily accessible to general readers. Including Griswold's accounts is essential in an assemblage of "lives" of Poe, because they have spawned so much commentary about Poe and his writings, and particularly because the lengthy "memoir" has not been available outside of the *Works*. One cannot delve far into Poe studies without encountering allusions to Griswold, so making convenient the "Ludwig" obituary and the "Memoir" should be of genuine service to the causes of Edgar Allan Poe.

I include such familiar accounts as those by Lowell and Willis, along with many more that may not be so well known. I omit such extended publications as Sarah Helen Whitman's *Edgar Poe and His Critics* (1860) because they have been edited and reprinted and so are more readily available.

The Brennan Farm in New York, where Poe lived from June 1844 through January 1845. Engraving from *The Life of Edgar Allan Poe* by William F. Gill, published in 1877.

An item in which Griswold's reliability is questioned, by the British journalist William Moy Thomas, is just one among often overlooked articles. Thomas's evaluation of Griswold's biographical accounts of Poe is objective, though the question of Griswold's veracity looms large; thus it forms a good corrective to such commentaries as Gilfillan's or Proctor's, because their acceptance of Griswold's portraiture is anything but objective.

In sum, many of the items that I assemble bear out the thought in a passage from Poe's tale, "The System of Dr. Tarr and Professor Fether (1845): "Believe nothing you hear, and only one half of what you see."[7] Numerous discrepancies over what those who knew Poe seem to have heard and saw, as attested by the contents of this book and in other materials that continue to engender enigmas, appear to be inseparable from widespread conceptions of Poe in person and of Poe as author. The speculative content in many other portrayals, by persons who had or had not known Poe himself, often read as if their authors had set out to write a short story—of scant friendliness toward the protagonist.

I am also aware that readers of this book may find objectionable my inclusion of some one or another item, as well as the omission of another. The maker of a book like this one is, however, cognizant that limitations of space prevent the inclusion of all possible writings on the topic and that the contents set forth in the following pages do illuminate the topic of Edgar Allan Poe in his own time.

The texts in this book are from those of the first or early printed versions. In preparing them for use here, I have emended only when an original text was incorrect or not clear without such emendations. I have let stand nineteenth-century spellings (Poe himself was an inconsistent speller at times) and misspellings. Punctuation, inconsistent uses of dashes and other punctuation along with capitalization are also let stand. Desiring to offer a readable text, I have not tried to overdo in modernizing or "correcting" the texts. Names of authors and titles of essays and other works are enclosed in brackets when they have not been supplied by the editor. Complete bibliographic information is given in a source note following each text.

A related matter may be clarified here. Poe was born on 19 January 1809. During his adult years, however, he often gave his birth date as 1811 or 1813. Therefore, such inaccurate dates may be found in some of the items included in the biographical materials.

I am grateful to the Inter-Library Loan staff at the University of Mississippi for excellent service in securing rare items. I am also grateful to my friends and former students, Melanie R. Anderson, Lorraine Dubuisson, and Travis D. Montgomery for ready assistance in expediting the typing of this project. To another friend, and former student, Professor Harry M. Bayne, Brewton-Parker College, I acknowledge gratitude for aid in securing several items of no easy access, as I do to Jeffrey A. Savoye, that stalwart of the Edgar Allan Poe Society of Baltimore, who also made access to some recondite documents far more simple than it might have been without his generous help. Professor Bayne has, moreover, enhanced the graphics in this book by bestowing a gift to me of an original portrait of Poe, painted by Zeke Addison, professor of art at Brewton-Parker College.

Likewise, I owe gratitude to Professors Kent P. Ljungquist, Worcester Polytechnic Institute, and Richard Fusco, St. Joseph's University, who have repeatedly facilitated my efforts on behalf of Poe. For technical assistance, great thanks go to Alex Movitz; to my daughter, Hattie E. Fisher; and to my wife, Julie A. Fisher. For their memorable patience, I thank Holly Carver, at the University of Iowa Press, and Joel Myerson, Emeritus Professor of English at the University of South Carolina and academic editor of the series.

Notes

1. All of my quotations from Poe's fiction follow the text in Mabbott. This passage appears in 3: 1145.

2. See Hammond, and Fisher (1985).

3. See Eddings, 213, 217n8; and Fisher (2008), 9, 109–110.

4. Wilde's comment, originally part of a review he published in the *Court and Society Review* (20 April 1887: 146) is conveniently reprinted in Ellmann, 65. After Wilde's death, his friend Robert Ross, writing to Adela Schuster, 23 December 1900, presumably quoting Wilde, changed "usually" to "always." See Hart-Davis, 756, 863.

5. Wilson, 314.

6. Quinn (1936), 434.

7. Mabbott, 3: 1007.

Chronology

1806	early April	David Poe, Jr., marries Elizabeth Arnold Hopkins, a widow, in Richmond
1807	30 January	Their first child, William Henry Leonard Poe, born in Boston
1809	19 January	Edgar Poe is born in Boston, to David Poe, Jr., and Elizabeth Arnold Hopkins Poe, traveling stage actors (William Henry Leonard Poe had remained with his grandparents, David Poe, Sr., and Elizabeth Cairnes Poe, in Baltimore)
1810		Rosalie Poe born in Norfolk, probably December
1811	Summer	Deserted by her husband, Elizabeth Poe continues on the stage, becomes ill
	20 September	Elizabeth Poe performs in Richmond
	8 December	Elizabeth Arnold Hopkins Poe dies (Presumably, David Poe, Jr., dies around the same time). Edgar taken as foster child of John and Frances Allan; Rosalie by Mr. and Mrs. William Mackenzie
1815	23 June	Hoping to strengthen his mercantile business Allan, with his wife, her sister, and Poe, sail for England
	August	The Allan entourage spend time in Scotland so Allan may see his family
	7 October	Allan and his group arrive in London

1816	April	Edgar enrolls in the school of the Dubourg sisters in Chelsea
1818	Late July	Poe enters the Manor House School of the Rev. John Bransby, Stoke Newington (Bransby and the school furnish partial inspiration for "William Wilson")
1820	16 June	The Allan family sail from Liverpool for New York
	28 July	They depart New York by steamboat for Richmond, arriving there 2 August
	September	Poe enters the school of Joseph H. Clarke, where he is a good student; befriends Robert Craig Stanard; meets Robert's mother, Jane Stith Stanard, who supposedly inspired Poe's poem, "To Helen" (1831)
1823	January	Poe enters William Burke's school
	28 April	Mrs. Stanard dies
	June	Poe swims the James River from Ludlam's Wharf to Warwick Bar, a six-mile distance, a considerable athletic feat
1825	March	John Allan inherits considerable wealth upon the death of his uncle, William Galt
		Poe enters the school of Dr. and Mrs. Ray Thomas
	Summer	Poe and a neighbor, Sarah Elmira Royster, fall in love
1826		Poe and Elmira plan marriage
	14 February	Poe enters the University of Virginia, is an excellent, but indifferent student
		Letters between Elmira and Poe intercepted, ending their relationship and causing each to suspect the motives of the other

		Because Allan did not provide sufficient funding, Poe gambles, drinks to excess, and runs up great debts
	21 December	Allan makes Poe return to Richmond; engagement to Elmira Royster broken shortly thereafter
1827	March	Allan and Poe quarrel; Poe leaves the Allan house
	26 May	Using the alias, Edgar A. Perry, Poe enlists in the Army, is stationed at Fort Independence, in Boston Harbor
	June–July	Calvin F. S. Thomas, Boston, publishes *Tamerlane and Other Poems*, by "a Bostonian"
	31 October	Poe's battery is sent to Fort Moultrie, on Sullivan's Island, off Charleston, South Carolina
1828	1 May	Poe is appointed artificer
	6 December	Sarah Elmira Royster marries Alexander B. Shelton
1829	28 February	Frances Allan dies
	2 March	Obtaining leave, Poe arrives in Richmond after Mrs. Allan's funeral
	15 April	After several letters to Allan concerning an appointment to West Point, and having secured a substitute for his Army service, Poe is officially discharged from the Army
	May	Poe writes "Alone" for the album of Lucy Holmes
	14 May	Poe meets William Gwynn, a Baltimore newspaper editor
	18 May	Gwynn excerpts "Al Aaraaf" in his newspaper, the *Federal Gazette and Baltimore Daily Advertiser*

	December	*Al Aaraaf, Tamerlane, and Minor Poems*, with Poe's name on the title page, published by Hatch & Dunning, Baltimore
1830	Late June	Poe enters the Military Academy at West Point
	11 September	Poe's "Sonnet—To Science" appears in the Philadelphia *Saturday Evening Post*
	5 October	John Allan marries Louisa Patterson
1831	January	Poe neglects his duties because he wishes to leave West Point
	Late January	Poe is court-martialed and sentenced to dismissal from West Point
	19 February	Poe leaves West Point, goes to New York City
	6 March	Poe's dismissal from West Point becomes official
	April	*Poems by Edgar A. Poe* published in New York by Elam Bliss
	April–May	Poe takes up residence in his Grandmother Poe's home, in Baltimore, where his aunt, Maria Poe Clemm, and her daughter Virginia also reside
1832	14 January	The Philadelphia *Saturday Courier* publishes Poe's tale, "Metzengerstein," one of five tales submitted for a prize contest, and Poe's first published fiction (Poe did not win the prize)
1833	7 October	The Baltimore *Saturday Visiter* publishes Poe's tale, "MS. Found in a Bottle," which took the prize for the best prose tale in a contest sponsored by the *Visiter* (Poe's poem, "The Coliseum," was also considered the finest verse submission, but, thinking that prizes for both poetry and prose should not go to the same writer, the judges awarded the poetry prize to another)

	26 October	The *Visiter* publishes "The Coliseum" and announces that "Tales of the Folio Club" is forthcoming (This projected book, however, was not accepted by any publisher because its content was considered too subtle for the average reader. Dismantling the manuscript, Poe published tales separately in magazines and literary annuals.)
1834	January	*Godey's Lady's Book* publishes Poe's tale, "The Visionary" (later titled "The Assignation")
	Mid-February	Poe visits John Allan for the last time; Allan is hostile to Poe
	27 March	John Allan dies without mentioning Poe in his will
	Early August	Thomas W. White, in Richmond, publishes the first issue of the *Southern Literary Messenger*; early issues appear irregularly
	Mid-April	Poe's tale, "Berenice," appears in the March *Messenger*; Poe subsequently publishes tales, poems, and reviews in the magazine
	Early August	Poe moves to Richmond
	December	Poe's scathing *Messenger* review of Theodore S. Fay's egregious novel, *Norman Leslie*, earns him hostility from the powerful New York City literary establishment, which continues during much of Poe's literary career
	11 December	Poe replies to John Pendleton Kennedy, who wrote to him about the minglings of comedy and tragedy in his tales, providing no decisive claim for either
1836	Late April–Early May	Poe's review, in the April *Messenger*, of poems by Joseph Rodman Drake and Fitz-Greene Halleck embodies his concepts of poetry, along with a response to those who attacked him as a critic

	16 May	Poe and Virginia Clemm, first cousins, marry
1837	3 January	Having had disagreements with White, who could not tolerate Poe's drinking, Poe leaves the *Messenger*
	Late January	The first installment of Poe's novel, *The Narrative of Arthur Gordon Pym*, appears in the January *Messenger*
	Early February	Poe, Virginia, and Mrs. Clemm arrive in New York City
	Early March	The second installment of *Pym* appears in the February *Messenger*
1838		Early this year Poe, Virginia, and Mrs. Clemm move to Philadelphia
1839	19 July	Poe writes to James Kirke Paulding, Secretary of the Navy, asking consideration for a political appointment
	30 July	*The Narrative of Arthur Gordon Pym*, expanded to book length, is published by Harper & Brothers, New York
	October	Wiley and Putnam's London branch publish an English edition of *Pym*
1838		Late in the year Poe helps Thomas Wyatt, an Englishman, prepare *The Conchologist's First Book* and *Synopsis of Natural History* (Poe was mistaken by some as the actual author of these books)
1839	11 May	William E. Burton hires Poe for editorial work on *Burton's Gentleman's Magazine*, where Poe publishes some of his own works
	Early December	*Tales of the Grotesque and Arabesque* published by Lea & Blanchard, Philadelphia; the two volumes carry an 1840 publication date

1840	January	Poe's novel about the West, "The Journal of Julius Rodman," begins serialization in *Burton's Gentleman's Magazine*
	Late May	Thinking that Burton has turned from the magazine to the theater, Poe sends out a prospectus for his own periodical, the *Penn Magazine* (which, however, never materializes)
	30 May	Burton sends Poe a note of dismissal from *Burton's*
1841	Early February	Poe accepts George R. Graham's offer to be the reviewer for *Graham's Magazine*
	Early March	Poe's tale, "The Murders in the Rue Morgue" appears in the April issue of *Graham's Magazine*, thus initiating the modern detective story; there is also an announcement of Poe's becoming an editor for the magazine
	Early May	Poe meets Rufus W. Griswold
	June–July	Poe and his friend, Frederick W. Thomas, another author, discuss possibilities for Poe's obtaining a political appointment in the administration of President John Tyler
1842	Late January	Virginia Poe suffers her first tubercular hemorrhage
	Early March	Poe and Charles Dickens, who visited Philadelphia 5–9 March, meet twice; Dickens says that he will try to interest an English publisher in bringing out *Tales of the Grotesque and Arabesque* (but, for whatever reason, no English firm publishes the book)
	1 April	Poe resigns from *Graham's*
	25 May	Poe writes to Frederick W. Thomas, hoping that through Thomas's assistance, he may gain employment as a Tyler presidential appointee
	21 September	Poe apologizes to Thomas for failing to in-

terview, in Washington, D.C., for a political appointment

	Late November	Poe writes to Thomas that he has not won a customs official appointment from Thomas Smith, administrator of such posts in Philadelphia
1843	Early January	Once again Poe mentions starting his own literary magazine, the *Stylus*, and enlists support (As with the proposed *Penn Magazine*, this one never materializes, though others expressed interest in the project for several years afterward)
	25 February	A biographical sketch of Poe is published in the *Philadelphia Saturday Museum*, a mammoth weekly; Poe apparently furnished notes for this account to Henry B. Hirst, who then composed the piece (This article contains misinformation that has crept into subsequent biographical accounts)
	Early March	The biography is reprinted in the 4 March *Saturday Museum*
	Mid-March	Poe travels to Washington, D.C., where he becomes drunk, thus adversely affecting his chance of gaining a Tyler political appointment
	21 June	The Philadelphia *Dollar Newspaper* publishes Part I of "The Gold-Bug," a tale that won that paper's prize contest
	28 June	Part II of "The Gold-Bug" appears in the *Dollar Newspaper* (The tale was widely reprinted and also dramatized by Silas S. Steele)
	Mid-July	William H. Graham, of Philadelphia, publishes *The Prose Romances of Edgar A. Poe* (containing "The Murders in the Rue Morgue" and "The Man That Was Used Up")
	21 November	Poe lectures on American poetry at the Wirt Institute, Philadelphia

	28 November	Poe lectures again on American poetry at the Franklin Lyceum, Wilmington, Delaware
	23 December	Poe again lectures on American poetry at the Newark Academy, Newark, Delaware
1844	31 January	Poe again lectures on American poetry at the Odd Fellows' Hall, Baltimore
	6 April	Poe and Virginia move from Philadelphia to New York City
	Early May	Mrs. Clemm joins the young couple in New York
	Early October	Nathaniel P. Willis hires Poe as his assistant for the *Evening Mirror*; Poe continues to contribute literary works and reviews to other periodicals
1845	January	Poe begins contributing to the *Broadway Journal*, a weekly published by Charles Frederick Briggs and John Bisco
1846	29 January	"The Raven" appears in the *Evening Mirror*; in his terse introduction to the poem, Nathaniel P. Willis acknowledges Poe as the author
	Early February	"The Raven" appears in the *American Review*, signed "Quarles"; Poe becomes extremely popular following publication of "The Raven"
	Early February	*Graham's Magazine* publishes a biographical sketch of Poe, by James Russell Lowell (to whom Poe supplied most of the information)
	21 February	Poe joins the staff of the *Broadway Journal*
	28 February	Poe lectures on American poetry and poets at the New York Society Library
	25 June	Wiley and Putnam, New York, publish Poe's *Tales*, Volume 2 in their "Library of American Books"; Poe later expresses annoyance that Evert Duyckinck, the editor for the firm, not Poe himself, selected the twelve tales for the volume

	12 July	Bisco announces that Poe has sole editorial charge of the *Broadway Journal*
	Early October	Poe borrows $30 from Thomas Dunn English to use as partial payment to John Bisco for his share of the *Broadway Journal*
	16 October	Poe appears at the Boston Lyceum, delivers brief remarks concerning poetry, then reads "Al Aaraaf"; and recites "The Raven"; he later admits that he had prepared no original poem but simply presented "Al Aaraaf" as "The Messenger Star"; controversial reports of his performance appear in area newspapers
	24 October	John Bisco sells his interest in the *Broadway Journal* to Poe, who becomes owner and editor
	Mid-November	Poe and Thomas H. Lane become partners on the *Broadway Journal*, Poe to handle editing, Lane financial matters
	19 November	Wiley and Putnam publish *The Raven and Other Poems*
1846	January	Wiley and Putnam's London branch brings out *The Raven and Other Poems*
	3 January	The *Broadway Journal* ceases publication because of financial difficulties; hereafter Poe has no forum under his own control for his writings
	Late February	Wiley and Putnam publish Poe's *Tales* and *The Raven and Other Poems* in a single volume
	April	"The Philosophy of Composition" appears in *Graham's Magazine*
	May	The Poe family moves to Fordham and Poe begins publishing his "Literati" sketches in *Godey's Lady's Book* (Reactions to those articles are generally negative)
	17 June	Nathaniel Hawthorne writes to Poe, supposing that the publishers have sent Poe a copy of

Mosses from an Old Manse; Hawthorne remarks that although he often disagrees with Poe's evaluations of his works, he respects Poe's honest opinions

23 June — Thomas Dunn English's scathing "Reply" [to Poe's "Literati" sketch of him], wherein he charges Poe with drunkenness and depravity, appears in the New York *Morning Telegraph*; later English persuades Hiram Fuller to reprint the "Reply" in the *Evening Mirror*

5 September — English, angry at Poe's hostile "Literati" article about him, targets Poe, as "Marmaduke Hammerhead," in Part Seven of his novel, *1844, or, The Power of the "S. F.*," serialized in the New York *Weekly Mirror* ("Hammerhead" appears, drunk or insane, in several later installments)

November — Mary Gove visits the Poe home in Fordham, is shocked by their poverty and Virginia's illness, enlists the help of Marie Louise Shew, who in turn makes others aware of this dire situation, such that the worst effects of poverty are eased

26 December — Nathaniel P. Willis, in the *Home Journal*, seeks help from persons to alleviate the Poe family's poverty and illness

1847   January — Sarah Anna Lewis visits the Poe home; her friendship continues

30 January — Virginia Poe dies

2 February — Virginia is buried in the cemetery of the Old Dutch Reformed Church, in the plot of John Valentine, owner of the cottage Poe is renting

17 February — Poe wins his suit for libel against Thomas Dunn English, for English's "Reply"

27 February — In the *Weekly Mirror*, Charles F. Briggs, in an installment of his serial novel, *The Trippings of Tom Pepper*, satirizes Poe as "Austin Wicks,"

		a literary critic, who becomes drunk and insulting
	February–March	Poe is ill
	November	Mary Gove visits the Poe cottage, remarks on Poe's poverty
	December	Poe's "Ulalume" appears in the *American Review*
1848	January	Poe again announces that he will produce the *Stylus*
	3 February	Poe lectures on "The Universe" at the New York Society Library
	3 June	In the *John-Donkey*, a comic periodical, Thomas Dunn English publishes "Hints to Authors: On the Germanesque," a satire on Poe the fiction writer; English includes, as illustrative of Poe's techniques, a parody of Poe's fiction from the Philadelphia *Irish Citizen*
	Mid-July	*Eureka: A Prose Poem* (an expansion of Poe's lectures on "The Universe") is published by George P. Putnam
	21 September	Poe visits the home of Mrs. Sarah Helen Whitman, in Providence, Rhode Island
	Late October	Poe goes to Lowell, Massachusetts, to lecture on American poets and poetry; he does not lecture, however, because of events relating to the presidential election (He initially stays at the home of Mrs. Jane Ermina Locke, a poet; then moves to the residence of Mrs. Annie Richmond rousing Mrs. Locke's displeasure)
	November	Poe again visits Mrs. Whitman, who permits a provisional engagement to him, though her mother, on whom she is financially dependent, disapproves of Poe
	23 December	Mrs. Whitman breaks their engagement

		because of Poe's drinking; he and Sarah never meet again
1849	22 January	Frederick Gleason, in Boston, invites Poe to contribute to his weekly newspaper, *The Flag of Our Union*
	30 June	Enroute to Richmond to lecture, Poe stops in Philadelphia and begins drinking; John Sartain, his host, is worried over Poe's irrationality
	14 July	Poe reaches Richmond
	Late July	Poe proposes to his early beloved, Sarah Elmira Royster, now Mrs. Shelton, a widow
	17 August	Poe lectures on "The Poetic Principle" at the Exchange Hotel in Richmond
	27 August	Poe joins the Sons of Temperance
	14 September	Poe lectures again on "The Poetic Principle" at the Norfolk Academy
	17 September	Poe returns from Norfolk to Richmond
	Late September	Poe's marriage proposal to Mrs. Shelton is accepted
	24 September	At the Exchange Hotel Poe lectures again on "The Poetic Principle"
	27 September	Poe leaves Richmond on a steamboat bound for Baltimore
	3 October	Poe is discovered, ill, in Baltimore; Poe's old friend, Joseph E. Snodgrass, and Poe's cousin, Henry Herring, take Poe to Washington College Hospital
	5 October	Neilson Poe, another cousin, visits the hospital, does not see Poe, but sends him necessities; Poe's condition remains critical
	7 October	Poe dies
	8 October	Poe is buried in the plot of his grandfather,

David Poe, Sr., in the graveyard of Westminster Presbyterian Church, Baltimore; few persons attend the funeral and burial

9 October   The New York *Daily Tribune* publishes Rufus W. Griswold's malicious obituary; for many years this slanderous notice and Griswold's expansion of it in his edition of Poe's *Works* (1850) were accepted as accurate accounts of Poe's life and character

[Letter about Poe's West Point Matriculation] (1829)

John Allan

After taking him as a ward into his own home, John Allan hoped that Poe would enter Allan's own business firm in Richmond. Poe's inclinations toward a literary career, his indiscretions at the University of Virginia, and the temperamental differences between him and Allan serve as background for this letter from Allan regarding Poe's qualifications for entering the military academy at West Point.

John Allan to John H. Eaton, Secretary of War, 6 May 1829

Dr. Sir,—The youth who presents this, is the same alluded to by Lt. Howard, Capt. Griswold, Colo. Worth, our representative and the speaker, the Hon'ble Andrew Stevenson, and my friend Major Jno. Campbell.

He left me in consequence of some gambling at the University at Charlottesville, because (I presume) I refused to sanction a rule that the shopkeepers and others had adopted there, making Debts of honour of all indiscretions. I have much pleasure in asserting that he stood his examinations at the close of the year with great credit to himself. His history is short. He is the grandson of Quartermaster-General Poe, of Maryland, whose widow as I understand still receives a pension for the services or disabilities of her husband. Frankly, Sir, do I declare that he is no relation to me whatever; that I have many [in] whom I have taken an active interest to promote theirs; with no other feeling than that, every man is my care, if he be in distress. For myself I ask nothing, but I do request your kindness to aid this youth in the promotion of his future prospects. And it will afford me great pleasure to reciprocate any kindness you can show him. Pardon my frankness; but I address a soldier.

Reprinted in Harrison, 17: 372–373.

[Letter about Poe at West Point] (1884)

ALLAN B. MAGRUDER

The letter that follows, from a contemporary of Poe's at West Point, offers interesting portraiture of Cadet Poe, though some of the romanticizing of his circumstances must have come from the subject himself. To date, no evidential proof that Poe traveled in Europe or the Middle East or that he was a sailor has come to light. A sailor's life, perhaps with travel to some of the overseas regions, may have been actualities in the life of Poe's brother, William Henry Poe. References to travel to foreign countries appear in other biographical accounts based on information supplied by Poe. The letter's being written more than fifty years after Poe's time at West Point may also explain inaccuracies in the correspondent's memory.

Allan B. Magruder to George E. Woodberry, 23 April 1884

He was very shy and reserved in his intercourse with his fellow-cadets—his associations being confined almost exclusively to Virginians. He was by several years my senior, and had led a wild, adventurous life, traveling in Europe and the East, and was a seaman, I think, on board a whaler. He was an accomplished French scholar, and had a wonderful aptitude for mathematics, so that he had no difficulty in preparing his recitations in his class and obtaining the highest marks in these departments. He was a devourer of books, but his great fault was his neglect of and apparent contempt for military duties. His wayward and capricious temper made him at times utterly oblivious or indifferent to the ordinary routine of roll-call, drills, and guard duties. These habits subjected him often to arrest and punishment, and effectually prevented his learning or discharging the duties of a soldier.

Reprinted in Woodberry (1909), 1: 70.

[Letter about Commencement of Poe's Professional Literary Life] (1835)

JOHN P. KENNEDY

Having published three volumes of poems, which brought him no financial remuneration, and having gotten himself court-martialed and expelled from West Point, Poe traveled south, taking up residence in the home of his grandmother, Elizabeth C. Poe, who had become an invalid after a paralytic stroke. The period from 1831 to late 1833 remains vague because no great amount of evidence about Poe's activities has come to light. Seeking greater rewards for his literary endeavors, Poe turned to the writing of fiction. Poe's career as a writer of fiction speedily led to his attempting a book, "Tales of the Folio Club," in which he created a frame narrative structure featuring caricatures, chiefly of best-selling writers (though he apparently included himself) who constituted the Folio Club. The club members and the tales—each modeled upon a theme or technique of one of the caricatured club members—would have been comic creations, as would the interlarded critical debates concerning the merits and demerits of each tale. No publisher would accept the work, however, because the humor was considered too rarefied for the average reader, thus leading to poor sales.

John P. Kennedy to Thomas W. White, 13 April 1835

DEAR SIR,—Poe did right in referring to me, He is very clever with his pen—classical and scholar-like. He wants experience and direction, but I have no doubt he can be made very useful to you. And, poor fellow! He is *very* poor. I told him to write something for every number of your magazine, and that you might find it to your advantage to give him some permanent employ. He has a volume of very bizarre tales in the hands of ———, in Philadelphia, who for a year past has been promising to publish them. This young fellow is highly imaginative, and a little given to the terrific. He is at work upon a tragedy, but I have turned him to drudging upon whatever may make money, and I have no doubt you and he will find your account in each other.

Reprinted in Ingram (1891), 95.

[Letter about Poe's Drinking and the *Messenger*] (1835)

Thomas W. White

Poe continued to experiment with the Folio Club book project into 1836. In 1835, thanks to a recommendation from John P. Kennedy, Poe had been hired as a staff member for the *Southern Literary Messenger*, in Richmond, Virginia, though his employment there was checkered by his tendency to overindulge in alcohol when he was under stress, as this letter indicates. Poe must have overcome his drinking problem for a time, such that White maintained him in an editorial position with the *Messenger*, thus affording the young man satisfactory prospects. Poe married his young cousin, Virginia Clemm, and embarked on what seemed to be a pleasant literary career.

Thomas W. White to E. A. Poe, Esq., 29 September 1835

Dear Edgar,—Would that it were in my power to unbosom myself to you, in language such as I could on the present occasion, wish myself master of. I cannot do it—and therefore must be content to speak to you in my plain way.

That you are sincere in all your promises, I firmly believe. But, Edgar, when you once again tread these streets, I have my fears that your resolve would fall through,—and that you would again sip the juice, even till it stole away your senses. Rely on your own strength, and you are gone! Look to your Maker for help, and you are safe!

How much I regretted parting with you, is unknown to anyone on this earth, except myself. I was attached to you—and am still,—and willingly would I say return, if I did not dread the hour of separation very shortly again.

If you could make yourself contented to take up your quarters in my family, or in any other private family where liquor is not used, I should think there were hopes of you.—But, if you go to a tavern, or to any other place where it is used at table, you are not safe. I speak from experience.

You have talents, Edgar,—and you ought to have them respected as well as yourself. Learn to respect yourself, and you will very soon find that you are respected. Separate yourself from the bottle, and bottle companions, for ever!

Tell me if you can and will do so—and let me hear that it is your fixed purpose never to yield to temptation.

If you should come to Richmond again, and again should be an assistant in my office, it must be expressly understood by us that all engagements on my part would be dissolved, the moment you get drunk.

No man is safe who drinks before breakfast! No man can do so, and attend to business properly. . . .

Reprinted in Harrison, 17: 20–21.

[Letter about Mixed Modes
in Poe's Early Tales] (1836)

JOHN P. KENNEDY

These responses to Poe as a fiction writer, by older, established authors John P. Kennedy and James Kirke Paulding, recognize Poe's accomplishments in humor. Paulding's 17 March letter may have spurred Poe to begin writing *The Narrative of Arthur Gordon Pym.*

John P. Kennedy to Poe, 9 February 1836

My dear Poe . . . I am greatly rejoiced at your success not only in Richmond, but every where. My predictions have been more than fulfilled in regard to the public favour for your literary enterprises. Let me beg you to set down this praise for its value, as nothing, but an incentive to the utmost care and labour for improvement. You are strong enough now to be criticized. Your fault is the love of the extravagant. Pray beware of it. You find a hundred *intense* writers for one *natural* one. Some of your *bizareries* have been mistaken for satire—and admired too in that character. They deserved it, but *you* did not, for you did not intend them so. I like your grotesque—it is of the very best stamp, and I am sure you will do wonders for yourself in the comic, I mean the serio tragic comic. Do you easily keep pace with the demands of the magazine? Avoid, by all means, the appearance of flagging. I like the critical notices very well. . . .

Reprinted in Harrison, 17: 28.

[Epistolary Response with Comment on Humor] (1836)

Edgar A. Poe

Edgar A. Poe to John P. Kennedy, 11 February 1836

. . . You are nearly, but not altogether right in relation to the satire in some of my Tales. Most of them were *intended* for half banter, half satire— although I might not have fully acknowledged this to be their aim even to myself. "Lionizing" and "Loss of Breath" were satires properly speaking— at least so meant—the one of the rage for lions, and the facility of becoming one—the other of the extravagancies of Blackwood. I find no difficulty in keeping up with the demands of the Magazine. . . .

Reprinted in Harrison, 17: 29.

[*Harper's* Rejection of "Tales of the Folio Club"] (1836)

James Kirke Paulding

James Kirke Paulding to Thomas W. White, 3 March 1836

Dear Sir,—I duly received the Book containing the Tales by Mr. Poe heretofore published in the "Messenger," and have delayed writing to you on the subject until I could communicate the final decision of the Messrs. Harpers as to their publication. . . . They say that the stories have so recently appeared before the Public in the "Messenger" that they would be no novelty—but most especially they object that there is a degree of obscurity in their application, which will prevent ordinary readers from comprehending their drift, and consequently from enjoying the fine satire they convey. It requires a degree of familiarity with the various kinds of knowledge which they do not possess, to enable them to relish the joke: the dish is too refined for them to banquet on. They desire me, however, to state to Mr. Poe that if he will lower himself a little to the ordinary comprehension of the generality of readers, and prepare a series of original Tales, or a single work, and send them to the Publishers, previous to their appearance in the "Messenger," they will make such arrangements with him as will be liberal and satisfactory. . . . I hope Mr. Poe will pardon me if the interest I feel in his success should prompt me to take this occasion to suggest to him to apply his fine humor, and his extensive acquirements, to more familiar subjects of satire; to the faults and foibles of our own people, their peculiarities of habits and manners, and above all, to the ridiculous affectations and extravagancies of the fashionable English Literature of the day which we copy with such admirable success and servility. His quiz on Willis, and the Burlesque of "Blackwood," were not only capital, but what is more, were understood by all. For Satire to be relished, it is necessary that it should be leveled at something with which readers are familiar. . . .

Reprinted in Harrison, 17: 377–378.

[Letter Advising Poe to Compose a Novel] (1836)

JAMES KIRKE PAULDING

James Kirke Paulding to Mr. Edgar A. Poe, 17 March 1836

. . . I think it would be worth your while, if other engagements permit, to undertake a Tale in a couple of volumes, for that is the magical number. There is a great dearth of good writers at present both in England and in this country, while the number of readers and purchasers of Books, is daily increasing, so that the demand is greater than the supply, in mercantile phrase. . . . I am of the opinion that a work of yours, would at least bring you a handsome remuneration, though it might not repay your labours, or meet its merits. Should you write such a work, your best way will be to forward the MS directly to the Harpers, who will be I presume governed by the judgment of their Reader, also from long experience can tell almost to a certainty what will succeed. . . .

Reprinted in Harrison, 17: 31–32.

[Letter Justifying Poe's Critical Practices] (1836)

Lydia H. Sigourney

Lydia H. Sigourney, another well-established author and editor by the time Poe emerged on the literary scene, responded to his uncertainties about the nature of his literary criticism. Poe's critiques, chiefly in the form of book reviews, were often savage, and although they drew much attention to the *Messenger*, they occasionally alarmed Thomas W. White, the owner, as well as making for Poe many enemies who were connected with or powerful in the literary world of early nineteenth-century America, thus paving the way for later onslaughts by his detractors.

Lydia H. Sigourney to E. A. Poe, Esq., 11 June 1836

My Dear Sir,—Yours of the 4th was this morning received, and I hasten to assure you that your apprehension of having forfeited my good-will, is entirely groundless.—It is surely a hard case, if a critic may not express his opinions, freely, and even severely, in this land of freedom. All that an author can expect, in such a case, is to explain, if he supposes there has been ought of misconception. This I ventured to do.—But to cherish vindictiveness, is quite another affair, & I assure you, forms no part of my creed. There is surely, enough of controversy abroad in our land, without its few literati lifting up the tomahawk, and scalping-knife against each other. Even if I cherished some lingerings of resentment, which I by no means acknowledge, you would have entirely removed every such somber shadow, by your favorable review of Mellen's poems. . . .

I send at your request, what I happen to have by me,—and as you will have it to be a peace offering, you can thus view it, though there is in reality, no truce to be made between us. Do not, however, assume a more lenient style with regard to me, in consequence of any little aid I may have afforded the "Messenger," since no traffick in civilities is as valuable in my opinion as sincerity.

Reprinted in Harrison, 17: 37–38.

[10]

[Letter Seeking Political Appointment] (1841)

EDGAR A. POE

This exchange of letters between Poe and his friend, Frederick W. Thomas, a writer who held a small political office and who was friendly with the sons of President John Tyler and persons connected with the Tyler administration, makes evident Poe's desire, intense for a time, to seek a political appointment instead of devoting his energies solely to literary pursuits, particularly those that were somewhat controlled by editors, whose eye was ever attentive to public taste. Thanks to Poe's ultimately becoming drunk and ill just when he should have been interviewing for political office, he never did gain political employment.

Edgar A. Poe to Frederick W. Thomas, 26 June 1841

Would to God I could do as you have done! Do you seriously think that an application to Tyler would have a good result? My claims, to be sure, are few. I am a Virginian, at least I call myself one, for I have resided all my life, until within the last few years, in Richmond. My political principles have always been, as nearly as may be, with the existing administration, and I battled with right good will for Harrison when opportunity offered. With Mr. Tyler I have some slight personal acquaintance—although this is a matter which he has possibly forgotten. For the rest, I am a literary man, and see a disposition in Government to cherish letters. Have I any chance?

Reprinted in Harrison, 17: 91–92.

[Letter Encouraging Poe's Political Desires] (1841)

Frederick W. Thomas

> Poe's earlier friendship with John Pendleton Kennedy, mentioned here, was indeed a means of his entering the literary world of early nineteenth-century America, an assistance Poe never forgot.

Frederick W. Thomas to Poe, 1 July 1841

My dear Poe,—Yours of 26 June I received yesterday. I trust, my dear friend, that you can obtain an appointment. President Tyler I have not seen except in passing in his carriage—never having called at the White House since the death of Harrison except to see the sons of the President, and then they were not in—couldn't you slip in here and see the President yourself—or if you would prefer it I will see him for you—but perhaps your application had better be made through someone who has influence with the executive. I have heard you say that J. P. Kennedy has a regard for you—he is here a Congressman and would serve you—would he not? My employment is merely temporary. I had a letter of introduction to the Secretary of the Treasury, from my friend Governor Corwin of Ohio, merely introducing me as a "literary character"—and I did not then expect to ask office, but finding that publishing was at a low ebb, I waited on Mr. Ewing and told him frankly how I was situated, and that I should like to be making something; he with great kindness installed me here. There are thousands of applicants. My duty is to schedule their claims and present them to the Secretary. He reads the schedule and makes his decision, unless he has doubts about the matter, and then he sends on the papers. Let me hear from you in this matter of yours. . . .

Reprinted in Harrison, 17: 92–93.

[Additional Comments on Political Aspirations] (1841)

EDGAR A. POE

✹✹✹

Edgar A. Poe to Frederick W. Thomas, 4 July 1841

I wish to God I could visit Washington—but the old story, you know—I have no money—not even enough to take me there, saying nothing of getting back. It is a hard thing to be poor—but as I am kept so by an honest motive, I dare not complain. Your suggestion about Mr. Kennedy is well timed; and here, Thomas, you can do me a true service. Call upon Mr. Kennedy—you know him I believe—if not, introduce yourself, he is a perfect gentleman, and will give you a cordial welcome. Speak to him of my wishes, and urge him to see the Secretary of War in my behalf—or one of the other Secretaries or President Tyler. I mention in particular the Secretary of War, because I have been to W. Point, and this may stand me in some stead. I would be glad to get almost any appointment—even a $500 one—so that I may have something independent of letters for a subsistence. To coin one's brain into silver, at the nod of a master, is to my thinking the hardest task in the world. Mr. Kennedy has been at all times a true friend to me—he was the first true friend I ever had—I am indebted to him for life itself. He will be willing to help me, I know—but needs urging, for he is always head and ears in business. Thomas, may I depend upon you?

Reprinted in Harrison, 17: 93–94.

[Letter about Poe's Political Qualifications] (1841)

FREDERICK W. THOMAS

Frederick W. Thomas to Poe, 7 July 1841

My Dear Poe, . . . Congress was now in session last night until twelve o'clock, and it may be a day or two before I see Kennedy. I wrote you that I had never seen the President. I shall see him on Friday, as his son has invited me to dine with him. If I had address now I might bring you up in a quiet way and pave the way—but as I have not, I must make the genius of Friendship my guide . . . to make all right in your behalf. There are thousands of applicants, but I think the wants of a man like you, who asks only for a clerkship, should not be neglected. You will eventually succeed if you should not at first.

I know very few of the "bigbugs" here, having kept myself to myself, but I think I have skill enough to commit your merits to those, who, though not women, will be more skilful advocates of your claims.

Reprinted in Harrison, 17: 94–95.

"Autographs" (1842)

[ANONYMOUS]

> This item provides useful information regarding a segment of Poe's writings that may no longer be deemed among his most significant creations, but that certainly attracted notice from his contemporaries. Poe's turning to a popular mode—and the awareness of readers that he was doing so—attests to his having gained stature in American authorship.

The November and December numbers of "Graham's Magazine" contain engraved fac-similes of the signatures of the most distinguished American authors, with very sprightly comments by Mr. E. A. Poe, and we understand that they have excited a great deal of interest. The collecting of autographs has been a great rage among people of fashion for some years past in England, and even among the learned it seems to have succeeded to the old passion of book collecting. . . . The fondness for these trifles seems to be extending to this country [cites several notable American autograph collectors and collections]. Autographs have engaged the curiosity of some of the most eminent persons of the time.

"Autographs." *New-York Mirror: A Weekly Gazette of Literature and Fine Arts*, 1 January 1842: 3.

[Letter about Poe's Possible Custom House Appointment] (1842)

Frederick W. Thomas

Although Poe continued to produce literary publications, he also continued to seek political employment, as is revealed in the following exchange.

Frederick W. Thomas to Edgar A. Poe, Esq., 21 May 1842

My Dear Poe,—I fear you have been reproaching me with neglect in not answering yours of March 13th before. If you have you have done me an injustice.

I knew it would be of no avail to submit your proposition to Robert Tyler, with regard to any pecuniary aid which he might extend to your undertaking, as he has nothing but his salary of $1500 and his situation requires more than its expenditure. In a literary point of view he would gladly aid you, but his time is so taken up with political and other matters that his contributions would be few and far between.

I therefore thought I could aid you better by interesting him in you personally without your appearing, as it were, personally in the matter. In consequence I took occasion to speak of you to him frequently in a way that friendship and a profound respect for your genius and acquirements dictated. He thinks of you as highly as I do.

Last night I was speaking of you, and took occasion to suggest that a situation in the Custom House, Philadelphia, might be acceptable to you, as Lamb (Charles) had held a somewhat similar appointment, etc., and as it would leave you leisure to pursue your literary pursuits. Robert replied that he felt confident that such a situation could be obtained for you in the course of two or three months at farthest, as certain vacancies would then occur.

What say you to such a place? Official life is not laborious, and a situation that would suit you and place you beyond the necessity of employing

[16]

your pen, he says, he can obtain for you there. Let me hear from you as soon as convenient upon this subject.—I assure you, Poe, that not an occasion has offered when in the remotest way I thought I could serve you that I did not avail myself of it—but I would not write upon mere conjecture that something available was about to occur. So my motives must be my apology, my friend, for my long silence. . . .

Reprinted in Harrison, 17: 108–110.

[Letter about Reasons for Leaving *Graham's*] (1842)

EDGAR A. POE

❧✦❧

Edgar A. Poe to Frederick W. Thomas, 25 May 1842

My Dear Thomas,—Through an accident I have only just now received yours of the 21st. Believe me, I never dreamed of doubting your friendship, or of reproaching you for your silence. I knew you had good reasons for it; and, in this matter, I feel that you have acted for me more judiciously, by far, than I should have done for myself. You have shown yourself, from the first hour of our acquaintance, that *rara avis in terris*—"a true friend." Nor am I a man to be unmindful of your kindness.

What you say respecting a situation in the Custom House here gives me new life. Nothing could more precisely meet my views. Could I obtain such an appointment, I would be enabled thoroughly to carry out all my ambitious projects. It would relieve me of all care as regards a mere subsistence, and thus allow me time for thought, which, in fact, is action. I repeat that I would ask for nothing farther or better than a situation such as you mention. If the salary will barely enable me to live I shall be content. Will you say as much for me to Mr. Tyler, and express to him my sincere gratitude for the interest he takes in my welfare?

The report of my having parted company with Graham is correct; although in the forthcoming June number there is no announcement to that effect; nor had the papers any authority for the statement made. My duties ceased with the May number. I shall continue to contribute occasionally. Griswold succeeds me. My reason for resigning was disgust with the namby-pamby character of the Magazine—a character which it was impossible to eradicate. I allude to the contemptible pictures, fashion-plates, music, and love-tales. The salary, moreover, did not pay me for the labour which I was forced to bestow. With Graham, who is really a very gentlemanly, although an exceedingly weak, man, I had no misunderstanding. I am rejoiced to say that my dear little wife is much better, and I have strong hope of her ultimate recovery. She desires her kindest regards—as also Mrs. Clemm.

I have moved from the old place—but should you pay an unexpected visit to Philadelphia, you will find my address at Graham's. I would give the world to shake you by the hand; and have a thousand things to talk about which would not come within the compass of a letter. Write immediately upon receipt of this, if possible, and do let me know something of yourself, your own doings and prospects: see how excellent an example of egotism I set you. Here is a letter nearly every word of which is about myself of my individual affairs. You say White—little Tom. I am anxious to know what he said about things in general. He is a *character* if ever one was. God bless you—

Reprinted in Harrison, 17: 110–111.

From *The Poets and Poetry of America* (1842)

RUFUS W. GRISWOLD

Rufus W. Griswold stands as one of the foremost anthologists of American literature in the earlier years of the nineteenth century. This account of Poe, in the first edition of *The Poets and Poetry of America*, though it is repeatedly factually inaccurate (for example, Poe was born in 1809, not 1811, but he often gave misleading birthdates), was the first published biographical sketch of Poe. According to Griswold's practice in negotiating with authors included in his anthologies, Poe himself furnished the information for this piece which served as a headnote in that volume. The contents in this sketch contrast to those in many others, which contributed to the long-standing impression— based on his obituary, signed "Ludwig," and the lengthy memoir in his edition of Poe's *Works*—that Griswold initiated the hostility that dominated many biographical accounts published after Poe's death. But when this sketch appeared, none of the animosity that Griswold was later to sustain toward Poe and his memory had commenced. The exact fate of Poe's father remains undetermined; Poe himself was never adopted by John Allan; the travel on the European continent has never been verified; John Allan died in his fifties, not at sixty-five. Along with subsequent accounts for which Poe supplied information, this one helped to establish what may well be designated the enigma of Poe or the Poe legend. Albeit this sketch contains nothing about the quality or technique of Poe's poems themselves, it did give Poe prominence as an American poet, a classification that he himself would have relished.

Edgar A. Poe.
Born, 1811.

THE family of Mr. POE is one of the oldest and most respectable in Baltimore. DAVID POE, his paternal grandfather, was a quartermaster-general in the Maryland line during the Revolution, and the intimate friend of LAFAYETTE, who, during his last visit to the United States, called personally upon the general's widow, and tendered her his acknowledgments for the services rendered to him by her husband. His great-grandfather, JOHN POE, married, in England, JANE, a daughter of Admiral JAMES MCBRIDE, noted in British naval history, and claiming kindred with some of the most illustrious English families. His father and mother died within a few weeks of each other, of consumption, leaving him an orphan, at two years of age. Mr. JOHN ALLAN, a wealthy gentleman of Richmond, Virginia, took a fancy to him, and persuaded General POE, his grandfather, to suffer him to adopt him. He was brought up in Mr. ALLAN's family; and as that gentleman had no other children, he was regarded as his son and heir. In 1816 he accompanied Mr. and Mrs. ALLAN to Great Britain, visited every portion of it, and afterward passed four or five years in a school kept at Stoke Newington, near London, by the Reverend Doctor BRANSBY. He returned to America in 1822, and in 1825 went to the Jefferson University, at Charlottesville, in Virginia, where he led a very dissipated life, the manners of the college being at that time extremely dissolute. He took the first honours, however, and went home greatly in debt. Mr. ALLAN refused to pay some of his debts of *honour*, and he hastily quitted the country on a Quixotic expedition to join the Greeks, then struggling for liberty. He did not reach his original destination, however, but made his way to St. Petersburg, in Russia, where he became involved in difficulties, from which he was extricated by Mr. MIDDLETON, the American consul at that place. He returned home in 1829, and immediately afterward entered the military academy at West Point. In about eighteen months from that time, Mr. ALLAN, who had lost his first wife while POE was in Russia, married again. He was sixty-five years of age, and the lady was young; POE quarelled with her, and the veteran husband, taking the part of his wife, addressed him an angry letter, which was answered in the same spirit. He died soon after, leaving an infant son the heir to his vast property, and bequeathed POE nothing. The army, in the opinion of the young cadet, was not a place for a poor man, so he left West Point abruptly, and determined to maintain himself by authorship. The proprietor of a weekly literary gazette in Baltimore offered two premiums, one for the best prose story, and the other for the best poem. In due time POE sent in two articles, and the examining committee, of whom Mr. KENNEDAY [Kennedy], the author of "Horse-Shoe Robinson," was one, awarded to him both the premiums, and took occasion to insert in the gazette a card under their signatures, in which he was very highly praised. Soon after this, he became associated with

Mr. THOMAS W. WHITE in the conduct of the "Southern Literary Messenger," and he subsequently wrote for the "New York Review," and for several foreign periodicals. He is married, and now resides in Philadelphia, where he is connected with a popular monthly magazine.

From *The Poets and Poetry of America*, edited by Rufus W. Griswold, 387.

From "Poets and Poetry of Philadelphia . . ." (1843)

[Edgar A. Poe and Henry B. Hirst]

In early 1843, when materials for a biography were requested by a mammoth weekly, the *Philadelphia Saturday Museum*, Poe first asked his friend, Frederick W. Thomas, to prepare a sketch. Thomas refused, so Poe supplied information to Henry B. Hirst, for what follows. Along with accounts Poe supplied to other writers, this sketch contains much misinformation, but it was excerpted and reprinted. Along with Griswold's memoirs published after Poe's death, it formed a strong foundation for the romanticized portraits of Poe that continue to circulate even today. The *Museum* biography is significant because it offers materials, some apparently no longer extant, used by Poe to bolster his literary reputation, most notably that of a poet, though he also reprinted (not always accurately) encomiums to his abilities in fiction writing and criticism. He probably downplayed comment regarding his criticism because it had occasioned considerable hostility from authors whose writings he gave negative notice and from others who disliked the savage tone in several of his reviews.

FOR THE MATERIALS of the present biography, we are indebted, partly to information derived from the late Thomas W. White, Proprietor of the "Southern Literary Messenger," but, principally, to memoranda furnished by the well known author of "Clinton Bradshaw,"—Frederic W. Thomas, Esq.—who has enjoyed a better opportunity of intimate acquaintance with the subject of our sketch, than, perhaps, any other in America.

EDGAR ALLAN POE is descended from one of the oldest and most respectable families in Baltimore. His great-grandfather, John Poe, married, in England, Jane, a daughter of the British Admiral McBride, and through her, the family claim connexion with many of the noblest in England.—His paternal grandfather, General David Poe, of Baltimore, was Quartermaster General in the "Maryland Line," during the Revolution. General Poe, was, in the true sense of the word, a patriot. To furnish provisions, forage, and clothing for the destitute Government troops, he stripped himself of his entire patrimony. For this he never instituted a claim, nor for services rendered to the United States as an officer; but for actual money loaned, he claimed $40,000. Owing to technical informalities in the vouchers (which consisted principally of letters from WASHINGTON and LA FAYETTE) he received no portion of the sum. The Maryland Legislature, however, subsequently allowed his widow a pension, and in the preamble of the act, expressed their satisfaction of the *equity* of the claim, while they deplored the *legal* insufficiency of the proofs to support it. General Poe was one of the most intimate friends of La Fayette, who, during his memorable visit to America, called upon the widow, publicly acknowledged the obligations of the country to her husband, expressed his astonishment at finding her in comparative indigence, and his strong indignation at the narrow-minded policy of the Government. We gather a few particulars of this interview from the late "Baltimore Gazette," and other papers of the time. General La Fayette affectionately embraced Mrs. Poe, exclaiming at the same time, in tears, "the last time I embraced you madame, you were younger and more blooming than now." He visited, with his staff, the grave of General Poe, in the "First Presbyterian Church-yard," and, kneeling on the ground, kissed the sod above him, and, weeping, exclaimed "*Ici repose un coeur noble!*"—here lies a noble heart!—a just tribute to the memory of a good, if not a great man.

Mr. Poe's father was David Poe, Jr., the fourth son of the General. He studied law for several years in the office of William Gwyn, the *quondam* proprietor of the "Baltimore Gazette." When very young he became enamored of Miss Elizabeth Arnold, a lady of great beauty, and extraordinary talents and accomplishments, who made the stage her profession for some time previous. The attachment resulted in an elopement and marriage, to the great displeasure of his father's family, who afterwards, however, became reconciled. By this lady, Mr. David Poe had three children, Henry, Edgar and Rosalie. Both parents died of consumption within a few weeks of each other, while on a visit to Richmond, Va. This circumstance excited much interest, and the youngest children (Edgar and Rosalie) were adopted, the one by Mr. John Allan, a very wealthy gentleman of Richmond, and the other by Mr. William McKenzie of the same city.

Mr. Allan's principal recommendation was his wealth. His income was large, some $20 or $30,000 *per annum*. He treated his young *protégé* with as much kindness as his gross nature admitted, and, as he had no children, made a point of informing everyone that he intended to make him his sole heir. He took a species of pride in the precocious talents evinced by his adopted son, and gave him an expensive education.

In 1816 or 17, Edgar accompanied Mr. Allan and his wife to England, of which, and of Scotland, they made the tour. He remained in England five years, during which time he went to school, chiefly to Reverend Dr. Bransby, at Stoke Newington. A faithful description of this school and its principal, is introduced in Mr. Poe's tale of "William Wilson," which forms a part of the collection entitled, "Tales of the Grotesque and Arabesque." Upon his return to America, he went to various academies, and finally to the University of Virginia, (Jefferson's) at Charlottesville. The manners of the Institution, at that time, were exceedingly dissolute, and he fell in with the general course. He managed, however, to maintain a position with the Professors. He attended lectures at random, and spent his time partly in the debating societies, where he soon grew noted as a debater, partly in solitary rambles among the mountains of the Blue Ridge, and partly in covering the walls of his dormitory with crayon drawings, caricaturing the Faculty. This dissipated course of life brought with it, however, a natural disgust, and, towards the close of his university career, arousing himself to better things, he took the first honors of the college, without any difficulty, and returned home.

His good resolutions, however had come somewhat too late, for he had already become involved in difficulties, which resulted in his leaving home. With a young friend, Ebenezer Burling, he endeavored to make his way, with scarcely a dollar in his pocket, to Greece, with the wild design of aiding in the Revolution then taking place. Burling soon repented his folly, and gave up the design when he had scarcely entered on the expedition: Mr. Poe persevered, but did not succeed in reaching the scene of action; he proceeded, however, to St. Petersburgh, where, through deficiency of passport, he became involved in serious difficulties, from which he was finally extricated by the American Consul. He returned to America, only in time to learn of the severe illness of Mrs. Allan, who, in character, was the reverse of her husband, and whom he sincerely loved. He reached Richmond on the night after her burial.

Mr. Allan's house now became doubly displeasing to him; deprived of her who had, in all cases, endeavored to make it a happy home. Mr. Allan's manners, however, had become somewhat softened, and he professed, if he did not feel, an entire reconciliation. Mr. Poe now resolved to enter the

West Point Academy, and, as his application was backed by Chief Justice
Marshall, Andrew Stevenson, Gen. Scott, and many other gentlemen of the
highest distinction, to say nothing of Mr. Allan, he found no difficulty in
obtaining a letter of appointment. At West Point his stay was brief. At first
he was delighted with everything, busied himself in study, and "headed"
every class; but after the lapse of some ten months, he heard of Mr. Allan's
marriage with Miss Patterson, of Richmond, a lady young enough to be his
granddaughter. She was a relative of Gen. Scott's, and lived at Belleville,
the residence of Mrs. Mayo, the General's mother-in-law. Upon the birth of
the first child, Mr. Poe made up his mind that the heirship was at an end,
and as he considered the army no place for a poor man, he determined to
resign. At West Point it is necessary, in order to achieve such a step, to obtain permission from the parent or guardian. For this permission he wrote
to Mr. Allan, who flatly refused it; this refusal Mr. Poe represented to Col.
Thayer, the Superintendent of the post, who declined interfering with the
rules, or to accept the resignation. It was about this period that Poland
made the desperate and unfortunate struggle for independence, against the
combined powers of Russia, Austria and Prussia, which terminated in the
capitulation of Warsaw, and the annihilation of the kingdom.—All our cadet's former chivalric ardor had now returned, and with tenfold vigor. He
burned to be a participant in the affray. But to do this, it was doubly necessary to leave West Point. There was one resource yet left him: he positively
refused to do duty of any kind, disobeyed all orders, and, keeping closely
to his quarters, amused himself with his old tricks—caricaturing, and Pas-
quinading the Professors. There was a gentleman named Joseph Locke,
who had made himself especially obnoxious, through his pertinacity in
reporting the pranks of the cadets. At West Point, a "report" is no every
day matter, but a very serious thing. Each "report" counts a certain number against the offender—is charged to his account—and, when the whole
exceeds a stated sum, he is liable to dismissal. Mr. Poe, it appears, wrote a
long lampoon against this Mr. Locke, of which the following are the only
stanzas preserved: [text of "As for Locke, he is all in my eye" follows].

The result of all this was just what he intended. For some time Colonel
Thayer, to whose good offices the young cadet had been personally recommended by General Scott, overlooked these misdemeanors. But at length,
the matter becoming too serious, charges were instituted against him for
"Neglect of duty, and disobedience of orders;" (nothing was said about the

lampoons) and he was tried by a Court Martial. There were specifications innumerable, to all of which, by way of saving time, he pleaded "guilty," although some of them were monstrously absurd. In a word he was cashiered *nem. con.* and went on his way rejoicing.

But not to Poland. The capitulation had been effected, and that unfortunate country was no more. He repaired to Baltimore where, shortly afterwards, he learned of the death of Mr. Allan, who had left him nothing. His widow even refused him possession of his library—a valuable one. To be sure, he never treated this lady with a whit more respect than that to which he thought her, as a woman, entitled.

A circumstance now occurred of great moment as regards Mr. Poe's subsequent literary career. "The Baltimore Visiter," a weekly paper, edited by a Mr. John Hewitt, or Hewlett, offered a premium for the best prose tale; also one for the best poem. This system of premium offering was not then as now. The Committee, in this case, were men of the highest literary, as well as social respectability, if not of profound talents—John P. Kennedy, author of "Horse Shoe Robinson," J. H. B. Latrobe, and Dr. James H. Miller. To neither of these gentlemen was Mr. P. at that time, personally or by reputation known. He offered a poem, ("The Coliseum," published in Mr. Griswold's book) and six tales. These articles, with Mr. P's name prefixed, were written in a remarkably neat and peculiar manuscript, bearing a close resemblance to brevier type, and, the name being entirely new to the committee, it was thought that some person who could merely *write* and punctuate well, had been attempting an imposition—in short that the articles were copies from some of the foreign magazines—so little did their spirit resemble the usual character of American compositions. Nevertheless, *both* premiums were awarded to the unknown writer, (although, among the competitors were many of the most celebrated names in our literature,) and the committee took occasion to pay him some extraordinary compliments, over their own signatures, in the "Visiter."

They said, among other things, that *all* the tales offered by him, were far *better than the best* offered by others, adding that they "thought it a duty to call public attention to them in that marked manner, since they possessed a singular force and beauty, and were eminently distinguished by a wild, vigorous and poetical imagination, a rich style, a fertile invention, and varied and curious learning."

Shortly after this, Mr. Poe was invited by Mr. White to edit the "Southern Literary Messenger" which was then in its seventh month, with about four hundred subscribers. He remained with this journal until the end of its second year, by which time its circulation had increased to between three and four thousand; which latter number, it is believed, the Magazine never afterwards exceeded—if it did not immediately and permanently decrease upon Mr. P's secession. The success of the "Messenger" has been on all hands justly attributed to his exertion in its behalf, but, especially, to the skill, honesty and audacity of the criticism under the editorial head. The review of "Norman Leslie" may be said to have introduced a new era in our critical literature. The article afforded even a ludicrous contrast to the mere *glorifications* which had heralded and attended that miserable abortion. It was followed up, continuously, by others of the same force and character. Of the review of "Drake and Halleck" Mr. J. K. Paulding says, in a letter now upon our table, "I think it one of the finest pieces of criticism ever published in this country." None of these articles, however, were comparable, either in severity, or analytical ability, to many of those which subsequently established, (during Mr. Poe's brief connection with that journal) the character of "Graham's Magazine."

About this period was commenced "The New York Quarterly Review," by Professors Anthon and Henry, with Dr. Hawks. Receiving a flattering invitation from its proprietors, Mr. P. was induced to abandon "The Messenger" (in which he had no pecuniary interest) and remove to New York. Dr. Hawks says:—"I wish you to fall in with your *broad-axe* amidst this miserable literary trash which surrounds us. I believe you have the will, and I know well you have the ability." This Review, however, has since deceased: perhaps the old adage about "too many cooks" had something to do with its decline. There was assuredly no lack of talent or learning, whatever there might have been of independence, in its conductors. The long article on "Stephens' Travels in Arabia Petrea," which attracted so much attention in the "New York Review," some years ago, and in which the traveller's misconceptions of the biblical prophecies were exposed, as well as some important mistranslations in Ezekiel and Isaiah, was the composition of Mr. Poe.

At the end of a year, the subject of our memoir removed to Philadelphia, where he has since constantly resided. He here formed an association, not altogether satisfactory to himself, with the proprietor of the "Gentleman's Magazine," the journal which was subsequently merged in "Graham's." With Mr. Graham, (with whom he has always maintained the most friendly

[28]

relations,) he remained as critical editor, for a period of some fourteen or fifteen months; but is not to be considered responsible, (as some have held him) either for the external appearance or the general internal character of that periodical.

It has often been a subject for wonder that with the prëeminent success which has attended his editorial efforts, Mr. Poe has never established a magazine, in which he should have more than a collateral interest, and we are now happy to learn that such is, at length, his intention. By reference to another page of our paper, it will be seen that he has issued the prospectus of a Monthly, to be entitled "THE STYLUS," for which, it is needless to say, we predict the most unequivocal success. In so saying, we but endorse the opinion of every literary man in the country, and fully agree with Fitz Greene Halleck, that, however eminent may be the contributors engaged, it is, after all, "on his own fine taste, sound judgment, and great general ability for the task, that the public will place the firmest reliance."

We have already spoken of Mr. Poe as a critic and, on this head, it is unnecessary to say more. His analytical reputation is universal.

"As a critic," says the St. Louis Bulletin, [and so say we] "notwithstanding the dignity of the two Quarterlies, we have ranked him *first*. If various and general powers on almost every subject, combined with an acumen that seems intuitive, and which shrinks from no responsibility, deserve success, then will he be successful." But as imagination is a loftier faculty than mere taste or judgment, so it is upon his tales, perhaps, that, in the end, his reputation will mainly depend. In 1840 Messrs. Lea & Blanchard published his "Tales of the Grotesque and Arabesque," a work which elicited encomiums of the most extraordinary character, from the greatest variety of the highest sources. Indeed, to append here only a few of these commendations, will be the best comment we can possibly make, upon the merits and reputation of the author. We glean some of them from the late magazines and papers now lying before us, and some from the Publisher's appendix affixed, by Messrs, [*sic*] Lea and Blanchard to the volumes themselves. It will be seen that our extracts are totally distinct from the common newspaper *puff*, and are of such nature that Mr. Poe's bitterest enemy, (if he have *one* in the world) will find it impossible to question or gainsay them—since they embody the already published, personal, and not merely editorial or anonymous opinions, of almost every *noted literary man in America*.

Of "William Wilson," MR. WASHINGTON IRVING says:—"It is managed in a highly picturesque style, and its singular and mysterious interest is ably sustained throughout. In point of mere style, it is, perhaps, even superior to 'House of Usher.' It is simpler. In the latter composition, he seems to have been distrustful of his effects, or, rather, too solicitous of bringing them forth fully to the eye, and thus, perhaps, has laid on too much coloring. He has erred, however, on the safe side, that of exuberance, and the evil side might easily be remedied, by relieving the style of some of its epithets" [since done.] "There would be no fear of injuring the graphic effect, *which is powerful.*" The italics are Mr. Irving's own.

Judge BEVERLY TUCKER, author of "George Balcombe," says:—"Mr. Poe possesses an extraordinary faculty. He paints the 'palpable obscure' with strange power; throwing over his pictures a sombre gloom which is *appalling.* The images are dim, but distinct—shadowy, but well defined. The outline, indeed, is all we see; but there they stand, shrouded in darkness, and fright us with the mystery which defies farther scrutiny. . . . Original thoughts come to him thronging unbidden; *crowding* themselves upon him in such numbers, as to require the rod of his own Master of Ceremonies, *Criticism,* to keep them in order. . . . His genius and history remind me of Coleridge."

Mr. JAMES E. HEATH, the original editor of the "Messenger," says:— "There can be but one opinion in regard to the force and beauty of his style. . . . A gentleman of fine endowments, possessing a taste classical and refined, an imagination affluent and splendid, and withal a singular capacity for minute and mathematical detail. . . . Morella will unquestionably prove that he has great powers of imagination, and a command of language never surpassed. We doubt if anything in the same style can be cited, which contains more terrific beauty than this tale."

Professor H. W. LONGFELLOW says:—"All that I have seen from his pen inspires me with a high idea of his power, and I think him destined to stand among the first of romance writers—if such, indeed, be his aim."

Mr. NATHANIEL HAWTHORNE, author of "Twice Told Tales," says:— "Mr. Poe gained ready admission [into the Hall of Fantasy] on account of his imagination, but was threatened with ejection as belonging to the obnoxious class of critics."

Mr. N. P. WILLIS says:—"Mr. Poe's contribution, 'The Tell-Tale Heart' is very wild and very readable, and is the only thing in the number which most people would read and remember.— . . . In 'Ligeia' there is a fine march of description which has a touch of the D'Israeli quality."

The opinion of Mr. FITZ-GREENE HALLECK, we have already quoted, and that of Mr. JOHN NEAL we will quote elsewhere.

Mr. JAMES RUSSELL LOWELL says:—"This species of *physical* remorse is strikingly depicted in Mr. Thomas Hood's 'Dream of Eugene Aram,' and with no less strength by the powerful imagination of Mr. Poe, in his story of 'The Tell-Tale Heart'."

"Mr. L. F. TASISTRO says:—"There is not one of the Tales published in the volumes before us, in which we do not find the development of great intellectual capacity, with a power for vivid description, an opulence of imagination, a fecundity of invention, and a command over the elegances of diction, which have seldom been displayed, even by writers who have acquired the greatest distinction in the Republic of Letters. . . . A succession of richly colored pictures in the magic lantern of invention."

Mr. FREDERICK W. THOMAS, author of "Clinton Bradshaw," says:—"I think 'The Murders in the Rue Morgue,' the most ingenious thing of the kind on record. It is managed with a tact, ability, and subtlety that are absolutely *marvellous*. I do not know what to make of his intellectuals."

Mr. PARK BENJAMIN says:—"We have always been admirers of Mr. Poe's talents. Under his supervision the 'Southern Literary Messenger' acquired its high character. His productions display great power and originality, and bear the stamp of a thoroughly educated mind. In a recent number of this Magazine (Graham's), there appeared a narrative which we intend to copy, on account of its philosophical spirit, and extraordinary interest, entitled 'The Murders of [*sic*] the Rue Morgue'. . . . We regard this gentleman as one of the best writers of the English language now living. His style is singularly pure and idiomatic. He never condescends to affectations but writes with a nervous clearness that inspires the reader with a perpetual confidence in his power."

Mr. M. M. NOAH says:—" 'Bon-Bon,' by Edgar A. Poe, is equal to anything Theodore Hook ever wrote. . . . 'The House of Usher' would have been considered a *chef-d'-oeuvre*, even if it had appeared in the pages of Blackwood."

Mrs. SIGOURNEY says:—"That powerful pen whose brilliant and versatile creations I have so often admired."

Mr. EPES SARGENT, author of "Velasco," says:—"I have always been an ardent admirer of his varied and surpassing talents."

Mr. W. G. SIMMS has paid him some very high compliments in "The Magnolia," which we are now unable to obtain.

Mr. JOHN P. KENNEDY, author of "Horse-Shoe Robinson," says:—"These tales are eminently distinguished by a wild, vigorous, and poetical imagination, a fertile invention, a rich style, and varied and curious learning."

Mr. JOHN L. CAREY, of the "Baltimore American," says:—"The impress of genius is stamped upon them all. . . . Without particularising others, we will observe, of the story called 'William Wilson,' that it embodies a profounder meaning than will be gathered from regarding it as a purely fanciful invention."

Mr. G. G. FOSTER, of the "St. Louis Bulletin," says:—"He is one of the very few writers who blend philosophy, common sense, humor, and poetry smoothly together. He places his hands upon the wild steeds of his imagination, and they plunge furiously through storm and tempest, or, at his bidding, glide noiselessly along the quiet and dreamy lake, or among the whispering bowers of thought and feeling. . . . With an acuteness of observation, a vigorous and effective style, and an independence that defies control, he unites a fervid fancy, and a most beautiful enthusiasm. His is a high destiny."

The "BALTIMORE METHODIST" says:—"Mr. Poe is a gentleman of the finest abilities. For freshness of thought, vigor of imagination, and force of description, he stands *alone* among the Magazine writers of the age. This is saying a great deal for him, but it is no more than all are willing to award."

The "N.Y. TIMES AND STAR" says:—"Mr. Poe, in our opinion, is the most truly original writer we have in America."

The "NORFOLK HERALD" says:—"The author of the 'Lunar Hoax,' is indebted to the 'Hans Pfaall' of Mr. Poe, for the conception, and, in a great measure, for the execution of his discoveries."

Mr. GEORGE H. CALVERT, of the "Baltimore American," says:—" 'The Duc de L'Omelette,' is one of those light, spirited, and fantastic inventions, of which we have had specimens before in the 'Messenger,' betokening a fertility of imagination, and power of execution, that would under sustained effort, produce creations of enduring character."

The "N.Y. COURIER AND ENQUIRER" says:—"Mr. Poe is one of those original philosophical writers, of whom we have so few in America, and his articles always produce a deep and thrilling interest."

The "SOUTHERN LITERARY MESSENGER," says:—"The production of a talented and powerful writer . . . The possession of high powers of invention and imagination—of genius is undoubtedly his—His compositions are, many of them, in Literature, like Martin's in the Fine Arts. His serious sketches all bear the marks of bold, fertile genius. There is the dark cloud hanging over all—there are the dim, misty, undefined shapes in the back-ground. But, amid all these, arise huge and magnificent columns, flashing lamps, rich banquetting vessels, gleaming tiaras, and sweet, expressive faces. But the writings of Mr. Poe are well-known to the readers of the Messenger."

Mr. H. HAINES, of the "Petersburg Constellation," says:—"Of the diamonds which sparkle beside the more sombre gems, commend us, thou Spirit of Eccentricity, forever and a day, to the 'Duc de L'Omelette,' the best of the kind we have ever read, or expect to read."

Mr. HORACE GREELEY, of the "N. Y. Tribune," says of "The Tell-Tale Heart,"—"Mr. Poe contributes a strong and skilful, but in our minds, over-strained and repulsive analysis of the feelings and promptings of an insane homicide. The painting of the terror of the victim, while he sat upright in his bed, feeling that death was near him, is most powerful and fearfully vivid."

Coming to our own city, Mr. JOSEPH C. NEAL says:—"A writer who adds to the most extensive acquirements, a remarkable vigor and originality of mind . . . These 'grotesque and arabesque' delineations are full of variety—now irresistibly quaint and droll, and again marked with all the deep and painful interest of the German school. In every page the reader will note matter unlike the production of any other writer. He follows in nobody's track. His imagination seems to have a domain of its own to revel in."

Mr. MORTON MCMICHAEL says:—"Mr. Poe is a writer of rare and various abilities. He possesses a fine perception of the ludicrous, and his humorous stories are instinct with the principle of mirth. He possesses, also, a mind of unusual grasp, a vigorous power of analysis, and an acuteness of perception which have given him high celebrity as a critic. These same faculties, moreover, aided by an unusually active imagination, and directed by familiar study of metaphysical writings, have led him to produce some of the most vivid scenes of the wild and wonderful which can be found in English literature."

Professor JOHN FROST says:—"'William Wilson,' by Mr. Poe, reminds us of Godwin and Brockden Brown. . . . We must say that we derive no small enjoyment from a delineation like this. We like to see the evidences of study and thought, as well as of inspiration, in the design, and of careful and elaborate handling in the execution, not less than of grand and striking effect in the *tout ensemble*. 'The Fall of the House of Usher' is what we denominate a stern and sombre, but at the same time, a noble and imposing picture, such as could be drawn only by a master-hand.—Such things are not produced by your slip-shod amateurs in composition." And again:

"To say we have read these tales attentively, is not enough. We have *studied* them. They are, in every way, worthy of such distinction, and whoever shall give them a careful study and a philosophical analysis, will find in them the evidences of an original, vigorous and independent mind, stored with rich and various learning, and capable of successful application to a great variety of subjects. As a writer of fiction, Mr. Poe passes 'from grave to gay, from lively to severe,' with an ease and buoyance not less wonderful than the unfailing vigor of his style, and the *prodigious* extent of his resources for illustration and embellishment. He is capable of great things, and beautiful and interesting as the Tales before us are, we deem them much less remarkable as actual performances, than as evidences of ability for more serious and sustained efforts. They seem to us the playful effusions of a remarkable—of a powerful intellect. He has placed himself in the foremost rank of American writers."

Mr. P. P. COOKE, author of "Florence Vane," and one of the finest critics in America, says:—"In the first place I must say, what I firmly believe, that his mere *style* is the *very best among the first of the living writers*; and I regard style as something more than the mere manners of communicating ideas. 'Words are used by the wise as counters, by the foolish as coin,' is the aphorism of a person who never appreciated Jeremy Taylor or Sir Thomas Browne. . . . He does not, to be sure, use his words, as those fine old glowing rhetoricians did, as tints of the pencil—as colors of a picture—but he moulds them into exquisitely artful excellence; a care which is pleasantly perceptible, and accomplishing an effect which I can only characterize as the visible presentation, instead of the mere expression, of his ideas. . . . I consider the *skill* of one portion of 'Eiros and Charmion' *unapproachable*. 'Tales of the Grotesque and Arabesque' expresses admirably the character of his wild stories, and *as* tales of the grotesque and arabesque, they have certainly never been equalled."

In conclusion, (it is absolutely necessary to bring these extracts to a close,) Mr. JAMES K. PAULDING says:—"'Lionizing,' by Edgar A. Poe, is the happiest travestie of the coxcombical egotism of travelling scribblers, I have ever seen . . . *Mr. Poe is decidedly the best of all our young writers, and I don't know but that I may say of all our old ones.*"

[34]

To which Professor CHARLES ANTHON pointedly adds— "*facile princeps.*"

We have only to remark here, that *all the best* of Mr. Poe's Prose Tales have been published *since* the issue of the volumes which elicited these extraordinary comments, and a thousand of similar character from men of less note, or purely editorial. A complete collection of his Tales is a *desideratum* in our Literature.

But notwithstanding his success as a prose writer, it is as a poet we now wish chiefly to consider him. He wrote verses as soon as he could write at all. His most poetical publication, however, was "Al Aaraaf, Tamerlane, and Minor Poems. By a Virginian." Of this, the first edition was published in pamphlet form in Boston, before he had completed his fifteenth year. Some of his best pieces, among others the subjoined lines to Helen, were composed two years previously [text of "To Helen" follows].

These lines, by a boy of fourteen, will compare favorably with any written, at any age, *by any poet whatsoever.*

A second edition of the volume was published in Baltimore, by Hatch and Dunning, we believe in 1827; a third during the author's cadetship at West Point. Of these editions, the two first attracted but little attention, on account of their slovenly printing and their modes of publication—John Neal, however, whose judgment will not be disputed, said of them that "they put him in mind of no less a poet than Shelley." The critic quoted from "Al Aaraaf," in support of his opinion the following [text of "Spirit's Invocation" follows].

This we conceive to be a truly wonderful poem to have emanated from the pen of a boy of fourteen. Ligeia, (a Greek word signifying canorous, or high-sounding,) is intended as a personification of Music, and the picture, which we have italicised, of the Spirit soaring, is surpassed by no American poet. From "Al Aaraaf!" we select only three more passages; and they might be quoted as gems even from Keats [texts of "Ours Is a World of Words" and "Sonnet—To Science" follow].

In speaking of this sonnet and the preceding extracts, John Neal says: "And again the old-fashioned truth and strength of the following!—Of a truth, we ought to overlook much in one capable of so much simplicity and power." Elsewhere in the same review, he says: "If the young author now before us should fulfil his destiny, as they would say on the other side of the water, he will be *foremost* in the rank of *real* poets." [The italics are Mr. Neal's.] Speaking of "Tamerlane," from which we have foreborne to quote, he says: "As a whole, it is much the best; for there is breadth and depth in it, a certainty of purpose, and a loftiness of look, throughout, which are wanting in 'Al Aaraaf,' *wonderful* as some of the passages of the latter are." Again, "But the grandest and sweetest of all is the following," which we quote, with his own Italics [text of "Romance" follows].

In closing this review, Mr. Neal makes this remarkable prophecy:—"Our author, if he be just to his peculiar gift, (for it *is* a gift here,) will be distinguished among the *most* distinguished."

The last which we shall quote of the "Minor Poems," is one in which the *skill* of the composition, when the age of the writer is considered, is by no means its least remarkable feature [text of "To the River—" follows].

In leaving these to note the poems of his maturer years, we are wonderstruck not more at the genius of the poet, than at his poetical reputation. We can only say that, in our opinion, and in every one's, he *has* fulfilled his destiny, and Mr. Neal's prediction. With the true intellect of the land, Mr. Poe stands among the first—*if not the first*. As a critic, and a tale-writer, he is *certainly* unequalled in America. As a poet, the following poems (which he has not even taken the trouble to collect) exhibit him second to none; not even excepting Mr. Longfellow [texts of "The Conqueror Worm," "Lenore," "Sonnet—To Zante," "The Sleeper," "To One in Paradise," "Sonnet—Silence," "Israfel," "Song of the Newly-Wedded," "To One Departed," "The Coliseum," and "The Haunted Palace" follow].

As an essayist, Mr. Poe has been equally successful. His most noted compositions, in this way, are a treatise on Maelzel's Automaton, published in the "Southern Literary Messenger," in which, by an ingenious train of reasoning *à priori*, he proves it *not* a pure machine; the "Philosophy of Furniture;" "A New Theory of English Versification;" several most remarkable papers on "Secret Writing;" and the celebrated "Chapters on Autography," published in the "Messenger" and in "Graham's."

The circumstances connected with the papers on secret writing, are of too extraordinary a nature, and have too obvious a bearing upon Mr. Poe's reputation for *analysis*, to be omitted in a biography like this. In a work entitled "Sketches of conspicuous living characters of France," by Mr. Robert Walsh, Jr., Berryer, the French minister, is said to have displayed the highest ingenuity in the solution of a cipher addressed by the Duchess de Berri, to the legitimists of Paris, but of which she had neglected to furnish the key. Berryer discovered this key to be the phrase—*"Le Gou-*

vernement Provisoire," and the work in question extolled the acumen of the decipherer—. In a review of the book, Mr. Poe maintained not only that he could unriddle any similar secret, but that "human ingenuity could construct *no* secret writing which human ingenuity could not resolve." The challenge elicited a flood of cryptographs *which were promptly and without exception deciphered*—of course to the profound astonishment of the writers—not one of whom, perhaps, would have hesitated to staking his existence that his secret was absolutely insoluble without the key.

For many months the pages of "Graham" contained these cryptographs, with the editor's solutions. In order to convey an intelligible idea of the task undertaken, we append one of the least difficult of the ciphers solved with the correspondence which accompanied it. "F. W. Thomas" is the author of the "Clinton Bradshaw," and the cryptograph in question was solved *by return of mail.*

MY DEAR SIR:—The enclosed cryptograph is from a friend of mine (Dr. Frailey) who thinks he can puzzle you. If you decipher it, then you are a magician, for he has used, as I think, the greatest art in making it.

Your friend,
F. W. Thomas

> £ 7i A itagi niinbiiit thitvuiaib9g h auehbiif b ivgiht itau 🐦 gvuiitiif 4 t$btzihtbo £iiiiadb9 iignit£d iz ta5ta whbo ttbibtiii†it9 A iti if X hti 4 ithtt 🐦 i‡ bnniathubii iSt b eaovuhoSu vtt7diboif * iti nihd6Xht na3ig an choo$ht u‡tnvotigg2 iibtvo$if b Eaovu£avg iinoht$h7 niau iti vtheiigbo iit6 A itagi t7iitig h fifvti iti gvugidviti bubodbub9 A tiiiaditiavg nbttg iStavi fvuhiiu £thnhiti niiiit8 † bni 4 iiiu£$i ht d£bo evodbiSa ‡ nbiivihiti uavtib£g ibei—it dbuvo$if ia niafvti uvgtvnvobi buai9g uii iti £giSv9 iz gvuiiti A uu iiubisg ibg tai—it iStavi tbvgi iti itiui A iz intiuiiibo taovutg an dvaihfh¶ iavitbog ¶f a ititvghbgight ittauh$h7g ht t7eiigb9bo £iiitavigi.

Washington, July 6th, 1841

MY DEAR SIR,

This morning I received yours of yesterday, deciphering the "cryptograph" of my friend, Doctor Frailey. You requested that I would obtain the Dr's. acknowledgment of your solution. I have just received the enclosed from him.

Doctor Frailey had heard me speak of your having deciphered a letter which our mutual friend, Dow, wrote upon a challenge from you last year, at my lodgings in your city, when Aaron Burr's correspondence in cipher was the subject of our conversation. You laughed at what you termed Burr's shallow artifice, and said you could decipher any such cryptography easily. To test you on the spot, Dow withdrew to the corner of the room, and wrote a letter in cipher, which you solved in a much shorter time than it took him to indite it.

As Doctor Frailey seemed to doubt your skill to the extent of my belief in it, when your article on "Secret Writing" appeared in the last number of your Magazine, I showed it to him. After reading it, he remarked that he thought he could puzzle you, and the next day he handed me the cryptograph which I transmitted to you. He did not tell me the key. The uncommon nature of his article of which I gave you not the slightest hint, made me express to you my strong doubts of your ability to read it. I confess that your solution, so speedily and correctly made, surprised me. I congratulate myself that I do not live in an age when the black art is believed in, for, innocent as I am of all knowledge of cryptography, I should be arrested as an accessory before the fact, and though I escaped, it is certain that you would have to die that death, and alas! I fear upon my testimony.

Your friend,

F. W. THOMAS

Edgar A. Poe, Esq.
WASHINGTON, July 6, 1841

DEAR SIR,

It gives me pleasure to state, that the reading by Mr. Poe, of the cryptograph which I gave you a few days since for transmission to him is correct.

I am the more astonished at this, since for various words of two, three and four letters, a distinct character was used for each, in order to prevent the discovery of some of those words, by their repetition in a cryptograph of any length and applying them to other words. I also used a distinct character for the terminations *tion* and *sion*, and substituted in every word where it was possible, some of the characters above alluded to. Where the same word of two of those letters occurred frequently, the letters of the key phrase and the characters were alternately used, to increase the difficulty.

As ever, yours, & c.

CHAS. S. FRAILEY

TO F. W. THOMAS, ESQ.

The key phrase employed by Dr. Frailey in the construction of this cipher, was—"But find this out and I give it up." Under this the alphabet was written, letter beneath letter. In this way, it will be found that many of the secret characters represent not one, but *several* of the natural alphabet. For example, *n*, in the cipher, stands either for *b* or *m* or *y*, and the decipherer is left to guess when it means the one and when the other. The question is, how could he ever ascertain that it meant *either*? Again, t stands for either c, h, n, or x, while i represents e, j, t, r, and w. When we consider these difficulties, with the other embarrassments mentioned in the letter (arbitrary marks used for *whole words!*) and when we consider, also, the nonsensical nature of the meaning concealed, which we give below, we can regard the solution (*by return of mail, too!*) as little less than miraculous.

In one of those peripatetic circumrotations I obviated a rustic whom I subjected to catechetical interrogation respecting the nosocomical characteristics of the edifice to which I was approximate.—With a volubility uncongealed by the frigorific powers of villatic bashfulness, he ejaculated a voluminous replication from the universal tenor of whose contents I deduce the subsequent amalgamation of heterogeneous facts. Without dubiety incipient pretension is apt to terminate in final vulgarity, as parturient mountains have been fabulated to produce muscupular abortions. The institution the subject of my remarks, has not been without cause the theme of the ephemeral columns of quotidian journals, and enthusiastic encomiations in conversational intercourse.

Before the publication of Mr. P's solution, reward was offered for the deciphering of the riddle. It stood in the Magazine for several months, and met the eyes of more than 100,000 readers—but was solved by none.

This cryptograph, however, was simplicity itself, in comparison with others resolved by the subject of our memoir.

Besides the works mentioned, he is the author of "Arthur Gordon Pym," published anonymously by the Harpers—a book which ran through many English editions;—a System of Conchology, very successful, with his own name;—a large and expensively illustrated work on Natural History, in part a translation, and in part a re-arrangement of the French system of Milne Edouarde, and Achille Lecompte;—also, a work of fiction, in two volumes, under a *nom-de-plume*, never acknowledged;—also, two papers on American topics, for a Parisian critical journal—with one or two anonymous articles in a British periodical, and several also anonymous, in an American Quarterly.

In his youth, Mr. Poe was noted for gymnastic feats, to an extent almost beyond the credible; and it is believed, that, to this day, he remembers such achievements with greater pride, than any subsequent mental triumphs. At one period he was known to leap the distance of twenty-one feet, six inches, on a dead level, with a run of twenty yards. A most remarkable swim of his, is, also, on record in the columns of the "Richmond Enquirer," and other Richmond papers. It took place in his fifteenth year. He swam on a hot July day, against a three-knot tide, from Ludlam's wharf, on James River, to Warwick—a distance of seven miles and a half—fully equal to thirty miles in still water. The impossibility of resting, even for a moment, by floating, in a task such as this, renders it Herculean, and the feat has never been equalled by anyone, properly authenticated. Byron's paddle across the Hellespont, was mere child's play in comparison, and, indeed, would never have been thought worthy of mention, by any true swimmer, or by any other than a lord and a dandy. Mr. Poe's swim was undertaken for a wager, at first sportively, and then seriously urged. No one had the faintest idea that he would make good his boast. He was accompanied, in boats, by a number of gentlemen, then youths, of Richmond. Among the survivors of the party, are Dr. Robert H. Cabell and Messrs.: Robert Saunders and Robert Stannard, Jr.—all gentlemen of the highest respectability, and even of distinction, now residing in Richmond. They relate that, upon reaching the goal at Warwick, Mr. P., before getting out of the water, offered to double the wager that he would *swim back to the point of starting*, but that, owing to the extreme exhaustion of the rowers, the experiment was, of necessity, declined.

In 1836, Mr. Poe married Virginia, youngest daughter of Mr. William Clemm, of Baltimore, and, through her, is closely connected with many of the best families in Maryland.

He is now but little more than thirty years of age; in person, he is somewhat slender, about five feet, eight inches, in height, and well-proportioned; his complexion is rather fair; his eyes are grey and restless, exhibiting a marked nervousness: while the mouth indicates great decision of character; his forehead is extremely broad, displaying prominently the organs of Ideality, Causalty, Form, Constructiveness, and Comparison, with small Eventuality and Individuality. His hair is nearly black, and partially curling. Our portrait conveys a tolerably correct idea of the man.

From "Poets and Poetry of Philadelphia. Number II. Edgar Allan Poe." *Philadelphia Saturday Museum*, 4 March 1843: 1 (reprinted from the 26 February issue, which seems to be no longer extant).

"Mr. Poe's Lecture" (1843)

GEORGE LIPPARD

In late 1843 Poe turned lecturer, perhaps following the example of his friend, Frederick W. Thomas, who spoke about eloquence to a Baltimore audience, to supplement his meager income. Poe's first lectures were delivered in Delaware and Philadelphia. The only report of the Delaware event—Philadelphia *Spirit of the Times*, 6 January 1844 (p. 1)—which took place in November 1843, is that Poe's comments on American poetry were "good, but rather severe." Poe went on to lecture, most notably on topics of poetry and poetics, during the next half-dozen years. The best known of these public appearances is probably the one at the Boston Lyceum in late 1845, along with those in Richmond and Norfolk not long before his death. The Boston Lyceum event—at which Poe, intoxicated, delivered remarks on poetry, then read "Al Aaraaf," instead of the original poem requested for this event; and which earned Poe great disapprobation from most quarters—may today be the best known among these appearances because of coverage devoted to it in *Poe's Literary Battles*, by Sidney P. Moss (1963). In the wake of Poe's performance at the Boston Lyceum, many area newspapers featured deprecatory accounts. Evaluations of the last lectures, in Virginia, tended to be more supportive. George Lippard's review of Poe's Philadelphia lecture, a portion of which follows here, implicitly supplies cause for Griswold's later vilification of Poe.

THE SUBJECT, "American Poetry," was handled in a manner, that placed all the pseudo-critics, the Rev. Mr. Rufus Griswold, Esq. among others, to the blush, and showed the audience, how a man born a poet, could describe the true nature and object, as well as the principles of poetry. The sentences of the Lecturer were vigorous, energetic and impassioned, his criticism scathingly severe in some cases, and deservedly eulogistic in others. Ex-Judge Conrad, received a merited compliment from Mr. Poe, who recited the whole of his version of the Lord's Prayer, and Mr. Morris of the Inquirer, was noticed with cordial approbation. As a general thing, the Lecture was received with the most enthusiastic demonstrations of applause, and it was agreed by all, that it was second to none, if not all lectures ever delivered before the Wirt institute.

From George Lippard, "Mr. Poe's Lecture," *Citizen Soldier* [Philadelphia], 29 November 1843: 316.

"For the *Delaware State Journal*" (1844)

ACADEMICUS

> Poe lectured again, on 23 December 1843, to an audience at the Newark
> Academy, Delaware, which event was detailed at length by "Academicus,"
> whose identity remains uncertain.

. . . THE LECTURE WAS an eloquent production eloquently delivered by Edgar A. Poe. . . . His theme was the *"Poetry of America"*—itself a topic particularly appropriate to one who has himself acquitted so honorable a place among the Poets of the land, and who has proven himself to possess in no small degree the high qualifications he demands in his brethren of the inspired pen. Mr. Poe is also well known as a fearless and perhaps somewhat severe *critic* of American Poesy and has not unfrequently brought down upon himself the wrath of many of the "genus irritable." His right however to speak freely is one which by his own writings he has *earned*, and holds by the acknowledged law of Parnassus:

"Let such teach others who themselves excel
And *censure freely* who have written well."

It is perfectly impossible to convey to a reader from the fragments preserved by not very faithful memory, any worthy impression of the rich tide of thought and imagery with which our Lecturer charmed his audience for almost *two* hours. . . . My design is more humble and will aim only to give to your readers a general sketch of the outlines of the discourse, with, however, the privilege reserved of enlarging a little upon some of its more interesting and prominent points.

After a graceful exordium and prospective apology for the foreseen necessary length of remarks designed to cover so wide a field, our Lecturer approached the body of his theme. The proper criterion by which we may safely judge of the present state of the poetic art in America and of the comparative excellence of the productions of our different bards first occupied his attention. In this part of the subject the system of *puffery* at present common with our newspapers, magazines, and even dignified reviews was most clearly and indignantly exposed and condemned. Editors of newspapers building up large Libraries for which they pay by wholesale and indiscriminate puffs of works whose title pages they have hardly had time to copy.—Authors reviewing and praising their own writings, or securing the bespoken praises of a friend—booksellers and publishers promoting the sale of their goods by measures equally corrupt, all received their full share of severe rebuke. The severities as well as the flatteries of the critical press were shown in many instances to spring from personal feelings and interests and the general proposition was well maintained, *that the criticism of the American press, corrupt and venal as it has become, was not a fair mirror of the defects or of the excellences of American Poetry.* While on the subject of criticism our Lecturer was especially witty and sarcastic in reference to a peculiar style of reviewing not unknown in New England, 'yclept the "*Transcendental.*" The wonderful involutions and dislocations by which good English words were made to wrap up the fancies of their mis-users until the little sense that was intended was forever buried like the roman nymph, under the mass of its ornaments, were capitally parodied and exposed. In this connection also, the doctrine was advanced and by a very finely conducted argument enforced:—that the *prime office of criticism was to detect and correct what was faulty*, and not to point out or praise what was good.

After showing the incompetency of our criticism, as at present managed, to present a true picture of American Poetry, our Lecturer turned to an inspection of the works themselves of our poets—and especially to the several "*collections*" of American poetry which have successively appeared as *representing* the state of the art in our country. After a cursory examination and criticism of some five or six such "collections" in the order of their publication, the late compilation of Rev. Rufus W. Griswold, styled the "*Poets and Poetry of America*," was introduced—as the last and best— tho' by no means unobjectionable. This book and its author were handled by the critical Lecturer in not the most gentle manner. Many names had been inserted which Apollo would have refused and some (such as Morris and Conrad) left out, which the muses have acknowledged. The selections from those admitted have been made with a miserable want of judgment— the worst specimens being often chosen instead of the best,—and an extravagant proportion of space allotted to personal friends—altho' inferior poets—(as in the case of Mr. Hoffman)—while superior merit has been put off with a single page. After thus preparing the way, some eight or ten of our lady poets were introduced one by one and dismissed to their appropriate seats in the temple of Fame, after whom, came the *five* steel plate faces of Mr. Griswold's frontispiece, in their order—Dana, Bryant, Halleck, Sprague and Longfellow.

The whole was closed with a highly philosophical and eloquent discourse on the true end and province of poetry and condemnation of what the Lecturer was pleased to term *"didacticism"* of modern Poetry.

Such, Mr. Editor, is a brief sketch of one of the most interesting and instructive lectures I have ever had the pleasure of hearing. I have attempted but the merest skeleton,—for the life and beauty you must supply if you can, of Mr. Poe's ever ready and ever beautiful imagery, and glowing diction. It would afford me pleasure to devote an hour or two to a review of some of the topics presented in the Lecture. The doctrines of the *office of criticism*—and of the *End and Province of Poetry* are those upon which I would most like to dilate: but the time is not now. Perhaps I may sometime again, if an opportunity should offer, attempt to sustain an appeal from the decisions pronounced by our Lecturer on these two topics.

We have some hopes of having another Lecture from Mr. Poe on the first Friday of January. . . .

From Academicus, "For the Delaware State Journal." *Delaware State Journal*, 2 January 1844: 2.

"Lecture by Mr. Poe" (1844)

GEORGE LIPPARD

Poe lectured again in Philadelphia, and George Lippard's forecast of this event reveals Poe's growing prominence in several areas of the contemporary literary milieu. Lippard also places Poe as one whose work highlights causes of a genuinely national literature.

IT IS WITH sincere pleasure we perceive that the excellent lecture lately delivered before the Wm Wirt Institute by Edgar A. Poe, will be repeated this evening at the lecture Room of the Philadelphia Museum. The subject "American Poetry," was handled in the lecture, in an able, effective and original manner, calling forth the most enthusiastic demonstrations of applause from the audience. Mr. Poe is rapidly adding to his towering fame as Poet, Author, Critic, in this new capacity of lecturer; and all friends of a correct and healthy national literature hail with delight, the appearance of an able and eloquent advocate of the right and caustic censor of the wrong. We hope in a short time, to have it in our power to welcome the appearance of a sound Magazine, devoted to all the higher objects of American Literature, edited, owned and controlled by Mr. Poe, and do most heartily bid him "God-speed" in the cause.

George Lippard, "Lecture by Mr. Poe." *Citizen Soldier* [Philadelphia], January 1844: 18.

[Letter Detailing Life in New York City] (1844)

EDGAR A. POE

> This excerpt of Poe's letter to his mother-in-law, Maria Clemm, relating to the family's moving to New York City, offers glimpses into Poe's family life and the concern for money that continually worried that household. His itemizing the expenses incurred in travel from Philadelphia to New York, and for food provided at the boarding house to which he proposed to bring her, indicates how greatly money and food signified to those who often went on scanty rations. Virginia's frail health was an understandable concern for the family. (Poe never wrote the biographical sketch of James Russell Lowell that he mentions as "Lowell's article," though Lowell published one about Poe for *Graham's Magazine* in February 1845.)

Edgar A. Poe to Maria Clemm, 7 April 1844

My dear Muddy,—We have just this minute done breakfast, and I now sit down to write you about everything. I can't pay for the letter, because the P. O. won't be open to-day.—In the first place, we arrived safe at Walnut Street wharf. The driver wanted to make me pay a dollar, but I wouldn't. Then I had to pay a boy a levy to put the trunks in the baggage car. In the meantime I took Sis in the Depôt Hotel. It was only a quarter past 6, and we had to wait till 7. We saw the Ledger & Times—nothing in either—a few words of no account in the Chronicle.—We started in good spirits, but did not get here until nearly 3 o'clock. We went in the cars to Amboy about 40 miles from N. York, and then took the steamboat the rest of the way.— Sissy coughed none at all. When we got to the wharf it was raining hard. I left her on board the boat, after putting the trunks in the Ladies' Cabin, and set off to buy an umbrella and look for a boarding house. I met a man selling umbrellas and bought one for 62 cents. Then I went up Greenwood St. and soon found a boarding house. It is just before you get to Cedar St. on the West side going up the left hand side. It has brown stone steps with a porch with brown pillars. "Morrison" is the name on the door. I made a bargain in a few minutes and then got a hack and went for Sis. I was not gone more than ½ an hour, and she was quite astonished to see me back so soon. She didn't expect me for an hour. There were other ladies waiting on board—so she wasn't very lonely.—When we got to the house we had to wait about ½ an hour before the room was ready. The house is old and looks buggy. . . . Last night, for supper, we had the nicest tea you ever drank, strong & hot—wheat bread & rye bread—cheese—tea-cakes (elegant) a great dish (2 dishes) of elegant ham, and 2 of cold veal, piled up like a mountain and large slices—3 dishes of the cakes, and everything in the greatest profusion. No fear of starving here. The landlady seemed as if she couldn't press us enough, and we were at home directly. Her husband is living with her—a good-natured old soul. There are 8 to 10 boarders—2 or 3 of them ladies— 2 servants.—For breakfast we had excellent-flavored coffee, hot & strong— not very clear & no great deal of cream—veal cutlets, elegant ham & eggs & nice bread and butter. I never sat down to a more plentiful or nicer breakfast. I wish you could have seen the eggs—and the great dish of meat. I ate the first hearty breakfast I have eaten, since I left our little home. Sis is delighted, and we are both in excellent spirits. She is now busy mending my pants which I tore against a nail. I went out last night and bought a skein of silk, a skein of thread, 2 buttons, a pair of slippers & a tin pan for the stove. The fire kept in all night—We have now got $4 and a half left. Tomorrow I am going to try & borrow $3—so that I may have a fortnight to go upon. I feel in excellent spirits & haven't drunk a drop—so that I hope to get out of trouble. The very instant I scrape together enough money I will send it on. You can't imagine how much we both do miss you. Sissy had a hearty cry last night, because you and Catterina weren't here. We are resolved to get 2 rooms the first moment we can. In the meantime it is impossible we could be more comfortable or more at home than we are. It looks as if it was going to clear up now.—Be sure and go to the P. O. & have my letters forwarded. As soon as I write Lowell's article, I will send it to you & get you the money from Graham. . . .

Reprinted in Harrison, 17: 165–167.

[Early Criticism of Poe's Works] (1845)

LAWRENCE LABREE

The following items by Lawrence Labree, no mean literary critic, indicate Poe's visibility in the mid-1840s. Suggesting a literary debt for "The Gold-Bug," in the first review, is ironic, given Poe's repeated charges of plagiarism by other authors. The second item alludes to Poe's defense of James Russell Lowell against John Wilson's ("Christopher North's") strictures and errors in regard to Lowell and his poems. Poe the equally acid critic is commended for his attack on Wilson's imperfect perceptions. Poe's comments appeared in his "Editorial Miscellany," *Broadway Journal*, 4 October 1845: 199–200. The third item acclaims Poe as one of America's foremost poets, notably because of "The Raven."

"New Books"

TALES: by Edgar A. Poe. Mr. Poe has acquired the reputation of a powerful and vigorous writer, though occasionally delighting in biting sarcasm and highly-strained and unreasonable criticism. But in this instance he has given the public a pleasant volume of tales rather above the medium of that style of writing, each one of which possesses the power of holding the reader to the end—tales of absorbing interest. By and bye, however, we shall take the liberty of pointing out a close similarity of the main incident in the "Gold Bug" with another in a story published some years ago called "The Pirate's Treasure."

Lawrence Labree, "New Books," *Rover*, 28 June 1845: 240.

"Literary: 'Old Kit' and James Russell Lowell"

In the September number of *Blackwood*, we have another ferocious growl from the Editor toward a young American Author, which we are happy to see is meeting with a just response. Among others, Mr. Poe, has taken up the gauntlet, and reciprocates his savageisms with proper severity. That Mr. L. erred, is perfectly apparent. He goes abroad with a broadaxe, when he should leave it at home.

Lawrence Labree, "Literary: 'Old Kit' and James Russell Lowell," *Illustrated Magazine of Literature and Art*, 11 October 1845: 64.

Lawrence Labree

"Literary: 'The Raven' and Other Poems. By Edgar A. Poe"

It bothers us some how to rate the author; still the contents of this volume are creditable to American Literature. We have but few poets whose works we care to see in "book form," and Mr. Poe is one of these. His "Raven" is more remarkable for its mechanical construction than for its spirit of poetry, though any one who has read it several times over, as we have, must confess it to have some merit. The public are indebted to Mr. Poe for this offering from his muse.

Lawrence Labree, "Literary: 'The Raven' and Other Poems. By Edgar A. Poe," *Illustrated Magazine of Literature and Art*, 6 December 1845: 192.

From "A Failure" (1845)

CORNELIA WELLS WALTER

Poe again turned to lecturing on 16 October 1845, when he appeared before the Boston Lyceum. Contrary to the invitation, Poe did not prepare an original poem for the occasion. His performance was not met with the enthusiasm accorded to his earlier lecturing in Delaware and Pennsylvania, perhaps because he was intoxicated and, after offering comments about poetry, read "Al Aaraaf," which reading baffled and disappointed most of the audience. The audience were doubtless already tired from listening to Caleb Cushing's long speech, delivered before Poe's talk and reading. At any rate, many reports of Poe's debacle enlivened columns of Boston area newspapers. Poe replied to the journalistic attacks of Cornelia Walter and her collaborator, Henry N. Hudson. Poe himself commented that he had intended to quiz the Bostonians, for which he received additional lambastings in the columns of the *Transcript* and other newspapers. Poe's debacle was instrumental in undermining his credibility in northeastern literary circles, and, once the *Broadway Journal* slipped from his control, in early 1846, he had no ready forum to respond to attacks from his enemies.

A FAILURE. The anniversary exercises before the Boston Lyceum last evening were heavy and uninteresting, and illy adapted to an introductory to a course of lectures. . . .

When the orator [Caleb Cushing] had concluded, an officer of the society introduced to the assembly a gentleman, who, as we understood him to say, possessed a *raven*-ous desire to be known as the author of a particular piece of poetry on a celebrated croaking bird well known to ornithologists. The poet immediately arose; but if he uttered poesy in the first instance, it was certainly of the most prosaic order. The audience listened in amazement to a singularly didactic exordium, and finally commenced the noisy expedient of removing from the hall, and this long before they had discovered the style of the measure, or whether it was rhythm or blank verse. We believe, however, it was a prose introductory to a poem on the "Star discovered by Tycho Brahe," considered figuratively as the "Messenger of the Deity," out of which idea Edgar A. Poe had constructed a sentimental and imaginative poem. The audience now thinned so rapidly and made so much commotion in their departure that we lost the beauties of the composition. We heard the prefatory exordium, however, (which we took to be in *prose*) and our thoughts ran as follows.

> Twixt truth and poesy they say there is a mighty schism
> I'd like to be a moral man, and preach *"didacticism"*
> But as truth and taste do not agree and I do surely know it,
> Let truth and morals go and be a *critic* and a poet

From Cornelia Wells Walter, "A Failure," *Boston Evening Transcript*, 17 October 1845: [2].

From "Edgar A. Poe" in
Boston Evening Transcript (1845)

P.

IN OUR PAPER of yesterday we referred to the poem of this gentleman before the Lyceum, without attempting to analyze his capacity as a writer either of prose or of poetry. The following communication from a correspondent who was present at the late anniversary celebration makes good our omission. . . .

Mr. Poe. On Thursday evening, for the first time, we had a taste of this gentleman's quality in a poem delivered before the Boston Lyceum. Mr. Poe introduced his poem with a sort of apologetic preface, the chief merit of which was its great length. His idea of poetry as developed in his introduction, is, like his poetry itself, certainly very novel; and, as according to his theory, there never has been and never can be any such thing as originality, novelty is of course the best thing we can expect . . . All who have heard him must confess that he has more of novelty and less of originality than any other writer of any distinction living. We differ somewhat from this new poet and philosopher; and should be inclined to classify writers under the heads of original, sensible and novel, giving Mr. Poe any place he may choose in the latter class, and not believing he would accept of a place in either of the others. A man may obviously be original (if there be any such thing as originality) in the utterance of truth, how old soever that truth may be; and, on the other hand, as most truth is somewhat old, we naturally seek for novelty beyond as below the region of truth. All this is admirably exemplified in Mr. Poe. Indeed, his theory of poetry is that *it has nothing to do with truth*, and is concerned only with beauty; that it is not addressed to the intellect at all, but only to the taste. Whether his theory be devised to explain his poetry, or his poetry be written to exemplify his theory, certainly no one will question the intimate correspondence between them. His poetry, accordingly, has neither truth nor falsehood in it; is not chargeable indeed, with having any ideas whatever; but is simply beautiful. His poem of Thursday evening, *at whatever age it may have been written, and for what purpose soever he may have given it in Boston,* was fully equal to anything we have ever seen from him.

Mr. Poe's system of criticism is adequate and applicable to nobody's poetry but his own. No poetry, we presume, but his has ever been written of which his criticisms can give the solution; or, if written, it has not survived the day of its birth. As a critic, indeed, his chief merit is that "he puts himself for all mankind" and writes for nobody's sense or understanding but his own. Mr. Poe, we are told, has a great horror of plagiarism. It is about the only literary vice of which he is guilty, and no one can charge him with plagiarism without charging somebody else. All his productions are eminently *new*; he abounds in "novel combinations," and all of them are replete with the same kind of life as a watch.

P.

From P., "Edgar A. Poe," *Boston Evening Transcript*, 18 October 1845: [2].

"Quizzing the Bostonians" (1845)

[ANONYMOUS]

IN "E. A. POE'S POEMS," *second edition*, published in New York in 1831, is the entire poem recently delivered before the Lyceum of this city, and for the attempt of speaking before which association the author made an apology as regards his *capacity*. This *capacity*, it seems, has been deteriorating since Mr. Poe was ten years of age, his best poems having been written before that period. Mr. Poe may have quizzed *the* Bostonians in his own estimation, but *one* Bostonian was not quizzed who had the above-named book of poems in his pocket during the late delivery of the "Messenger Star," and who sat quietly reading it in the gallery, prepared to act *the prompter* if its author by any unaccustomed bewilderment of memory should have lost the cue!

"Quizzing the Bostonians," *Boston Evening Transcript*, 30 October 1845: [2].

"Mr. Poe's Poem" (1845)

[ANONYMOUS]

> Not all responses to Poe's October appearance at the Boston Lyceum were
> negative, as this comment in the *Boston Courier* demonstrates (though the
> columnist was apparently unaware that "Al Aaraaf" had been published).
> This notice also includes awareness of Poe's debt to Milton, though the anal-
> ogy to Keats has not received responses from Poe specialists. I print this
> report after those from the *Transcript* in order to keep all the wholly hostile
> reactions separate from this more sympathetic reaction.

ON THURSDAY EVENING, Mr. Poe delivered his poem before the Boston Lyceum, to (what we should have conceived, from first appearances) a highly
intelligent and respectable audience. He prefaced it with twenty minutes
of introductory prose; showing that there existed no such thing as didactic
poetry, and that all *real* poetry must proceed and emanate directly from
truth, dictated by a pure taste. The poem, called the "Messenger Star," was
an elegant and classic production, based on the right principles, containing the essence of *true* poetry, mingled with a gorgeous imagination, exquisite painting, every charm of metre, and a graceful delivery. It strongly
reminded us of Mr. Horne's "Orion," and resembled it in the majesty of
its design, the nobleness of its incidents, and its freedom from the trammels of productions usual on these occasions. The delicious word-painting
of some of its scenes brought vividly to our recollection, Keats's "Eve of
St. Agnes," and parts of "Paradise Lost."

That it was not appreciated by the audience, was very evident, by their
uneasiness and continual exits in numbers at a time. Common courtesy,
we should think, would have suggested to them the politeness of hearing
it through, though it should have proved "Heathen Greek" to them; after,
too, the author had expressed his doubts of his ability, in preparing a poem
for a Boston audience.

That it was inappropriate to the occasion, we take the liberty to deny.
What is the use of repeating the "mumbling farce" of having invited a poet

to deliver a poem? We (too often) find a person get up and repeat a hundred or two indifferent couplets of words, with jingling rhymes and stale witticisms, with scarcely a line of *poetry* in the whole, and which will admit of no superlative to describe it. If we are to have a poem, why not have the "true thing," that will be recognized as such,—for poems being written for people that can appreciate them, it would be as well to cater for their tastes as for individuals who cannot distinguish between the true and false.

We hope Mr. Poe will publish his poem, and give an opportunity for those that were not present, to read and admire.

"Mr. Poe's Poem," *Boston Courier*, 18 October 1845: [2].

From *Memories of Many Men*
and of Some Women (1875)

M. B. FIELDS

Poe returned to the lecture platform in February 1848, his topic, the "Universe"—which was subsequently expanded and published as *Eureka* later in the year. This report, published long afterward, provides some idea of the impression Poe made on his audience.

EDGAR A. POE I remember seeing on a single occasion. He announced a lecture to be delivered at the [New York] Society Library building on Broadway, under the title of the "Universe." It was a stormy night, and there were not more than sixty persons present in the lecture room. I have seen no portrait of Poe that does justice to his pale, delicate, intellectual face, and magnificent eyes. His lecture was a rhapsody of the most intense brilliance. He appeared inspired, and his inspiration affected his scant audience almost painfully. He wore his coat tightly buttoned across his slender chest; his eyes seemed to glow like those of his own raven, and he kept us entranced for two hours and a half. The late Mr. Putnam, the publisher, told me that the next day the wayward, luckless poet presented himself to him with the manuscript of the "Universe." He told Putnam that in it he solved the whole problem of life; that it would immortalize the publisher as well as its author; and, what was of less consequence, that it would bring to him the fortune which he had so long and so vainly been seeking. . . . After poor Poe's death, the late Rufus W. Griswold, not altogether immaculate himself, treated his memory with undue severity. I had a correspondence upon the subject with his fellow-poet and old-time friend, N. P. Willis, who earnestly deprecated Griswold's harshness.

From M. B. Fields, *Memories of Many Men and of Some Women*, 224.

From "Hints to Authors" (1848)

[Anonymous]

The following parody of Poe's fiction writing demonstrates the ease with which many of Poe's contemporaries categorized his fiction as "German," that is, what we more commonly know as "Gothic." In Poe's day, such epithets designated fiction produced for little else but sheer lurid thrills to entertain unsophisticated readers. The article was several times reprinted from its first appearance in the Philadelphia *Irish Citizen* for January 1844. Signal characteristics of Poe's fiction—the protagonist who feels haunted, the sensational events affecting him—are well wrought in this successful parody, just as the article overall contributes to the image of Poe the author's customary themes. The effect of the parody approaches biography, by seeming to offer a specimen of Poe's typical intents and methods.

Hints to Authors.
On the Germanesque.

The Germanesque is a name, which, for want of a better, we have given to a species of tale or sketch of incident, which seems to be getting into vogue. As it may be—for popular taste is sometimes monstrous in its character—the rage, at one time or other, you shall be taught all the rules by which it is composed. They are few and easy to comprehend. Indeed, judging by the works and mind of its chief and almost only follower on this side of the Atlantic, it is a pure art, almost mechanical—requiring neither genius, taste, wit nor judgment—and accessible to every impudent and contemptible mountebank, who may choose to slander a lady, and then plead insanity to shelter himself from the vengeance of her relatives.

You must by all means choose a subject, which every one under ordinary management could comprehend. To mystify such a thing as this proves your genius. An ordinary man, in an ordinary disquisition upon a vegetable so ordinary as potatoes, would be easy to comprehend. What he wrote those who read would fathom at once. But if you write about such a matter, satisfy them that although you may be yourself the smallest of small potatoes, you and your productions are alike difficult of digestion.

Pay great attention to minutiae, and lay great stress on trifles. This makes the reader expect that the story will hinge upon these especially, and he becomes very thankful if he be disappointed. For instance—if your hero wear boots, give the exact height of their heels, the breadth of their toes, the name of their maker, and the number of pegs in their soles. Every one will conclude that you are possessed of an observation so rigorous that nothing can escape it, and think you qualified at least to search in a haystack for a lost needle.

You can frequently produce a great effect by writing the first part of your work with a certain design, which you change before you get to the end. This will make a very pretty confusion. But your best plan is to carry your work through without any design at all. Thus, neither yourself nor your reader will understand your intent; and to effect this delicious state of bewilderment is the true office of the Germanesque.

Preface your production by a number of quotations, from as many languages as possible. It is not necessary that these should have any reference to the subject, indeed, that they should have any meaning. Your purpose will be sufficiently answered, if you impress your reader with a belief that you are a profound linguist and an untiring reader.

The little sketch which follows combines the greater part of these requisites. It has been attributed to Mr. Poe. We are not sure that it is from the pen of that very distinguished writer; but if not his, is a palpable imitation of his style. You will do well to study its characteristics with great care before venturing upon the composition of the Germanesque.

Tale of a Gray Tadpole

"Muhazzin al zerdukkaut, munaskif al filfillee."
Jamee al Hukkaiaut.

"Al del Carpio freguenta 'l moro altiva
Le diga por merced—
Su nombre, y quien el por ser costumbre:
Bernaldo respondio, Bernaldo soy."
Espinosa, c. 2, 30, 1.

"Magnanimo signore, ogni vostro atto
Ho siempre con rajion laudato, e laudo."
Orlando Furioso, Car. xviii. stan. 1.

"Mihi an Beate Martin." *Plautus*.

"Nolus volus." *Gen Taylor, Ord. Capt. May.*

"Quel heure est il? Une heure apres midi."
Le Cid, par Corneille.

"Αβτδ." *Herodotus*, b. 1.

"Wir bekoomen trek schuyt."
Der Vrye Metsalaaren.

"Karl, der reiber, ist der mann." *Schiller.*

"Nid mugrell ond ceiliogwdd."
Gr. ad. M. ab Dafydd.

"Akt 2¶co† l = + ÷ rm. Fy! O!! p ?"
Nokt Intwopi.

"Iak ptak oknem przszcznztzskczjzmnkscznlwy."
Spiewy Hystorycne.

"Oysters are quiescent, bibulatory of sea-water and
bearded. The human mind luxuriates in the vague and
mysteresque as a pike in a fish-pond. Hence springs that
longing after the immortal which pervades the universe.
Hence lovers engrave the names of their heart's idols
upon gate-posts, with their jack-knives."—*Lord Bacon.*

There are strange antipathies and stranger attachments. It may be said of
a female infant, in the language of JAN CHODSKWICZSZNSKI, the well-known
Pole—"*Ona luba mleka.*" By the addition of the English words "and water," the remark may be applied to the writings of the great EPPIE SARGENT;
and at the same time refer to the taste of her admirers. Now, while many
admire, there are benighted few who detest both the writings of the divine
MISS EPPIE SARGENT, and the milk-and-water to which they may be likened.
They prefer for their reading, MRS. RADCLIFFE and the Newgate Calendar,
and refresh their inner man by that peculiar draught known as "cold with-

out." There is no accounting for this peculiar state of things. The calculus of probabilities fails us. Cryptography affords no solution. It would baffle the analytical powers of my friend, the Chevalier DUPIN. BABINGTON MACAULAY might write a disquisition on the matter, and CARLYLE might pen a book—but "*cui* bono?" They are both asses. I have said so in one of my reviews, and I ought to know.

From my infancy to the present time, I have possessed a dislike to tadpoles. Now, *per se*, the tadpole is not an object of dislike. Indeed, it is rather graceful than otherwise. The rotundity of body, with its gradual and progressive diminution at one extremity into a beautiful caudal appendage, gratifies the eyes of all lovers of the curvilinear and picturesque. But tadpoles are disgusting from their associations. They do not always remain in a state of tadpoledom. They emerge as it were into another nature. From graceful, gliding creatures, they pass into squatting, croaking, winking, leaping, diving and discontented frogs. The mind of the looker-on is obliged to travel to the future, and contemplate their probable destiny. A vision of innumerable mud-puddles crosses the fancy—green slime makes its appearance—and the ear is offended with pond-concerts, conducted with a scanty supply of musical knowledge, and in violation of the first principles of harmony.

But to my story.

Underneath the house in which I lived, there was a cellar. This was divided. The front part was arranged for the purpose of holding wood, coal, refrigerators, mice, and the usual appurtenances of such apartments. The back part was a kitchen—of the kind denominated by the unthinking vulgar, a cellar-kitchen. This communicated with the yard by means of steps. These steps were partly outside of the house, in a kind of area, six feet broad by fifteen long. The area was paved with damp bricks, and in its northeast corner, about six inches from the wall, stood a water cask, filled by means of a conductor leading from a rain-spout above.

I know not what peculiar impulse drove me to the spot. I have thought of it since, as I think of it now, with a vain attempt to penetrate the mystery. Be the cause what it may, that I did go there is undoubtedly true. I bent over the water-cask. It was, as I said before, filled; and just two inches from the bottom—I am certain it was two inches, for my eyes never deceive me—just two inches from the bottom, suspended there by a vibratory motion of his tail, was a large, grey tadpole, measuring five inches and four lines and three lines from the end of his tail to the tip of his snout.

I was horror struck. I stood over the cask with the upper part of my body bent to an angle of forty-five degrees, ten minutes, from the perpendicular. My eyes dilated to their utmost extent, and rolled painfully in their sockets. The left eye tried to catch the glance of the right—the right eye tried to catch the glance of the left. There I stood, motionless, transfixed for several minutes. I was shocked, and retired in a state of perfect disgust.

Again I stood over it. The tadpole, who had hitherto remained motionless, seemed to read my thoughts by a kind of mesmeric power. He curled his body until the end of his tail reached his nose, and remained there with a peculiar vibratory motion. The figure thus formed, although very strange, and strikingly arabesque, was nevertheless insulting, and inflamed my already excited temper to madness. Seizing a huge stick, I carefully poised it in a perpendicular position, over the spot where the reptile rested. I drove it as I thought with unerring aim. It descended vehemently—the water was agitated—dirt and bubbles arose to the surface. I congratulated myself on my success. I laughed.

The particles gradually subsided, the water became clear, and I looked in again. The laugh passed from the dexter to the sinister side of my mouth. Instead of the crushed, mangled and vile fragments of my enemy, I beheld the same tadpole as before—in the same spot—and in the same insulting position, with the tip of his tail applied to the end of his nose.

I sat down coolly and began to reflect. A thought stuck me. I drew a plug which was inserted at the base of the water-cask, for I knew if the waters escaped through the aperture thus made, my enemy would be drawn along with them. The result showed the greatness of my judgment.

At first the waters flowed fastly, then slower—but before their entire subsidence, the vainly-resisting reptile was borne out, and cast floundering upon the wet, brick floor. He waggled about, and looked piteously in my face. I had no pity. There was no remorse at my heart. With a fury at which my conscience now shudders, I raised my right foot, which is fifteen inches in length and seven in breadth, and with one stroke destroyed the wretch who had tormented me. I trampled on him again and again in a perfect fury of hatred. I fairly revelled in destructive joy.

Now that I had succeeded, a strange thirst came over me. I hastened to the hydrant in the yard, and setting the water in motion applied my mouth to the end of the spout. I sucked the water in greedily, till I was fully sated.

The peculiar sensation of thirst had now passed, and I sat down on the pavement to reflect. I began to speculate on the possibility of my head becoming one of HENSON's flying machines, and had actually thought of getting a tumbler of brandy by way of steam, when I saw a strange profile on the opposite fence.

Wonderful! The appearance assumed a definity—a fixity—a certainty. Madness! horror! There on the wall before me was a grey, gigantic, strange tadpole, with a ferocious glare. I knew it. I knew it for the tadpole I had slain. I sat like a statue of Pagan Rome, white, chiseled and motionless. I was haunted by a merciless fiend.

From "Hints to Authors," *John-Donkey*, 1 June 1848: 364–365.

[Untitled Headnote to Reprint of "Ulalume"] (1849)

[EVERT A. DUYCKINCK]

> The opinion of Evert Duyckinck, a prestigious person in the New York City publishing world during the 1840s and 1850s, should not be regarded lightly. His comment on "Ulalume" is as relevant to biography as to analytical criticism of Poe's writings.

THE FOLLOWING FASCINATING POEM, which is from the pen of Edgar A. Poe, has been drifting about in the newspapers under anonymous or mistaken imputation of authorship,—having been attributed to N. P. Willis. We now restore it to its proper author. It originally appeared without name in the *American Review*. In peculiarity of versification, and a certain cold moonlight witchery, it has much of the power of the author's "Raven" [text of "Ulalume" follows].

Untitled headnote to reprint of Poe's poem "Ulalume," *Literary World*, 3 March 1849: 202.

From "Mr. Poe's Lecture" (1849)

[ANONYMOUS]

In late 1849 Poe traveled to Virginia, in part to lecture on poetry, in part to arrange for his marriage to his childhood sweetheart, Sarah Elmira Royster, now the widowed Mrs. Alexander Shelton. The accounts of his lecturing, in Norfolk and Richmond, furnish insights into his final appearances on the platform, an aspect of his career that is often overlooked as of significance to biography or critical approaches to Poe and his ideas.

MR. POE DELIVERED a lecture on "The Poetic Principle," with various citations, at the Lecture Room of the Academy, on Friday evening. The main proposition of the lecture, was that there could not be a long poem—that a long metrical composition must tire and cease to be a poem. Milton's Paradise Lost and the Iliad were cited in illustration, which he said were but a succession of brilliant poetic scintillations—a collection of short poems. Mr. Poe entered into an analysis of the poem proper, and pointed out the defects as well as beauties of celebrated poets. There should not be too much brevity, nor should there be undue expansion in poetical compositions. In elucidation of his opinions, Mr. Poe recited with fine effect, extracts from the poetic effusions of Longfellow, Bryant, Willis, and Edward Pinkney, who he said was born too far South to be appreciated by the North American Quarterly Review—and from the works of Shelly [sic], Byron, Moore, Hood and others. Those of Longfellow and Pinkney, were particularly remarkable for beauty of rhythm as well as of sentiment. These recitations were received with rounds of applause from the intelligent audience.

Mr. Poe concluded the lecture by reciting by request, his brilliant fantasy, "The Raven,"—The audience seemed highly gratified with the intellectual repast which had been laid before them.

From "Mr. Poe's Lecture," *Norfolk Beacon*, 17 September 1849: [2].

[67]

From "Edgar A. Poe" in
Semi-Weekly Examiner (1849)

JOHN M. DANIEL

EDGAR A. POE lectured again last night on the "Poetic Principle," and concluded his lecture, as before, with his now celebrated poem of "The Raven." As the attention of many in this city [has been] directed to this singular performance, and as Mr. Poe's poems . . . have long been out of print, we furnish our readers, to-day, with the only correct copy ever published—which we are enabled to do by the courtesy of Mr. Poe himself.

"The Raven" has taken rank over the whole world of literature as the very first poem as yet practiced on the American continent. There is indeed but one other—the "Humble Bee" of Ralph Waldo Emerson [though "The Raven" is superior] as a work of pure *art*.—They hold the same relation the one to the other that a masterpiece of painting holds to a splendid piece of mosaic. But while this poem maintains a rank so high among all persons of catholic and generally cultivated taste, we can conceive the wrath of many who will read it for the first time in the columns of this newspaper. Those who have formed their taste in the Poe and Dryden school, whose earliest poetical acquaintance is Milton, and whose latest Hammond and Cowper—with a small sprinkling of Moore and Byron—will not be apt to relish on first sight a poem tinged so deeply with the dyes of the nineteenth century. The poem will make an impression on them which they will not be able to explain—but that will irritate them. Criticism and explanation are useless with such. Criticism cannot reason people into an attachment. . . . The worth of "The Raven" is not in any "moral," nor is its charm in the construction of its story. Its great and wonderful merits consist in the strange, beautiful, and fantastic imagery and colors with which the simple subject is clothed. . . . Added to these is a versification indescribably sweet and wonderfully difficult. . . . To all who have a strong perception, of tune there is a music in it which haunts the ear long after reading. These are great merits, and the Raven is a gem of art. It is stamped with the image of true genius—and genius in its happiest hour. It is one of those things an author never does but once [text of "The Raven" follows].

From John M. Daniel, "Edgar A. Poe," Richmond *Semi-Weekly Examiner*, 25 September 1849: [2].

[Note Requesting Assistance for Poe] (1849)

Joseph P. Wilson

> What happened between the time Poe left Richmond in late September and his being discovered, very ill, in Baltimore on 3 October, remains unknown. On 3 October Poe's longtime acquaintance, Dr. Joseph E. Snodgrass, received this note.

Joseph P. Wilson to Joseph E. Snodgrass, 3 October 1849

There is a gentleman, rather the worse for wear, at Ryan's Fourth Ward Polls, who goes under the cognomen of Edgar A. Poe, and who appears in great distress. He says he is acquainted with you, and I assure you he is in need of immediate assistance.

Joseph P. Wilson

Letter from Joseph P. Wilson to Joseph E. Snodgrass, 3 October 1849, reprinted in Woodberry (1909), 2: 344.

[Letter from Poe's Attending Physician] (1849)

John J. Moran

> Dr. Snodgrass called at Ryan's, and Mr. Herring, Poe's relative, who had
> also been summoned, came to the scene. Between them they put Poe into
> a carriage, and he was taken to the Washington Hospital, where he was ad-
> mitted, still unconscious, at 5 P.M. Neilson Poe was also notified, visited the
> hospital, and sent whatever was necessary. Poe remained in an alarming de-
> lirium, with intervals of apparent sanity, until he died on Sunday 7 October
> about 5 P.M. Dr. John J. Moran, who attended Poe's last illness, subsequently
> provided his own recollections of the writer's final days in this letter to
> Mrs. Clemm, though because of their sensational details they are at best sus-
> pect for accuracy.

John J. Moran to Maria Clemm, 15 November 1849

My dear Madam:—I take the earliest opportunity of responding to yours of
the 9th . . .

When brought to the hospital he was unconscious of his condition—who
brought him or with whom he had been associating. He remained in this
condition from five o'clock in the afternoon—the hour of his admission—
until three next morning. This was on the 3rd October.

To this state succeeded tremor of the limbs, and at first a busy but not violent or active delirium—constant talking—and vacant converse with spectral and imaginary objects on the walls. His face was pale and his whole
person drenched with perspiration. We were unable to induce tranquility
before the second day after his admission.

Having left orders with the nurses to that effect, I was summoned to his
bedside so soon as consciousness supervened, and questioned him in reference to his family, place of residence, relatives, etc. But his answers were
incoherent and unsatisfactory. . . . Wishing to rally and sustain his now
fast sinking hopes, I told him I hoped that in a few days he would be able
to enjoy the society of his friends here and I would be most happy to con-

tribute in every possible way to his ease and comfort. At this he broke out with much energy, and said the best thing his best friend could do would be to blow out his brains with a pistol—that when he beheld his degradation he was ready to sink into the earth, etc. Shortly after giving expression to these words Mr. Poe seemed to doze, and I left him for a short time. When I returned I found him in a violent delirium, resisting the efforts of the nurses to keep him in bed. This state continued until Saturday evening. [On Sunday morning around 3 a.m.] a very decided change began to affect him. Having become enfeebled from exertion he became quiet and seemed to rest for a short time; then gently moving his head, he said, *"Lord help my poor soul,"* and expired! . . .

Respectfully yours,

J. J. Moran, *Res. Phys.*

Reprinted in Woodberry (1909), 2: 346–348.

"Death of Edgar Allan Poe" in
New York Daily Tribune (1849)

"Ludwig" [Rufus Wilmot Griswold]

> Rufus W. Griswold wrote this obituary and published it over a pseudonym, as if he was reluctant to publish a negative portrait of Poe using his own name. Because Griswold was a respected editor, his biographical information went largely unchallenged for decades, albeit Poe did have champions. Those champions were often so intent on countering Griswold, however, that they veered into slavish admiration for Poe and his writings. Their accounts often contain as many inaccuracies as Griswold's, which have done little to represent Poe's literary art in any sophisticated way. This item, the infamous "Ludwig" obituary, is Griswold's first posthumous vilification of Poe and was seemingly supported by what the earlier excerpt from Griswold's *The Poets and Poetry of America* (1842) had outlined, thus giving the obituary an air of unimpeachable accuracy.

EDGAR ALLAN POE is dead. He died in Baltimore the day before yesterday. This announcement will startle many, but few will be grieved by it. The poet was well known, personally or by reputation, in all this country; he had readers in England, and in several of the states of Continental Europe; but he had few or no friends; and the regrets for his death will be suggested principally by the consideration that in him literary art has lost one of its most brilliant but erratic stars.

The family of Mr. Poe—we learn from Griswold's "Poets and Poetry of America," from which a considerable portion of the facts in this notice are derived—was one of the oldest and most respectable in Baltimore. David Poe, his paternal grandfather, was a Quartermaster-General in the Maryland line during the Revolution, and the intimate friend of Lafayette, who, during his last visit to the United States, called personally upon the General's widow, and tendered her acknowledgments for the services rendered to him by her husband. His great-grandfather, John Poe, married in England,

Jane, a daughter of Admiral James McBride, noted in British naval history, and claiming kindred with some of the most illustrious English families. His father and mother,—both of whom were in some way connected with the theater, and lived as precariously as their more gifted and more eminent son—died within a few weeks of each other, of consumption, leaving him an orphan, at two years of age. Mr. John Allan, a wealthy gentleman of Richmond, Virginia, took a fancy to him, and persuaded his grandfather to suffer him to adopt him. He was brought up in Mr. Allan's family; and as that gentleman had no other children, he was regarded as his son and heir. In 1816 he accompanied Mr. and Mrs. Allen [sic] to Great Britain, visited every portion of it, and afterward passed four or five years in a school kept at Stoke Newington, near London, by Rev. Dr. Bransby. He returned to America in 1822, and in 1825 went to the Jefferson University, at Charlottesville, in Virginia, where he led a very dissipated life, the manners of the college being at that time extremely dissolute. He took the first honors, however, and went home greatly in debt. Mr. Allan refused to pay some of his debts of *honor*, and he hastily quitted the country on a Quixotic expedition to join the Greeks, then struggling for liberty. He did not reach his original destination, however, but made his way to St. Petersburg, in Russia, when he became involved in difficulties, from which he was extricated by the late Mr. Henry Middleton, the American Minister at that Capital. He returned home in 1829, and immediately afterward entered the Military Academy at West-Point. In about eighteen months from that time, Mr. Allan, who had lost his first wife while Mr. Poe was in Russia, married again. He was sixty-five years of age, and the lady was young; Poe quarreled with her, and the veteran husband, taking the part of his wife, addressed him an angry letter, which was answered in the same spirit. He died soon after, leaving an infant son the heir to his property, and bequeathed Poe nothing.

The army, in the opinion of the young cadet, was not a place for a poor man; so he left West-Point abruptly, and determined to maintain himself by authorship. He printed, in 1827, a small volume of poems, most of which were written in early youth. Some of these poems are quoted in a reviewal by Margaret Fuller, in *The Tribune* in 1846, and are justly regarded as among the most wonderful exhibitions of the precocious development of genius. They illustrated the character of his abilities, and justified his anticipations of success. For a considerable time, however, though he wrote readily and brilliantly, his contributions to the journals attracted little attention, and his hopes of gaining a livelihood by the profession of literature were nearly ended at length in sickness, poverty and despair. But in 1831, the proprietor of a weekly gazette, in Baltimore, offered two premiums, one for the best story in prose, and the other for the best poem.—In due time Poe sent in two articles, and he waited anxiously for the decision. One of the Committee was the accomplished author of "Horseshoe Robinson," John P. Kennedy, and his associates were scarcely less eminent than he for wit and critical sagacity. Such matters are usually disposed of in a very off hand way: Committees to award literary prizes drink to the payer's health, in good wines, over the unexamined MSS, which they submit to the discretion of publishers, with permission to use their names in such a way as to promote the publisher's advantage. So it would have been in this case, but that one of the Committee, taking up a little book in such exquisite calligraphy as to seem like one of the finest issues of the press of Putnam, was tempted to read several pages, and being interested, he summoned the attention of the company to the half-dozen compositions in the volume. It was unanimously decided that the prizes should be paid to the first of geniuses who had written legibly. Not another MS. was unfolded. Immediately the "confidential envelop" was opened, and the successful competitor was found to bear the scarcely known name of Poe.

The next day the publisher called to see Mr. Kennedy, and gave him an account of the author that excited his curiosity and sympathy, and caused him to request that he should be brought to his office. Accordingly he was introduced: the prize money had not yet been paid, and he was in the costume in which he had answered the advertisement of his good fortune. Thin, and pale even to ghastliness, his whole appearance indicated sickness and the utmost destitution. A tattered frock-coat concealed the absence of a shirt, and the ruins of boots disclosed more than the want of stockings. But the eyes of the young man were luminous with intelligence and feeling, and his voice, and conversation, and manners, all won upon the lawyer's regard. Poe told his history, and his ambition, and it was determined that he should not want means for a suitable appearance in society, nor opportunity for a just display of his abilities in literature. Mr. Kennedy accompanied him to a clothing store, and purchased for him a respectable suit, with changes of linen, and sent him to a bath, from which he returned with the suddenly regained bearing of a gentleman.

[75]

The late Mr. Thomas W. White had then recently established *The Southern Literary Messenger*, at Richmond, and upon the warm recommendation of Mr. Kennedy, Poe was engaged, at a small salary—we believe of $500 a year—to be its editor. He entered upon his duties with letters full of expressions of the warmest gratitude to his friends in Baltimore, who in five or six weeks were astonished to learn that with characteristic recklessness of consequences, he was hurriedly married to a girl as poor as himself. Poe continued in this situation for about a year and a half, in which he wrote many brilliant articles, and raised the *Messenger* to the first rank of literary periodicals.

He next moved to Philadelphia, to assist William E. Burton in the editorship of the *Gentleman's Magazine*, a miscellany that in 1840 was merged in *Graham's Magazine*, of which Poe became one of the principal writers, particularly in criticism, in which his papers attracted much attention, by their careful and skillful analysis, and generally caustic severity. At this period, however, he appeared to have been more ambitious of securing distinction in romantic fiction, and a collection of his compositions in this department, published in 1841, under the title of "Tales of the Grotesque and Arabesque," established his reputation for ingenuity, imagination and extraordinary power in tragical narration.

Near the end of 1844 Poe removed to New-York, where he conducted for several months a literary miscellany called "The Broadway Journal." In 1845 he published a volume of "Tales" in Wiley and Putnam's Library of American Books, and in the same series a collection of his poems. Besides these volumes he was the author of "Arthur Gordon Pym," a romance; "A New Theory of Versification;" "Eureka," an essay on the spiritual and material universe: a work which he wished to have "judged as a poem;" and several extended series of papers in the periodicals, the most noticeable of which are "Marginalia," embracing opinions of books and authors; "Secret Writing," "Autography," and "Sketches of the Literati of New-York."

His wife died in 1847, at Fordham, near this City, and some of our readers will remember the paragraphs in the papers of the time, upon his destitute condition. His wants were supplied by the liberality of a few individuals. We remember that Col. Webb collected in a few moments fifty or sixty dollars for him at the Union Club; Mr. Lewis, of Brooklyn, sent a similar sum from one of the Courts, in which he was engaged when he saw the statement of the poet's poverty; and others illustrated in the same manner the effect of such an appeal to the popular heart.

Since that time Mr. Poe has lived quietly, and with an income from his literary labors sufficient for his support. A few weeks ago he proceeded to Richmond in Virginia, where he lectured upon the poetical character, &c.; and it was understood by some of his correspondents here that he was this week to be married, most advantageously, to a lady of that city: a widow, to whom he had been previously engaged while a student in the University.

The character of Mr. Poe we cannot attempt to describe in this very hastily written article. We can but allude to some of its more striking phases.

His conversation was at times almost supra-mortal in its eloquence. His voice was modulated with astonishing skill, and his large and variably expressive eyes looked repose or shot fiery tumult into theirs who listened, while his own face glowed, or was changeless in pallor, as his imagination quickened his blood or drew it back frozen to his heart. His imagery was from the worlds which no mortal can see but with the vision of genius. Suddenly starting from a proposition exactly and sharply defined in terms of utmost simplicity and clearness, he rejected the forms of customary logic, and by a crystalline process of accretion, built up his occular demonstrations in forms of gloomiest and ghastliest grandeur, or in those of the most airy and delicious beauty—so minutely, and distinctly, yet so rapidly, that the attention which was yielded to him was chained till it stood among his wonderful creations—till he himself dissolved the spell, and brought his hearers back to common and base existence, by vulgar fancies or by exhibitions of the ignoblest passion.

He was at all times a dreamer—dwelling in ideal realms—in heaven or hell—peopled with creatures and the accidents of his brain. He walked the streets, in madness or melancholy, with lips moving in indistinct curses, or with eyes upturned in passionate prayers, (never for himself, for he felt, or professed to feel, that he was already damned), but for their happiness who at the moment were objects of his idolatry—or, with his glances introverted to a heart gnawed with anguish, and with a face shrouded in gloom, he would brave the wildest storms; and all night, with drenched garments and arms wildly beating the winds and rains, he would speak as if to spirits that at such times only could be evoked by him from the Aidenn close by whose portals his disturbed soul sought to forget the ills to which his constitution subjugated him—close by that Aidenn where were those he loved—the Aidenn which he might never see, but in fitful glimpses, as its gates opened to receive the less fiery and more happy natures whose destiny to sin did not involve the doom of death.

He seemed, except when some fitful pursuit subjected his will and engrossed his faculties, always to bear the memory of some controlling sorrow. The remarkable poem of *The Raven* was probably much more nearly than has been supposed, even by those who were very intimate with him, a reflexion and an echo of his own history. He was that bird's

> —unhappy master,
> Whom unmerciful disaster
> Followed fast and followed faster,
>   Till his songs the burden bore—
> Till the dirges of his hope, the
>   Melancholy burden bore
> Of "Nevermore," of "Nevermore."

Every genuine author in a greater or less degree leaves in his works, whatever their design, traces of his personal character: elements of his immortal being, in which the individual survives the person. While we read the pages of the *Fall of the House of Usher*, or of *Mesmeric Revelations*, we see in the solemn and stately gloom which invests one, and in the subtle metaphysical analysis of both, indications of the idiosyncrasies,—of what was most remarkable and peculiar—in the author's intellectual nature. But we see here only the better phases of this nature, only the symbols of his juster action, for his harsh experience had deprived him of all faith in man or woman. He had made up his mind upon the numberless complexities of the social world, and the whole system with him was an imposture. This conviction gave a direction to his shrewd and naturally unamiable character. Still, though he regarded society as composed altogether of villains, the sharpness of his intellect was not of that kind which enabled him to cope with villainy, while it continually caused him by overshots to fail of the success of honesty. He was in many respects like Francis Vivian in Bulwer's novel of "The Caxtons." "Passion, in him, comprehended many of the worst emotions which militate against human happiness. You could not contradict him, but you raised quick choler; you could not speak of wealth, but his cheek paled with gnawing envy. The astonishing natural advantages of this poor boy—his beauty, his readiness, the daring spirit that breathed around him like a fiery atmosphere—had raised his constitutional self-confidence into an arrogance that turned his very claims to admiration into prejudice against him. Irascible, envious—bad enough, but not the worst, for these salient angles were all varnished over with a cold repellant cynicism, his passions vented themselves in sneers. There seemed to him no moral susceptibility; and, what was more remarkable in a proud nature, little or nothing of the true point of honor. He had, to a morbid excess, that desire to rise which is vulgarly called ambition, but no wish for the esteem or love of his species; only the hard wish to succeed—not shine, not serve—succeed, that he might have the right to despise a world which galled his self-conceit."

We have suggested the influence of his aims and vicissitudes upon his literature. It was more conspicuous in his later than his earlier writing. Nearly all that he wrote in the last two or three years—including much of his best poetry—was in some sense biographical; in draperies of his imagination, those who had taken the trouble to trace his steps, could perceive, but slightly concealed, the figure of himself.

There are perhaps some of our readers who will understand the allusions of the following beautiful poem. Mr. Poe presented it in MS. to the writer of these paragraphs, just before he left New-York recently, remarking that it was the last thing he had written [text of "Annabel Lee" follows].

We must omit any particular criticism of Mr. Poe's works. As a writer of tales it will be admitted generally, that he was scarcely surpassed in ingenuity of construction or effective painting. As a critic, he was more remarkable as a dissector of sentences than as a commentator upon ideas: he was little better than a carping grammarian. As a poet, he will retain a most honorable rank. Of his "Raven," Mr. Willis observes, that in his opinion "it is the most effective single example of fugitive poetry ever published in this country, and is unsurpassed in English poetry for subtle conception, masterly ingenuity of versification, and consistent sustaining of imaginative lift." In poetry, as in prose, he was most successful in the metaphysical treatment of the passions. His poems are constructed with wonderful ingenuity, and finished with consummate art. They illustrate a morbid sensitiveness of feeling, a shadowy and gloomy imagination, and a taste almost faultless in the apprehension of that sort of beauty most agreeable to his temper.

We have not learned of the circumstance of his death. It was sudden, and from the fact that it occurred in Baltimore, it is to be presumed that he was on his return to New-York.

"After life's fitful fever he sleeps well."

LUDWIG.

"Death of Edgar Allan Poe," *New York Daily Tribune*, 9 October 1849: 2.

From "Topics of the Month" (1849)

[C. F. BRIGGS]

This article, presumably by the Holden editor, which appeared two months after Poe's death, sounds a note of pity for Poe's shortcomings, thus bearing witness to viewpoints concerning him held by many in his era who were either unsympathetic, neutral, or uninformed as regarded the facts of his personal and professional life. As is typical of so much written about Poe, this article errs factually: for example, Mrs. Clemm had no such notion that Poe would never return. Moreover the article is self-contradictory when it mentions Poe's departing Richmond to return to his home.

THE PROMINENT TOPIC of conversation in literary circles, during the past month, has been the death of that melancholy man Edgar A. Poe. Mr. Poe left his home, in Westchester County, in this State, early in the Summer on a visit to the South, and we were told at the time that his mother-in-law, Mrs. Clemm, who was his sole companion, had no expectations of ever again seeing him return. He arranged all his papers so that they could be used without difficulty in case of his death, and told her if he never came back she would find that he had left everything in order. But there was no cause to apprehend that the termination of his career was so close at hand. He went to Richmond where he delivered a series of lectures and was well received by his old friends; he renewed his attachment to a wealthy widow in that city, whom he had known before his or her marriage, and was on his way home to make arrangements for his marriage to her, when he had a relapse of his besetting infirmities in Baltimore, and died miserably.

A biography of Mr. Poe is soon to be published with his collected writings, under the supervision of Rev. Rufus W. Griswold; but it will be a long while, if ever, before the naked character of the sad poet will be exposed to public gaze. There is generous disposition on the part of those who knew him intimately, to bury his failings, or rather personal characteristics, in the shade of forgetfulness; while nothing is dwelt upon but his literary productions. He was a psychological phenomenon, and more good than harm would result from a clear, unprejudiced analysis of his character. But when will any one be found bold enough to incur the risk of an imputation of evil motives, by making such a revelation as the task demands? Like all other writers, Mr. Poe developed himself in his literary productions, but to understand his writings it was necessary to be possessed of the key of his personal acquaintance. Knowing him thoroughly, you could thoroughly comprehend what he wrote, but not otherwise. He was an intellectual machine without a balance wheel; and all his poetry, which seems perfect in itself, and full of feeling, was mere machine work. It was not that spontaneous outgushing of sentiment, which the verse of great poets seems to be, but a carefully constructed mosaic, painfully elaborated, and designedly put together, with every little word in its right place, and every shade of thought toned down to its exact position. There is nothing of the "fine frenzy" about it, which marks the poetry of those who warble their native wood notes wild.—His poem, the Bells, is a curious example of his way of jingling words to make them sound like music:

> "Bell, bells,
> Bells, bells, bells, bells."

This was the burden of the song. Yet, ever and anon, in this strange jingling and clanging of words, there struck upon the ear sounds of real sadness, which touched the heart and produced the feeling caused by the strain of the true poet. But, was not Poe a true poet? That remains for the world to decide. If he was a poet, he cannot be deprived by criticism of his rightful fame. His merits as a critic were very slender, he was a minute detector of slips of the pen, and, probably, was unequalled as a proof reader. But such was his sensitiveness to small imperfections, that it incapacitated him from taking a comprehensive or liberal survey of a literary subject. He was of the Doctor Blair school of critics, and while measuring the lines of a poem was indifferent to their meaning. One of the strange points of his strange nature was to entertain a spirit of revenge towards all who did him a service. His pecuniary difficulties often compelled him to solicit aid, and he rarely, or never, failed to malign those who befriended him. It was probably this strange propensity which caused him to quarrel with his early benefactor, and forfeit the aid he might have received from that quarter. He was altogether a strange and a fearful being, and a true history of his life would be more startling than any of the grotesque romances which he was so fond of inventing. . . .

From "Topics of the Month," *Holden's Dollar Magazine*, December 1849: 765–766.

"To the Reader" (1850)

Maria Clemm

The following commentary, found in prefatory materials in Griswold's edition of Poe's *Works*, gives the impression that Poe himself designated Griswold as the editor to whom publication of his writings was entrusted. Challenges, notably by Thomas Ollive Mabbott and by Burton R. Pollin, have appeared, suggesting that perhaps Mrs. Clemm negotiated with Griswold in order to realize some pecuniary compensation for herself—adding yet another enigma to biographical information about Poe.

To the Reader.

The late Edgar Allan Poe, who was the husband of my only daughter, the son of my eldest brother, and more than a son to myself, in his long-continued and affectionate observance of every duty to me,—under an impression that he might be called suddenly from the world, wrote (just before he left his home in Fordham, for the last time, on the 29th of June, 1849) requests that the Rev. Rufus W. Griswold should act as his literary Executor, and superintend the publication of his works;—and that N. P. Willis, Esq., should write such observations upon his life and character, as he might deem suitable to address to thinking men, in vindication of his memory.

These requests he made with less hesitation, and with confidence that they would be fulfilled, from his knowledge of these gentlemen; and he many times expressed a gratification of such an opportunity of decidedly and unequivocally certifying his respect for the literary judgment and integrity of Mr. Griswold, with whom his personal relations, on account of some unhappy misunderstanding, had for years been interrupted.

In this edition of my son's works, which is published for my benefit, it is a great pleasure for me to thank Mr. Griswold and Mr. Willis for their prompt fulfilment of the wishes of the dying poet, in labors, which demanded much time and attention, and which they have performed without any other recompense than the happiness which rewards acts of duty and kindness. I add to these expressions of gratitude to them, my acknowledgments to J. R. Lowell, Esquire, for his notices of Mr. Poe's genius and writings which are here published.

MARIA CLEMM

From *The Works of the Late Edgar Allan Poe*, edited by Rufus W. Griswold, I: [iii].

"Edgar A. Poe" (1850)

James Russell Lowell

James Russell Lowell's earlier biographical sketch of Poe, composed largely from notes Poe himself sent (*Graham's Magazine* [February 1845]), was updated for inclusion in Griswold's edition of Poe's *Works*. Griswold omitted several passages that presented Poe in favorable contexts, but the resulting biographical sketch gives a sensible outline of Poe's life and career. In addition, an obituary notice by Nathaniel P. Willis, well-known author and editor, accompanied Lowell's sketch. Both articles present a far more balanced, sympathetic portrayal of Poe than we find in Griswold's obituary and the expansion of it as the "Memoir," which, along with these next two essays, appear as front matter in the first volume of the Griswold edition. Although Lowell's estimate is far more favorable than Griswold's, the latter had tampered with Lowell's text from *Graham's* to make the overall portrayal in that essay less complimentary to Poe. Griswold's "Memoir" and the essays by Lowell and Willis originally appeared in volume 3 of the Griswold edition of Poe's *Works*, but were later transferred to volume 1.

Edgar A. Poe.[1]
By James Russell Lowell.

The situation of American literature is anomalous. It has no centre, or, if it have, it is like that of the sphere of Hermes. It is divided into many systems, each revolving round its several suns, and often presenting to the rest only the faint glimmer of a milk-and-water way. Our capital city, unlike London or Paris, is not a great central heart, from which life and vigor radiate to the extremities, but resembles more an isolated umbilicus, stuck down as near as may be to the centre of the land, and seeming rather to tell a legend of former usefulness than to serve any present need. Boston, New York, Philadelphia, each has its literature almost more distinct than those of the different dialects of Germany; and the articulate rumor barely has reached us dwellers by the Atlantic.

Perhaps there is no task more difficult than the just criticism of contemporary literature. It is even more grateful to give praise where it is needed than where it is deserved, and friendship so often seduces the iron stylus of justice into a vague flourish, that she writes what seems rather like an epitaph than a criticism. Yet if praise be given as an alms, we could not drop so poisonous a one into any man's hat. The critic's ink may suffer equally from too large an infusion of nutgalls or of sugar. But it is easier to be generous than to be just, and we might readily put faith in that fabulous direction to the hiding-place of truth, did we judge from the amount of water which we usually find mixed with it.

Remarkable experiences are usually confined to the inner life of imaginative men, but Mr. Poe's biography displays a vicissitude and peculiarity of interest such as is rarely met with. The offspring of a romantic marriage, and left an orphan at an early age, he was adopted by Mr. Allan, a wealthy Virginian, whose barren marriage-bed seemed the warranty of a large estate to the young poet. Having received a classical education in England, he returned home and entered the University of Virginia, where, after an extravagant course, followed by reformation at the last extremity, he was graduated with the highest honors of his class. Then came a boyish attempt to join the fortunes of the insurgent Greeks, which ended at St. Petersburg, where he got into difficulties through want of a passport, from which he was rescued by the American consul, and sent home. He now entered the military academy at West Point, from which he obtained a dismissal on hearing of the birth of a son to his adopted father, by a second marriage, an event which cut off his expectations as an heir. The death of Mr. Allan, in whose will his name was not mentioned, soon after relieved him of all doubt in this regard, and he committed himself at once to authorship for a support. Previously to this, however, he had published (in 1827) a small volume of poems, which soon ran through three editions, and excited high expectations of its author's future distinction in the minds of many competent judges.

That no certain augury can be drawn from a poet's earliest lispings there are instances enough to prove. Shakespeare's first poems, though brimful of vigor and youth and picturesqueness, give but a very faint promise of the directness, condensation and overflowing moral of his maturer works. Perhaps, however, Shakespeare is hardly a case in point, his "Venus and Adonis" having been published, we believe, in his twenty-sixth year. Milton's Latin verses show tenderness, a fine eye for nature, and a delicate appreciation of classic models, but give no hint of the author of a new style

[87]

in poetry. Pope's youthful pieces have all the sing-song, wholly unrelieved by the glittering malignity and eloquent irreligion of his later productions. Collins' callow namby-pamby died and gave no sign of the vigorous and original genius which he afterwards displayed. We have never thought that the world lost more in the "marvellous boy," Chatterton, than a very ingenious imitator of obscure and antiquated dulness. Where he becomes original (as it is called) the interest of ingenuity ceases and he becomes stupid. Kirke White's promises were endorsed by the respectable name of Mr. Southey, but surely with no authority from Apollo. They have the merit of a traditional piety, which, to our mind, if uttered at all, had been less objectionable in the retired closet of a diary, and in the sober raiment of prose. They do not clutch hold of the memory with the drowning pertinacity of Watts; neither have they the interest of his occasional simple, lucky beauty. Burns, having fortunately been rescued by his humble station from the contaminating society of the "best models" wrote well and naturally from the first. Had he been unfortunate enough to have had an educated taste, we should have had a series of poems from which, as from his letters, we could sift here and there a kernel from the mass of chaff. Coleridge's youthful efforts give no promise whatever of that poetical genius which produced at once the wildest, tenderest, most original and most purely imaginative poems of modern times. Byron's "Hours of Idleness" would never find a reader except from an intrepid and indefatigable curiosity. In Wordsworth's first preludings there is but a dim foreboding of the creator of an era. From Southey's early poems, a safer augury might have been drawn. They show the patient investigator, the close student of history, and the unwearied explorer of the beauties of predecessors, but they give no assurances of a man who should add aught to stock of household words, or to the rarer and more sacred delights of the fire-side or the arbor. The earliest specimens of Shelley's poetic mind already, also, give tokens of that ethereal sublimation in which the spirit seems to soar above the regions of words, but leaves its body, the verse, to be entombed, without hope of resurrection, in a mass of them. Cowley is generally instanced as a wonder of precocity. But his early insipidities show only a capacity for rhyming and for the metrical arrangement of certain conventional combinations of words, a capacity wholly dependent on a delicate physical organization, and an unhappy memory. An early poem is only remarkable when it displays an effort of *reason*, and the rudest verses in which we can trace some conception of the ends of poetry, are worth all the miracles of smooth juvenile versification. A school-boy, one would say, might acquire the regular see-saw of Pope merely by an association with the motion of the play-ground tilt.

Mr. Poe's early productions show that he could see through the verse to the spirit beneath, and that he already had a feeling that all the life and grace of the one must depend on and be modulated by the will of the other. We call them the most remarkable boyish poems that we have ever read. We know of none that can compare with them for maturity of purpose, and a nice understanding of the effects of language and metre. Such pieces are only valuable when they display what we can only express by the contradictory phrase of *innate experience*. We copy one of the shorter poems, written when the author was only fourteen. There is a little dimness in the filling up, but the grace and symmetry of the outline are such as few poets ever attain. There is a smack of ambrosia about it [text of "To Helen" (1831) follows].

It is the *tendency* of the young poet that impresses us. Here is no "withering scorn," no heart "blighted" ere it has safely got into its teens, none of the drawing-room sansculotism which Byron had brought into vogue. All is limpid and serene, with a pleasant dash of the Greek Helicon in it. The melody of the whole, too, is remarkable. It is not of that kind which can be demonstrated arithmetically upon the tips of the fingers. It is of that finer sort which the inner ear alone can estimate. It seems simple, like a Greek column, because of its perfection. In a poem named "Ligeia," under which title he intended to personify the music of nature, our boy-poet gives us the following exquisite picture:

> Ligeia! Ligeia!
>   My beautiful one,
> Whose harshest idea
>   Will to melody run,
> *Say, is it thy will,*
>   *On the breezes to toss,*
> *Or, capriciously still,*
>   *Like the lone albatross,*
> *Incumbent on night,*
>   *As she on the air,*
> *To keep watch with delight*
>   *On the harmony there?*

John Neal, himself a man of genius, and whose lyre has been too long capriciously silent, appreciated the high merit of these and similar passages, and drew a proud horoscope for their author.

Mr. Poe had that indescribable something which men have agreed to call *genius*. No man could ever tell us precisely what it is, and yet there is none who is not inevitably aware of its presence and its power. Let talent writhe and contort itself as it may, it has no such magnetism. Larger of bone and sinew it may be, but the wings are wanting. Talent sticks fast to earth, and its most perfect works have still one foot of clay. Genius claims kindred with the very workings of Nature herself, so that a sunset shall seem like a quotation from Dante or Milton, and if Shakespeare be read in the very presence of the sea itself, his verses shall but seem nobler for the sublime criticism of ocean. Talent may make friends for itself, but only genius can give to its creations the divine power of winning love and veneration. Enthusiasm cannot cling to what itself is unenthusiastic, nor will he ever have disciples who has not himself impulsive zeal enough to be a disciple. Great wits are allied to madness only inasmuch as they are possessed and carried away by their demon, while talent keeps him, as Paracelsus did, securely prisoned in the pommel of its sword. To the eye of genius, the veil of the spiritual world is ever rent asunder, that it may perceive the ministers of good and evil who throng continually around it. No man of mere talent ever flung his inkstand at the devil.

When we say that Mr. Poe had genius, we do not mean to say that he has produced evidence of the highest. But to say that he possesses it at all is to say that he needs only zeal, industry, and a reverence for the trust reposed in him, to achieve the proudest triumphs and the greenest laurels. If we may believe the Longinuses and Aristotles of our newspapers, we have quite too many geniuses of the loftiest order to render a place among them at all desirable, whether for its hardness of attainment or its seclusion. The highest peak of our Parnassus is, according to these gentlemen, by far the most thickly settled portion of the country, a circumstance which must make it an uncomfortable residence for individuals of a poetical temperament, if love of solitude be, as immemorial tradition asserts, a necessary part of their idiosyncrasy.

Mr. Poe has two of the prime qualities of genius, a faculty of vigorous yet minute analysis, and a wonderful fecundity of imagination. The first of these faculties is as needful to the artist in words, as a knowledge of anatomy is to the artist in colors or in stone. This enables him to conceive truly, to maintain a proper relation of parts, and to draw a correct outline, while the second groups, fills up, and colors. Both of these Mr. Poe has displayed with singular distinctness in his prose works, the last predominating in his earlier tales, and the first in his later ones. In judging of the merit of an author, and assigning him his niche among our household gods, we have a right to regard him from our own point of view, and to measure him by our own standard. But, in estimating the amount of power displayed in his works, we must be governed by his own design, and, placing them by the side of his own ideal, find how much is wanting. We differ from Mr. Poe in his opinions of the objects of art. He esteems that object to be the creation of Beauty, and perhaps it is only in the definition of that word that we disagree with him. But in what we shall say of his writings, we shall take his own standard as our guide. The temple of the god of song is equally accessible from every side, and there is room enough in it for all who bring offerings, or seek an oracle.

In his tales, Mr. Poe has chosen to exhibit his power chiefly in that dim region which stretches from the very utmost limits of the probable into the weird confines of superstition and unreality. He combines in a very remarkable manner two faculties which are seldom found united; a power of influencing the mind of the reader by the impalpable shadows of mystery, and a minuteness of detail which does not leave a pin or a button unnoticed. Both are, in truth, the natural results of the predominating quality of his mind, to which we have before alluded, analysis. It is this which distinguishes the artist. His mind at once reaches forward to the effect to be produced. Having resolved to bring about certain emotions in the reader, he makes all subordinate parts tend strictly to the common centre. Even his mystery is mathematical to his own mind. To him x is a known quantity all along. In any picture that he paints, he understands the chemical properties of all his colors. However vague some of his figures may seem, however formless the shadows, to him the outline is as clear and distinct as that of a geometrical diagram. For this reason Mr. Poe has no sympathy with *Mysticism*. The Mystic dwells *in* the mystery, is enveloped with it; it colors all his thoughts; it affects his optic nerve especially, and the commonest things get a rainbow edging from it. Mr. Poe, on the other hand, is a spectator *ab extrà*. He analyzes, he dissects, he watches

[91]

—"with an eye serene,
The very pulse of the machine,"

for such it practically is to him, with wheels and cogs and piston-rods, all working to produce a certain end.

This analyzing tendency of his mind balances the poetical, and, by giving him the patience to be minute, enables him to throw a wonderful reality into his most unreal fancies. A monomania he paints with great power. He loves to dissect one of these cancers of the mind, and to trace all the subtle ramifications of its roots. In raising images of horror, also, he has a strange success: conveying to us sometimes by a dusky hint some terrible *doubt* which is the secret of all horror. He leaves to imagination the task of finishing the picture, a task to which only she is competent. . . .

Beside the merit of conception, Mr. Poe's writings have also that of form. His style is highly finished, graceful and truly classical. It would be hard to find a living author who had displayed such varied powers. As an example of his style we would refer to one of his tales, "The House of Usher," in the first volume of his "Tales of the Grotesque and Arabesque." It has a singular charm for us, and we think that no one could read it without being strongly moved by its serene and sombre beauty. Had its author written nothing else, it would alone have been enough to stamp him as a man of genius, and the master of a classic style. In this tale occurs, perhaps, the most beautiful of his poems.

The great masters of imagination have seldom resorted to the vague and the unreal as sources of effect. They have not used dread and horror alone, but only in combination with other qualities, as means of subjugating the fancies of their readers. The loftiest muse has ever a household and fireside charm about her. Mr. Poe's secret lies mainly in the skill with which he has employed the strange fascination of mystery and terror. In this his success is so great and striking as to deserve the name of art, not artifice. We cannot call his materials the noblest or purest, but we must concede to him the highest merit of construction.

As a critic, Mr. Poe was aesthetically deficient. Unerring in his analysis of dictions, metres, and plots, he seemed wanting in the faculty of perceiving the profounder ethics of art. His criticisms are, however, distinguished for scientific precision and coherence of logic. They have the exactness, and at the same time, the coldness of mathematical demonstrations. Yet

[92]

they stand in strikingly refreshing contrast with the vague generalisms and sharp personalities of the day. If deficient in warmth, they are also without the heat of partizanship. They are especially valuable as illustrating the great truth, too generally overlooked, that analytic power is a subordinate quality of the critic.

On the whole, it may be considered certain that Mr. Poe has attained an individual eminence in our literature, which he will keep. He has given proof of power and originality. He has done that which could only be done once with success or safety, and the imitation or repetition of which would produce weariness.

Note

1. The following notice of Mr. Poe's life and works was written at his own request, five years ago, and accompanied a portrait of him, published in *Graham's Magazine* for February, 1845. It is here reprinted with a few alterations and omissions. [Lowell's note. The original note was not numbered, but just asterisked.]

James Russell Lowell, "Edgar A. Poe." From *The Works of the Late Edgar Allan Poe*, edited by Rufus W. Griswold, I: vii–xiii.

"Death of Edgar A. Poe" (1850)

Nathaniel P. Willis

Death of Edgar A. Poe.[1]
By N. P. Willis.

The ancient fable of two antagonistic spirits imprisoned in one body, equally powerful and having the complete mastery by turns—of one man, that is to say, inhabited by both a devil and an angel—seems to have been realized, if all we hear is true, in the character of the extraordinary man whose name we have written above. Our own impression of the nature of Edgar A. Poe, differs in some important degree, however, from that which has been generally conveyed in the notices of his death. Let us, before telling what we personally know of him, copy a graphic and highly finished portraiture, from the pen of Dr. Rufus W. Griswold, which appeared in a recent number of the *Tribune* [excerpts from the Ludwig obituary follow].

Apropos of the disparaging portion of the above well-written sketch, let us truthfully say:—

Some four or five years since, when editing a daily paper in this city, Mr. Poe was employed by us, for several months, as critic and sub-editor. This was our first personal acquaintance with him. He resided with his wife and mother at Fordham, a few miles out of town, but was at his desk in the office, from nine in the morning till the evening paper went to press. With the highest admiration for his genius, and a willingness to let it atone for more than ordinary irregularity, we were led by common report to expect a very capricious attention to his duties, and occasionally a scene of violence and difficulty. Time went on, however, and he was invariably punctual and industrious. With his pale, beautiful and intellectual face, as a reminder of what genius was in him, it was impossible, of course, not to treat him always with deferential courtesy, and, to our occasional request that he would not probe too deep in a criticism, or that he would erase a passage colored too highly with his resentments against society and mankind, he readily and courteously assented—far more yielding than most men, we thought, on points so excusably sensitive. With a prospect of taking the lead in another periodical, he, at last, voluntarily gave up his employment with us, and, through all this considerable period, we had seen but one presentment of the man—a quiet, patient, industrious, and most gentlemanly person, commanding the utmost respect and good feeling by his unvarying deportment and ability.

Residing as he did in the country, we never met Mr. Poe in hours of leisure; but he frequently called on us afterwards at our place of business, and we met him often in the street—invariably the same sad-mannered, winning and refined gentleman, such as we had always known him. It was by rumor only, up to the day of his death, that we knew of any other development of manner or character. We heard, from one who knew him well, (what should be stated in all mention of his lamentable irregularities,) that, with a *single glass* of wine, his whole nature was reversed, the demon became uppermost, and, though none of the usual signs of intoxication were visible, his *will* was palpably insane. Possessing his reasoning faculties in excited activity, at such times, and seeking his acquaintances with his wonted look and memory, he easily seemed personating only another phase of his natural character, and was accused, accordingly, of insulting arrogance and bad-heartedness. In this reversed character, we repeat, it was never our chance to see him. We know it from hearsay, and we mention it in connection with this sad infirmity of physical constitution; which puts it upon very nearly the ground of a temporary and almost irresponsible insanity.

The arrogance, vanity and depravity of heart, of which Mr. Poe was generally accused, seem, to us, referable altogether to this reversed phase of his character. Under that degree of intoxication which only acted upon him by demonizing his sense of truth and right, he doubtless said and did much that was wholly irreconcilable with his better nature; but, when himself, and as we knew him only, his modesty and unaffected humility, as to his own deservings, were a constant charm to his character. His letters (of which the constant application for autographs has taken from us, we are sorry to confess, the greater portion) exhibited this quality very strongly. In one of the carelessly written notes of which we chance still to retain possession, for instance, he speaks of "The Raven"—that extraordinary poem which electrified the world of imaginative readers, and has become the type of a school of

[95]

poetry of its own—and, in evident earnest, attributes its success to the few words of commendation with which we had prefaced it in this paper. It will throw light on his sane character to give a literal copy of the note:—

"Fordham, April 20, 1849.

"*My dear Willis*:—The poem which I enclose, and which I am so vain as to hope you will like, in some respects, has been just published in a paper for which sheer necessity compels me to write, now and then. It pays well as times go—but unquestionably it ought to pay ten prices; for whatever I send it I feel I am consigning to the tomb of the Capulets. The verses accompanying this, may I beg you to take out of the tomb, and bring them to light in the Home Journal? If you can oblige me so far as to copy them, I do not think it will be necessary to say 'From the——,—that would be too bad;—and, perhaps, 'From a late —— paper,' would do.

"I have not forgotten how a 'good word in season' from you made 'The Raven,' and made 'Ulalume,' (which, by-the-way, people have done me the honor of attributing to you)—therefore I *would* ask you, (if I dared,) to say something of these lines—if they please you.

"Truly yours ever,
"Edgar A. Poe."

In double proof—of his earnest disposition to do the best for himself, and of the trustful and grateful nature which has been denied him—we give another of the only three of his notes which we chance to retain:—

"Fordham, January 22, 1848.

"*My dear Mr. Willis*:—I am about to make an effort at re-establishing myself in the literary world, and *feel* that I may depend upon your aid.

"My general aim is to start a Magazine, to be called '*The Stylus*;' but it would be useless to me, even when established, if not entirely out of the control of a publisher. I mean, therefore, to get up a Journal which shall be *my own*, at all points. With this end in view, I must get a list of, at least, five hundred subscribers to begin with:—nearly two hundred I have already. I propose, however, to go South and West, among my personal and literary friends—old college and West Point acquaintances—and see what I can do. In order to get the means of taking the first step, I propose to lecture at the Society Library, on Thursday, the 3d of February—and, that there may be no cause of *squabbling*, my subject shall *not be literary* at all. I have chosen a broad text—'The Universe.'

"Having thus given you *the facts* of the case, I leave all the rest to the suggestions of your own tact and generosity. Gratefully—*most* gratefully—

"Your friend always,
"Edgar A. Poe."

Brief and chance-taken as these letters are, we think they sufficiently prove the existence of the very qualities denied to Mr. Poe—humility, willingness to persevere, belief in another's kindness, and capability of cordial and grateful friendship! Such he assuredly was *when sane.* Such only he has invariably seemed to us, in all we have happened personally to know of him, through a friendship of five or six years. And so much easier is it to believe what we have seen and known, than what we *hear of* only, that we remember him but with admiration and respect—these descriptions of him, when morally insane, seeming to us like portraits, painted in sickness, of a man we have only known in health.

But there is another, more touching, and far more forcible evidence that there *was goodness* in Edgar A. Poe. To reveal it, we are obliged to venture upon the lifting of the veil which sacredly covers grief and refinement in poverty—but we think it may be excused, if so we can brighten the memory of the poet, even were there not a more needed and immediate service which it may render to the nearest link broken by his death.

Our first knowledge of Mr. Poe's removal to this city was by a call which we received from a lady who introduced herself to us as the mother of his wife. She was in search of employment for him, and she excused her errand by mentioning that he was ill, that her daughter was a confirmed invalid, and that their circumstances were such as compelled her taking it upon herself. The countenance of this lady, made beautiful and saintly with an evidently complete giving up of her life to privation and sorrowful tenderness, her gentle and mournful voice urging its plea, her long-forgotten but habitually and unconsciously refined manners, and her appealing and yet appreciative mention of the claims and abilities of her son, disclosed at once the presence of one of those angels upon earth that women in adversity can be. It was a hard fate that she was watching over. Mr. Poe wrote with fastidious difficulty, and in a style too much above the popular level to be well paid. He was always in pecuniary difficulty, and, with his sick wife, frequently in want of the merest necessities of life. Winter after winter, for years, the most touching sight to us, in this whole city, has been that tireless minister to genius, thinly and insufficiently clad, going from office to office with a poem, or an article on some literary subject, to sell—sometimes, simply pleading in a broken voice that he was ill, and begging for him—mentioning nothing but that "he was ill," whatever might be the reason for his writing nothing—and never, amid all her tears and recitals of distress, suffering one syllable to escape her lips that could convey a doubt of him, or a complaint, or a lessening of pride in his genius and good intentions. Her daughter died, a year and a half since, but she did not desert him. She continued his ministering angel—living with him—caring for him—guarding him against exposure, and, when he was carried away by temptation, amid grief and the loneliness of feelings unreplied to, and awoke from his self-abandonment prostrated in destitution and suffering, *begging* for him still. If women's devotion, born with a first love, and fed with human passion, hallow its object, as it is allowed to do, what does not a devotion like this—pure, disinterested and holy as the watch of an invisible spirit—say for him who inspired it?

We have a letter before us, written by this lady, Mrs. Clemm, on the morning in which she heard of the death of this object of her untiring care. It is merely a request that we would call upon her, but we will copy a few of its words—sacred as its privacy is—to warrant the truth of the picture we have drawn above, and add force to the appeal we wish to make for her:—

"I have this morning heard of the death of my darling Eddie. . . . Can you give me any circumstances or particulars . . . Oh! do not desert your poor friend in this bitter affliction. . . . Ask Mr. ―――― to come, as I must deliver a message to him from my poor Eddie. . . . I need not ask you to notice his death and to speak well of him. I know you will. But say what an affectionate son he was to me, his poor desolate mother."

To hedge round a grave with respect, what choice is there, between the relinquished wealth and honors of the world, and the story of such a woman's unrewarded devotion! Risking what we do, in delicacy, by making it public, we feel—other reasons aside—that it betters the world to make known that there are such ministrations to its erring and gifted. What we have said will speak to some hearts. There are those who will be glad to know how the lamp, whose light of poetry has beamed on their far-away recognition, was watched over with care and pain—that they may send to her, who is more darkened than they by its extinction, some token of their sympathy. She is destitute, and alone. If any, far or near, will send to us what may aid and cheer her through the remainder of her life, we will joyfully place it in her hands.

Note

1. These remarks were published by Mr. Willis, in the "Home Journal," on the Saturday following Mr. Poe's death. [Griswold's note]

Nathaniel P. Willis, "Death of Edgar A. Poe." From *The Works of the Late Edgar Allan Poe*, edited by Rufus W. Griswold, I: xiv–xx.

"Memoir of the Author" (1850)

Rufus Wilmot Griswold

Griswold's second account of Poe's life and career, an expansion of his vilifying "Ludwig" obituary, stands as testimony to the former's hostility toward his subject. Because the memoir appears in the first collective—though not complete—edition of Poe's writings, it has unfortunately borne authority, by one who presumably knew and understood Poe well. This supposition regarding Griswold's reliability in his portrayal of Poe ties in with what I call the Poe Legend, that tissue of innuendo and downright error that has dogged Poe's footsteps since his lifetime. I have commented—and in this volume have presented documents to demonstrate it—that Poe himself initiated some of the "facts" that surround his image and that continue to attract enthusiasts who want their Poe to be a figure who is colorful and mysterious—verging, perhaps, on the sensational. Of course Poe, in providing information, for example, to Griswold himself for the headnote in *The Poets and Poetry of America*, to Lowell for his article in the February 1845 *Graham's Magazine*, and to Henry B. Hirst for the *Saturday Museum* sketch, was never behindhand at supplying material that was favorable to himself.

Whether Poe himself passed on to Griswold incorrect or unclear information, whether Griswold forgot certain facts, or whether he had imperfect information from others, we may never know. Two passages in what follows merit clarification, however, because similar uncertainty and error have colored other accounts of Poe. First, Poe was born on 19 January 1809. Birthdates of 1811 or 1813 have crept into biographical works about him, whether from misinformation he himself furnished or from other causes of misunderstandings by others. Second, for the 1833 Baltimore *Saturday Visiter* cash prize competition Poe submitted verse and fiction. The submissions were anonymous, and so the judges awarded his poem, "The Coliseum," and his tale, "MS. Found in a Bottle," first in each category. When they discovered that the same author had written both, they felt that in all fairness they could award him only one prize. Poe responded that they should name both of his submissions prize winners, but give the cash for the poem to the second ranking candidate. The result was that "Song of the Winds," by "Henry Wilton," took the prize for poetry. When Wilton's identity proved to be John Hill

Hewitt, one of the owners of the *Visiter*, Poe became incensed, and shortly thereafter he assaulted Hewitt on a Baltimore street.

Griswold's animosity toward Poe has never been fully understood, although he seemed to think that Poe had unjustly evaluated *The Poets and Poetry of America*. Whatever the truth of the circumstances, once Griswold was given charge of preparing an edition of Poe's writings, he used his editor's capacity to deepen a negative portrayal of Poe. Whether, as has long been supposed, Poe actually requested that Griswold promote his writings after his death, or whether after Poe's decease his mother-in-law, Maria Clemm, turned over the responsibility for that edition—in hopes that she would benefit financially from the publication—remains unclear. The particulars really matter little; the outcome of Griswold's biographical portraiture does. Many in the nineteenth-century Euro-American literary world thought that Griswold was a credible biographer. After all, his editions of writers' works were, for their time, well done, presenting what appeared to be accurate primary texts, along with equally sound information about authors' lives. Nearly two centuries afterward, Griswold's presentation of Poe as well nigh diabolic continues to wend its way into subsequent reactions toward Poe's life and his writings, as if his personal life is present, in thinly veiled guise, in his creative and critical publications. Therefore Griswold's "Memoir," though largely erroneous, warrants inclusion in a book like this one. The notes to this section have been numbered and placed at the end, although in the original they appeared as unnumbered footnotes at the bottom of the page.

Preface.

Hitherto I have not written or published a syllable upon the subject of Mr. Poe's life, character, or genius, since I was informed, some ten days after his death, of my appointment to be his literary executor. I did not suppose I was debarred from the expression of any feelings or opinions in the case by the acceptance of this office, the duties of which I regarded as simply the collection of his works, and their publication, for the benefit of the rightful inheritors of his property, in a form and manner that would probably have been most agreeable to his own wishes. I would gladly have declined a trust imposing so much labor, for I had been compelled by ill health to solicit the indulgence of my publishers, who had many thousand dollars invested in an unfinished work under my direction; but when I was told by several of Mr. Poe's most intimate friends—among others by the family of S. D. Lewis, Esq., to whom in his last years he was under greater obligations than to any or to all others—that he had long been in the habit of expressing a desire that in the event of his death I should be his editor, I yielded to the apparent necessity, and proceeded immediately with the preparation of the two volumes which have heretofore been published. But I had, at the request of the Editor of "The Tribune," written hastily a few paragraphs about Mr. Poe, which appeared in that paper with the tele-graphic communication of his death; and two or three of these paragraphs having been quoted by Mr. N. P. Willis, in his Notice of Mr. Poe, were as a part of that Notice unavoidably reprinted in the volume of the deceased author's Tales. And my unconsidered and imperfect, but, as every one who knew its subject readily perceived, very kind article, was now vehemently attacked. A writer under the signature of "George R. Graham," in a sopho-morical and trashy but widely circulated Letter, denounced it as "the fancy sketch of a jaundiced vision," "an immortal infamy," and its composition a *"breach of trust."* And to excuse his five months' silence, and to induce a belief that he did not KNOW that what I had written was already published *before I COULD have been advised that I was to be Mr. Poe's executor,* (a con-dition upon which all the possible force of his Letter depends,) this silly and ambitious person, while represented as entertaining a friendship re-ally passionate in its tenderness for the poor author, (of whom in four years of his extremest poverty he had not purchased for his magazine a single line,) is made to say that in *half a year* he had not seen so noticeable an article,—though within a week after Mr. Poe's death it appeared in "The Tribune," in "The Home Journal," in three of the daily papers of his own city, and in "The Saturday Evening Post," of which he was or had been himself one of the chief proprietors and editors! And Mr. John Neal, too, who had never had even the slightest personal acquaintance with Poe in his life, rushes from a sleep which the public had trusted was eternal, to declare that my characterization of Poe (which he is pleased to describe as "poetry, exalted poetry, poetry of astonishing and original strength") is false and malicious, and that I am a "calumniator," a "Rhadamanthus," etc. Both these writers—John Neal following the author of the Letter signed "George R. Graham"—not only assume what I have shown to be false, (that the remarks on Poe's character were written by me *as his executor,*) but that there was a long, intense, and implacable enmity betwixt Poe and myself, which disqualified me for the office of his biographer. This scarcely needs an answer after the poet's dying request that I should be his editor; but the manner in which it has been urged, will, I trust, be a sufficient excuse for the following demonstration of its absurdity.

My acquaintance with Mr. Poe commenced in the spring of 1841. He called at my hotel, and not finding me at home, left two letters of introduction. The next morning I visited him, and we had a long conversation about literature and literary men, pertinent to the subject of a book, "The Poets and Poetry of America," which I was then preparing for the press. The following letter was sent to me a few days afterwards:

Philadelphia, March 29.

R. W. Griswold, Esq.: My Dear Sir:—On the other leaf I send such poems as I think my best, from which you can select any which please your fancy. I should be proud to see one or two of them in your book. The one called "The Haunted Palace" is that of which I spoke in reference to Professor Longfellow's plagiarism. I first published the "H. P." in Brooks's "Museum," a monthly journal at Baltimore, now dead. Afterwards, I embodied it in a tale called "The House of Usher," in Burton's magazine. Here it was, I suppose, that Professor Longfellow saw it; for about six weeks afterwards, there appeared in the "Southern Literary Messenger" a poem by him called "The Beleaguered City," which may now be found in his volume. The identity in title is striking; for by "The Haunted Palace" I mean to imply a mind haunted by phantoms—a disordered brain—and by the "Beleaguered City" Prof. L. means just the same. But the whole tournure of the poem is based upon mine as you will see at once. Its allegorical conduct, the style of its versification and expression—all are mine. As I understood you to say that you meant to preface each set of poems by some biographical notice, I have ventured to send you the above memoranda—the particulars of which (in a case where an author is so little known as myself) might not be easily obtained elsewhere. "The Coliseum" was the prize poem alluded to.

With high respect and esteem, I am your obedient servant, Edgar A. Poe.

The next is without date:

My Dear Sir:—I made use of your name with Carey & Hart, for a copy of your book, and am writing a review of it, which I shall send to Lowell for "The Pioneer." I like it decidedly. It is of immense importance, as a guide to what we have done; but you have permitted your good nature to influence you to a degree: I would have omitted at least a dozen whom you have quoted, and I can think of five or six that should have been in. But with all its faults—you see I am perfectly frank with you—it is a better book than any other man in the United States could have made of the materials. This I will say.

> With high respect, I am your obedient servant, Edgar A. Poe.

The next refers to some pecuniary matters:

> Philadelphia, June 11, 1843.

> *Dear Griswold*:—Can you not send me $5? I am sick, and Virginia is almost gone. Come and see me. Peterson says you suspect me of a curious anonymous letter. I did not write it, but bring it along with you when you make the visit you promised to Mrs. Clemm. I will try to fix that matter soon. Could you do anything with my *note*?

> Yours truly, E. A. P.

We had no further correspondence for more than a year. In this period he delivered a lecture upon "The Poets and Poetry of America," in which my book under that title was, I believe, very sharply reviewed. In the meantime advertisement was made of my intention to publish "The Prose Writers of America," and I received, one day, just as I was leaving Philadelphia for New-York, the following letter:

> New-York, Jan. 10, 1845.

> *Rev. Rufus W. Griswold: Sir*—I perceive by a paragraph in the papers, that your "Prose Writers of America" is in press. Unless your opinions of my literary character are entirely changed, you will, I think, like something of mine, and you are welcome to whatever best pleases you, if you will permit me to furnish a corrected copy; but with your present feelings you can hardly do me justice in any criticism, and I shall be glad if you shall simply say after my name: "Born 1811; published Tales of the Grotesque and the Arabesque in 1839; has resided latterly in New-York."

> Your obedient servant, Edgar A. Poe.

I find my answer to this among his papers:

> Philadelphia, Jan. 11, 1845.

> *Sir*:—Although I have some cause of quarrel with you, as you seem to remember, I do not under any circumstances permit, as you have repeatedly charged, my personal relations to influence the expression of my opinions as a critic. By the inclosed proof-sheets of what I had written before the reception of

your note, you will see that I think quite as well of your works as I did when I had the pleasure of being Your friend,

R. W. Griswold.

This was not mailed until the next morning; I however left Philadelphia the same evening, and in the course of the following day Poe and myself met in the office of "The Tribune," but without any recognition. Soon after he received my note, he sent the following to my hotel:

New-York, Jan. 16, 1845.

Dear Griswold—If you will permit me to call you so—your letter occasioned me first pain and then pleasure: pain, because it gave me to see that I had lost, through my own folly, an honorable friend:—pleasure, because I saw in it a hope of reconciliation. I have been aware, for several weeks, that my reasons for speaking of your book as I did, (of *yourself* I have always spoken kindly,) were based in the malignant slanders of a mischief-maker by profession. Still, as I supposed you irreparably offended, I could make no advances when we met at the "Tribune" office, although I longed to do so. I know of nothing which would give me more sincere pleasure than your accepting these apologies, and meeting me as a friend. If you *can* do this, and forget the past, let me know where I shall call on you—or come and see me at the "Mirror" office, any morning about ten. We can then talk over the other matters, which, to me at least, are far less important than your good will.

Very truly yours, Edgar A. Poe.

His next letter is dated February 24, 1845:

My dear Griswold:—A thousand thanks for your kindness in the matter of those books, which I could not afford to buy, and had so much need of. Soon after seeing you, I sent you, through Zieber, all my poems worth republishing, and I presume they reached you. I was sincerely delighted with what you said of them, and if you will write your criticism in the form of a preface, I shall be greatly obliged to you. I say this not because you praised me: everybody praises me now: but because you so perfectly understand me, or what I have aimed at, in all my poems: I did not think you had so much delicacy of appreciation joined with your strong sense; I can say truly that no man's approbation gives me so much pleasure. I send you with this another package, also through Zieber, by Burgess & Stringer. It contains, in the way of essay, "Mesmeric Revelation," which I would like to have go in, even if you have to omit the "House of Usher." I send also corrected copies of (in the way of funny criticism, but you don't like this) "Flaccus," which conveys a tolerable idea of my style; and of my serious manner "Barnaby Rudge" is a good specimen. In the tale line, "The Murders of the Rue Morgue," "The Gold Bug," and the "Man that was Used Up,"—far more than enough, but you can select to suit yourself. I prefer the "G. B." to the "M. in the R. M." I have taken a third interest in the "Broadway Journal," and will be glad if you could send me anything for it. Why not let me anticipate the book publication of your splendid essay on Milton?

Truly yours, Poe.

The next is without date:

Dear Griswold:—I return the proofs with many thanks for your attentions. The poems look quite as well in the short metres as in the long ones, and I am quite content as it is. In "The Sleeper" you have "Forever with unclosed eye" for "Forever with unopen'd eye." Is it possible to make the correction? I presume you understand that in the repetition of my Lecture on the Poets, (in N. Y.) I left out *all* that was offensive to yourself. I am ashamed of myself that I ever said anything of you that was so unfriendly or so unjust; but what I *did* say I am confident has been misrepresented to you. See my notice of C. F. Hoffman's (?) sketch of you.

Very sincerely yours, Poe.

On the twenty-sixth of October, 1845, he wrote:

My dear Griswold:—Will you aid me at a pinch—at one of the greatest pinches conceivable? If you will, I will be indebted to you for life. After a prodigious deal of manoeuvering, I have succeeded in getting the "Broadway Journal" entirely within my own control. It will be a fortune to me if I can hold it—and I can do it easily with a very trifling aid from my friends. May I count you as one? Lend me $50, and you shall never have cause to regret it.

Truly yours, Edgar A. Poe.

And on the first of November:

My dear Griswold:—Thank you for the $25. And since you will allow me to draw upon you for the other half of what I asked, if it shall be needed at the end of a month, I am just as grateful as if it were all in hand—for my friends here have acted generously by me. Don't have any more doubts of my success. I am, by the way, preparing an article about you for the B. J., in which I do you justice—which is all you can ask of any one.

Ever truly yours, Edgar A. Poe.

The next is without date, but appears to have been written early in 1849:

Dear Griswold:—Your uniform kindness leads me to hope that you will attend to this little matter of Mrs. L——, to whom I truly think you have done less than justice. I am ashamed to ask favors of you, to whom I am so much indebted, but I have promised Mrs. L—— this. They lied to you, (if you told —— what he says you told him,) upon the subject of my forgotten Lecture on the American Poets, and I take this opportunity to say that what I have always held in conversations about you, and what I believe to be entirely true, as far as it goes, is contained in my notice of your "Female Poets of America," in the forthcoming "Southern Literary Messenger." By glancing at what I have published about you, (Aut. in Graham, 1841; Review in Pioneer, 1843; notice in B. Journal, 1845; Letter in Int., 1847; and the Review of your Female Poets,) you will see that I have never hazarded my own reputation by a disrespectful word of you, though there were, as I long ago explained, in consequence of ——'s false imputation of that beastly article to you, some absurd jokes at your expense in the Lecture at Philadelphia. Come up and see me: the cars pass within a few rods of the New-York Hotel, where I have called two or three times without finding you in.

Yours truly, Poe.

I soon after visited him at Fordham, and passed two or three hours with him. The only letter he afterward sent me—at least the only one now in my possession—follows:

Dear Griswold:—I enclose perfect copies of the lines "For Annie" and "Annabel Lee," in hopes that you may make room for them in your new edition. As regards "Lenore," (which you were kind enough to say you would insert,) I would prefer the concluding stanza to run as here written. . . . It is a point of no great importance, but in one of your editions you have given my sister's age instead of mine. I was born in Dec. 1813; my sister, Jan. 1811. [The date of his birth to which he refers was printed from his statement in the memoranda referred to in the first of the letters here printed.— R. W. G.] Willis, whose good opinion I value highly, and of whose good word I have a right to be proud, has done me the honor to speak very pointedly in praise of "The Raven." I inclose what he said, and if you could contrive to introduce it, you would render me an essential favor, and greatly further my literary interests, at a point where I am most anxious they should be advanced.

Truly yours, E. A. Poe.

P. S.—Considering my indebtedness to you, can you not sell to Graham or to Godey (with whom, you know, I cannot with the least self-respect again have anything to do directly)—can you not sell to one of these men, "Annabel Lee," say for $50, and credit me that sum? Either of them could print it before you will need it for your book. *Mem.* The Eveleth you ask about is a Yankee impertinent, who, knowing my extreme poverty, has for years pestered me with unpaid letters; but I believe almost every literary man of any note has suffered in the same way. I am surprised that you have escaped.

Poe.

These are all the letters (unless I have given away some notes of his to autograph collectors) ever received by me from Mr. Poe. They are a sufficient answer to the article by John Neal, and to that under the signature of "George R. Graham," which have induced their publication. I did not undertake to dispose of the poem of "Annabel Lee," but upon the death of the author quoted it in the notice of him in "The Tribune," and I was sorry to learn soon after that it had been purchased and paid for by the proprietors of both "Sartain's Magazine," and "The Southern Literary Messenger."

R. W. G. New-York, September 2, 1850.

Memoir.

The family of Edgar A. Poe was one of the oldest and most reputable in Baltimore. David Poe, his paternal grandfather, was a Quartermaster-General in the Maryland line during the Revolution, and the intimate friend of Lafayette, who, during his last visit to the United States, called personally upon the General's widow, and tendered her acknowledgements for the services rendered to him by her husband. His great-grandfather, John Poe, married in England, Jane, a daughter of Admiral James McBride, noted in British naval history, and claiming kindred with some of the most illustrious English families. His father, David Poe, jr., the fourth son of the Quartermaster-General, was several years a law student in Baltimore, but becoming enamored of an English actress, named Elizabeth Arnold, whose prettiness and vivacity more than her genius for the stage made her a favorite, he eloped with her, and after a short period, having married her, became himself an actor. They continued six or seven years in the theatres of the principal cities, and finally died, within a few weeks of each other, in Richmond, leaving three children, Henry, Edgar, and Rosalie, in utter destitution.

Edgar Poe, who was born in Baltimore, in January, 1811, was at this period of remarkable beauty, and precocious wit. Mr. John Allan, a merchant of large fortune and liberal disposition, who had been intimate with his parents, having no children of his own, adopted him, and it was generally understood among his acquaintances that he intended to make him the heir of his estate. The proud, nervous irritability of the boy's nature was fostered by his guardian's well-meant but ill-judged indulgence. Nothing was permitted which could "break his spirit." He must be the master of his masters, or not have any. An eminent and most estimable gentleman has written to me, that when Poe was only six or seven years of age, he went to a school kept by a widow of excellent character, to whom was committed the instruction of the children of some of the principal families in the city. A portion of the grounds was used for the cultivation of vegetables, and its invasion by her pupils strictly forbidden. A trespasser, if discovered, was commonly made to wear, during school hours, a turnip or carrot, or something of this sort, attached to his neck as a sign of disgrace. On one occasion, Poe, having violated the rules, was decorated with the promised badge, which he wore in sullenness until the dismissal of the boys, when, that the full extent of his wrong might be understood by his patron, of whose sympathy he was confident, he eluded the notice of the schoolmistress, who would have relieved him of his esculent, and made the best of his way home, with it dangling at his neck. Mr. Allan's anger was aroused, and he proceeded instantly to the school-room, and after lecturing the astonished dame upon the enormity of such an insult to his son and to himself, demanded his account, determined that the child should not again be subjected to such tyranny. Who can estimate the effect of this puerile triumph upon the growth of that morbid self-esteem which characterized the author in after-life?

In 1816, he accompanied Mr. and Mrs. Allan to Great Britain, visited the most interesting portions of the country, and afterwards passed four or five years in a school kept at Stoke Newington, near London, by the Rev. Dr. Bransby. In his tale, entitled "William Wilson," he has introduced a striking description of the school and of his life there. He says:

"My earliest recollections of a school life, are connected with a large, rambling, Elizabethan house, in a misty-looking village of England, where were a vast number of gigantic and gnarled trees, and where all the houses were excessively ancient. In truth, it was a dream-like and spirit-soothing place, that venerable old town. At this moment, in fancy, I feel the refreshing chilliness of its deeply-shadowed avenues, inhale the fragrance of its thousand shrubberies, and thrill anew with undefinable delight, at the deep hollow note of the church-bell, breaking, each hour, with sullen and sudden roar, upon the stillness of the dusky atmosphere in which the fretted Gothic steeple lay embedded and asleep. It gives me, perhaps, as much of pleasure as I can now in any manner experience, to dwell upon minute recollections of the school and its concerns. Steeped in misery as I am—misery, alas! only too real—I shall be pardoned for seeking relief, however slight and temporary, in the weakness of a few rambling details. These, moreover, utterly trivial, and even ridiculous in themselves, assume, to my fancy, adventitious importance, as connected with a period and a locality when and where I recognise the first ambiguous monitions of the destiny which afterwards so fully overshadowed me. Let me then remember. The house, I have said, was old and irregular. The grounds were extensive, and a high and solid brick wall, topped with a bed of mortar and broken glass, encompassed the whole. This prison-like rampart formed the limit of our domain; beyond it we saw but thrice a week—once every Saturday afternoon, when, attended by two ushers, we were permitted to take brief walks in a body through some of the neighboring fields—and twice during Sunday, when we were paraded in the same formal manner to the morning and evening service in the one church of the village. Of this church the principal of our school was pastor. With how deep a spirit of wonder and perplexity was I wont to regard him from our remote pew in the gallery, as, with step solemn and slow, he ascended the pulpit! This reverend man, with countenance so demurely benign, with robes so glossy and so clerically flowing, with wig so minutely powdered, so rigid and so vast,—could this be he, who, of late, with sour visage, and in snuffy habiliments, administered, ferule in hand, the Draconian Laws of the academy? Oh, gigantic paradox, too utterly monstrous for solution! At an angle of the ponderous wall frowned a more ponderous gate. It was riveted and studded with iron bolts, and surmounted with jagged iron spikes. What impressions of deep awe did it inspire! It was never opened save for the three periodical egressions and ingressions already mentioned; then, in every creak of its mighty hinges, we found a plenitude of mystery—a world of matter for solemn remark, and for more solemn meditation. The extensive enclosure was irregular in form, having many capacious recesses. Of these, three or four of the largest constituted the playground. It was level, and covered with fine hard gravel. I well remember it had no trees, nor benches, nor anything similar within it. Of course it was in the rear of the house. In front lay a small parterre, planted with box and other shrubs; but through this sacred division we passed only upon rare occasions indeed—such as a first advent to school or final departure thence, or perhaps, when a parent or friend having called for us, we joyfully took our way home for the Christmas or Midsummer holidays. But the house!—how quaint an old building was this!—to me how veritably a palace of enchantment! There was really no end to its windings—to its incomprehensible subdivisions. It was difficult at any given time, to say with certainty upon which of its two stories one happened to be. From each room to every other there were sure to be found three or four steps either in ascent or descent. Then the lateral branches were innumerable—inconceivable—and so returning in upon themselves, that our most exact ideas in regard to the whole mansion were not very far different from those with which we pondered upon infinity. During the five years of my residence here, I was never able to ascertain with precision, in what remote locality lay the little sleeping apartment assigned to myself and some eighteen or twenty other scholars. The school room was the largest in the house—I could not help thinking, in the world. It was very long, narrow, and dismally low, with pointed gothic windows and a ceiling of oak. In a remote and terror-inspiring angle was a square enclosure of eight or ten feet, comprising the *sanctum*, 'during hours,' of our principal, the Reverend Dr. Bransby. It was a solid structure, with massy door, sooner than open which in the absence of the 'Dominie,' we would all have willingly perished by the *peine forte et dure*. In other angles were two other similar boxes, far less reverenced, indeed, but still greatly matters of awe. One of these was the pulpit of the 'classical' usher, one of the 'English and mathematical.' Interspersed about the room, crossing and recrossing in endless irregularity, were innumerable benches and desks, black, ancient, and time-worn, piled desperately with much-bethumbed books, and so beseamed with initial letters, names at full length, grotesque figures, and other multiplied efforts of the knife, as to have entirely lost what little of original form might have been their portion in days long departed. A huge bucket with water stood at one extremity of the room, and a clock of stupendous dimensions at the other.

"Encompassed by the massy walls of this venerable academy, I passed

[111]

yet not in tedium or disgust, the years of the third lustrum of my life. The teeming brain of childhood requires no external world of incident to occupy or amuse it; and the apparently dismal monotony of a school was replete with more intense excitement than my riper youth has derived from luxury, or my full manhood from crime. Yet I must believe that my first mental development had in it much of the uncommon—even much of the *outré*. Upon mankind at large the events of very early existence rarely leave in mature age any definite impression. All is gray shadow—a weak and irregular remembrance—an indistinct regathering of feeble pleasures and phantasmagoric pains. With me this is not so. In childhood I must have felt with the energy of a man what I now find stamped upon memory in lines as vivid, as deep, and as durable as the *exergues* of the Carthaginian medals. Yet in fact—in the fact of the world's view—how little was there to remember. The morning's awakening, the nightly summons to bed; the connings, the recitations; the periodical half-holidays and perambulations; the play-ground, with its broils, its pastimes, its intrigues; these, by a mental sorcery long forgotten, were made to involve a wilderness of sensation, a world of rich incident, an universe of varied emotions, of excitement the most passionate and spirit-stirring. '*Oh, le bon temps, que ce siècle de fer!*'"

In 1822, he returned to the United States, and after passing a few months at an Academy in Richmond, he entered the University at Charlottesville, where he led a very dissipated life; the manners which then prevailed there were extremely dissolute, and he was known as the wildest and most reckless student of his class; but his unusual opportunities, and the remarkable ease with which he mastered the most difficult studies kept him all the while in the first rank for scholarship, and he would have graduated with the highest honors, had not his gambling, intemperance, and other vices, induced his expulsion from the university.

At this period he was noted for feats of hardihood, strength and activity, and on one occasion, in a hot day of June, he swam from Richmond to Warwick, seven miles and a half, against a tide running probably from two to three miles and hour.[1] He was expert at fence, had some skill in drawing, and was a ready and eloquent conversationist and declaimer.

His allowance of money while at Charlottesville had been liberal, but he quitted the place very much in debt, and when Mr. Allan refused to accept some of the drafts with which he had paid losses in gaming, he wrote to him an abusive letter, quitted his house, and soon after left the country with the Quixotic intention of joining the Greeks, then in the midst of their struggle with the Turks. He never reached his destination, and we know but little of his adventures in Europe for nearly a year. By the end of this time he had made his way to St. Petersburgh, and our Minister in that capital, the late Mr. Henry Middleton, of South Carolina, was summoned one morning to save him from penalties incurred in a drunken debauch. Through Mr. Middleton's kindness he was set at liberty and enabled to return to this country.

His meeting with Mr. Allan was not very cordial, but that gentleman declared himself willing to serve him in any way that should seem judicious; and when Poe expressed some anxiety to enter the Military Academy, he induced Chief Justice Marshall, Andrew Stevenson, General Scott, and other eminent persons, to sign an application which secured his appointment to a scholarship in that institution.

Mrs. Allan, whom Poe appears to have regarded with much affection, and who had more influence over him than any one else at this period, died on the twenty-seventh of February, 1829, which I believe was just before Poe left Richmond for West Point. It has been erroneously stated by all Poe's biographers, that Mr. Allan was now sixty-five years of age, and that Miss Paterson, to whom he was married afterward, was young enough to be his grand-daughter. Mr. Allan was in his forty-eighth year, and the difference between his age and that of his second wife was not so great as justly to attract any observation.

For a few weeks the cadet applied himself with much assiduity to his studies, and he became at once a favorite with his mess and with the officers and professors of the Academy; but his habits of dissipation were renewed; he neglected his duties and disobeyed orders; and in ten months from his matriculation he was cashiered.

He went again to Richmond, and was received into the family of Mr. Allan, who was disposed still to be his friend, and in the event of his good behavior to treat him as a son; but it soon became necessary to close his doors against him forever. According to Poe's own statement he ridiculed the marriage of his patron with Miss Paterson, and had a quarrel with her; but a different story,[2] scarcely suitable for repetition here, was told by the friends of the other party. Whatever the circumstances, they parted in anger, and Mr. Allan from that time declined to see or in any way to assist him. Mr. Allan died in the spring of 1834, in the fifty-fourth year of his age, leaving three children to share his property, of which not a mill was bequeathed to Poe.

Soon after he left West Point Poe had printed at Baltimore a small volume of verses, ("Al Aaraaf," of about four hundred lines, "Tamerlane," of about three hundred lines, with smaller pieces,) and the favorable manner in which it was commonly referred to confirmed his belief that he might succeed in the profession of literature. The contents of the book appear to have been written when he was between sixteen and nineteen years of age; but though they illustrated the character of his abilities and justified his anticipations of success, they do not seem to me to evince, all things considered, a very remarkable precocity. The late Madame d'Ossoli refers to some of them as the productions of a boy of eight or ten years, but I believe there is no evidence that anything of his which has been published was written before he left the university. Certainly, it was his habit so constantly to labor upon what he had produced—he was at all times so anxious and industrious in revision—that his works, whenever first comprised, displayed the perfection of his powers at the time when they were given to the press.

His contributions to the journals attracted little attention, and his hopes of gaining a living in this way being disappointed, he enlisted in the army as a private soldier. How long he remained in the service I have not been able to ascertain. He was recognised by officers who had known him at West Point, and efforts were made, privately, but with prospects of success, to obtain for him a commission, when it was discovered by his friends that he had deserted.

He had probably found relief from the monotony of a soldier's life in literary composition. His mind was never in repose, and without some such resort the dull routine of the camp or barracks would have been insupportable. When he next appears, he has a volume of MS. stories, which he desires to print under the title of "Tales of the Folio Club." An offer by the proprietor of the Baltimore "Saturday Visiter," of two prizes, one for the best tale and one for the best poem, induced him to submit the pieces entitled "MS. found in a Bottle," "Lionizing," "The Visionary," and three others, with "The Coliseum," a poem, to the committee, which consisted of Mr. John P. Kennedy, the author of "Horse Shoe Robinson," Mr. J. H. B. Latrobe, and Dr. James H. Miller. Such matters are usually disposed of in a very off-hand way: Committees to award literary prizes drink to the payer's health in good wines, over unexamined MSS., which they submit to the discretion of publishers with permission to use their names in such a way as to promote the publishers' advantage. So perhaps it would have been in this case, but that one of the committee, taking up a little book remarkably beautiful and distinct in caligraphy, was tempted to read several pages; and becoming interested, he summoned the attention of the company to the half-dozen compositions it contained. It was unanimously decided that the prizes should be paid to "the first of geniuses who had written legibly." Not another MS. was unfolded. Immediately the "confidential envelope" was opened, and the successful competitor was found to bear the scarcely known name of Poe. The committee indeed awarded to him the premiums for both the tale and the poem, but subsequently altered their decision, so as to exclude him from the second premium, in consideration of his having obtained the higher one. The prize tale was the "MS. found in a Bottle." This award was published on the twelfth of October, 1833. The next day the publisher called to see Mr. Kennedy, and gave him an account of the author, which excited his curiosity and sympathy, and caused him to request that he should be brought to his office. Accordingly he was introduced; the prize money had not yet been paid, and he was in the costume in which he had answered the advertisement of his good fortune. Thin, and pale even to ghastliness, his whole appearance indicated sickness and the utmost destitution. A well-worn frock coat concealed the absence of a shirt, and imperfect boots disclosed the want of hose. But the eyes of the young man were luminous with intelligence and feeling, and his voice and conversation and manners all won upon the lawyer's regard. Poe told his history, and his ambition, and it was determined that he should not want means for a suitable appearance in society, nor opportunity for a just display of his abilities in literature. Mr. Kennedy accompanied him to a clothing store, and purchased for him a respectable suit, with changes of linen, and sent him to a bath, from which he returned with the suddenly regained style of a gentleman.

His new friends were very kind to him, and availed themselves of every opportunity to serve him. Near the close of the year 1834 the late Mr. T. W. White established in Richmond the "Southern Literary Messenger." He was a man of much simplicity, purity and energy of character, but not a writer, and he frequently solicited of his acquaintances literary assistance. On receiving from him an application for an article, early in 1835,

Mr. Kennedy, who was busy with the duties of his profession, advised Poe to send one, and in a few weeks he had occasion to enclose the following answer to a letter from Mr. White.

"Baltimore, April 13, 1835.

"*Dear Sir*: Poe did right in referring to me. He is very clever with his pen— classical and scholarlike. He wants experience and direction, but I have no doubt he can be made very useful to you. And, poor fellow! he is *very* poor. I told him to write something for every number of your magazine, and that you might find it to your advantage to give him some permanent employ. He has a volume of very bizarre tales in the hands of ——, in Philadelphia, who for a year past has been promising to publish them. This young fellow is highly imagina- tive, and a little given to the *terrific*. He is at work upon a tragedy, but I have turned him to drudging upon whatever may make money, and I have no doubt you and he will find your account in each other."

In the next number of the "Messenger" Mr. White announced that Poe was its editor, or in other words, that he had made arrangements with a gentleman of approved literary taste and attainments to whose especial management the editorial department would be confided, and it was de- clared that this gentleman would "devote his exclusive attention to the work." Poe continued, however, to reside in Baltimore, and it is probable that he was engaged only as a general contributor and a writer of critical notices of books. In a letter to Mr. White, under the date of the thirtieth of May, he says:

"In regard to my critique of Mr. Kennedy's novel I seriously feel ashamed of what I have written. I fully intended to give the work a thorough review, and examine it in detail. Ill health alone prevented me from so doing. At the time I made the hasty sketch I sent you, I was so ill as to be hardly able to see the paper on which I wrote, and I finished it in a state of complete ex- haustion. I have not, therefore, done anything like justice to the book, and I am vexed about the matter, for Mr. Kennedy has proved himself a kind friend to me in every respect, and I am sincerely grateful to him for many acts of generosity and attention. You ask me if I am perfectly satisfied with your course. I reply that I am—entirely. My poor services are not worth what you give me for them."

About a month afterward he wrote [to White]:

"You ask me if I would be willing to come on to Richmond if you should have occasion for my services during the coming winter. I reply that nothing would give me greater pleasure. I have been desirous for some time past of paying a visit to Richmond, and would be glad of any reasonable excuse for so doing. Indeed I am anxious to settle myself in that city, and if, by any chance, you hear of a situation likely to suit me, I would gladly accept it, were the salary even the merest trifle. I should, indeed, feel myself greatly indebted to you if through your means I could accomplish this object. What you say in the conclusion of your letter, in relation to the supervision of proof-sheets, gives me reason to hope that possibly you might find something for me to do in your office. If so, I should be very glad—for at present only a very small portion of my time is employed."

He continued in Baltimore till September. In this period he wrote several long reviewals, which for the most part were rather abstracts of works than critical discussions, and published with others, "Hans Pfaall," a story in some respects very similar to Mr. Locke's celebrated account of Herschell's Discoveries in the Moon. At first he appears to have been ill satisfied with Richmond, or with his duties, for in two or three weeks after his removal to that city we find Mr. Kennedy writing to him:

"I am sorry to see you in such plight as your letter shows you in. It is strange that just at this time, when everybody is praising you, and when fortune is beginning to smile upon your hitherto wretched circumstances, you should be invaded by these blue devils. It belongs, however, to your age and temper to be thus buffeted—but be assured, it only wants a little resolution to master the adversary forever. You will doubtless do well henceforth in literature, and add to your *comforts* as well as to your reputation, which it gives me great pleasure to assure you is everywhere rising in popular esteem."

But he could not bear his good fortune. On receiving a month's salary he gave himself up to habits which only necessity had restrained at Baltimore. For a week he was in a condition of brutish drunkenness, and Mr. White dismissed him. When he became sober, however, he had no resources but in reconciliation, and he wrote letters and induced acquaintances to call upon Mr. White with professions of repentance and promises of reformation. With his usual considerate and judicious kindness that gentleman answered him:

"*My dear Edgar*: I cannot address you in such language as this occasion and my feelings demand: I must be content to speak to you in my plain way. That you are sincere in all your promises I firmly believe. But when you once again tread these streets, I have my fears that your resolutions will fail, and that you will again drink till your senses are lost. If you rely on your strength you are gone. Unless you look to your Maker for help you will not be safe. How much I regretted parting from you is known to Him only and myself. I had become attached to you; I am still; and I would willingly say return, did not a knowledge of your past life make me dread a speedy renewal of our separation. If you would make yourself contented with quarters in my house, or with any other private family, where liquor is not used, I should think there was some hope for you. But, if you go to a tavern, or to any place where it is used at table, you are not safe. You have fine talents, Edgar, and you ought to have them respected, as well as yourself. Learn to respect yourself, and you will soon find that you are respected. Separate yourself from the bottle, and from bottle companions, forever. Tell me if you can and will do so. If you again become an assistant in my office, it must be understood that all engagements on my part cease the moment you get drunk. I am your true friend. T. W. W."

A new contract was arranged, but Poe's irregularities frequently interrupted the kindness and finally exhausted the patience of his generous though methodical employer, and in the number of the "Messenger" for January, 1837, he thus took leave of its readers:

"*Mr. Poe's* attention being called in another direction, he will decline, with the present number, the editorial duties of the Messenger. His Critical Notices for this month end with Professor Anthon's Cicero—what follows is from another hand. With the best wishes to the magazine, and to its few foes as well as many friends, he is now desirous of bidding all parties a peaceful farewell."

While in Richmond, with an income of but five hundred dollars a year, he had married his cousin, Virginia Clemm, a very amiable and lovely girl, who was as poor as himself, and little fitted, except by her gentle temper, to be the wife of such a person. He went from Richmond to Baltimore, and after a short time, to Philadelphia, and to New-York. A slight acquaintance with Dr. Hawks had led that acute and powerful writer to invite his contributions to the "New-York Review," and he had furnished for the second number of it (for October, 1837) an elaborate but not very remarkable article upon Stephens's then recently published "Incidents of Travel in Egypt, Arabia Petrea, and the Holy Land." His abilities were not of the kind demanded for such a work, and he never wrote another paper for this or for any other Review of the same class. He had commenced in the "Literary Messenger," a story of the sea, under the title of "Arthur Gordon Pym,"[3] and upon the recommendation of Mr. Paulding and others, it was printed by the Harpers. It is his longest work, and is not without some sort of merit, but it received little attention. The publishers sent one hundred copies to England, and being mistaken at first for a narrative of real experiences, it was advertised to be reprinted, but a discovery of its character, I believe prevented such a result. An attempt is made in it, by simplicity of style, minuteness of nautical descriptions, and circumstantiality of narration, to give it that air of truth which constitutes the principal attraction of Sir Edward Seaward's Narrative, and Robinson Crusoe; but it has none of the pleasing interest of these tales; it is as full of wonders as Munchausen, has as many atrocities as the Book of Pirates, and as liberal an array of paining and revolting horrors as ever was invented by Anne Radcliffe or George Walker. Thus far a tendency to extravagance had been the most striking infirmity of his genius. He had been more anxious to be intense than to be natural; and some of his *bizarréries* had been mistaken for satire, and admired for that quality. Afterward he was more judicious, and if his outlines were incredible it was commonly forgotten in the simplicity of his details and their cohesive cumulation.

Near the end of the year 1838 he settled in Philadelphia. He had no very definite purposes, but trusted for support to the chances of success as a magazinist and newspaper correspondent. Mr. Burton, the comedian, had recently established the "Gentleman's Magazine," and of this he became a contributor, and in May, 1839, the chief editor, devoting to it, for ten dollars a week, two hours every day, which left him abundant time for more important labors. In the same month he agreed to furnish such reviewals as he had written for the "Literary Messenger," for the "Literary Examiner," a new magazine at Pittsburgh. But his more congenial pursuit was tale writing, and he produced about this period some of his most remarkable and characteristic works in a department of imaginative composition in which he was henceforth alone and unapproachable. The "Fall of the House of Usher," and "Legeia [*sic*]," are the most interesting illustrations of his mental organization—his masterpieces in a peculiar vein of romantic creation. They have the unquestionable stamp of genius. The analyses of the growth of madness in one, and the thrilling revelations of the existence of a first wife in the person of a second, in the other, are made with consummate

[119]

skill; and the strange and solemn and fascinating beauty which informs the style and invests the circumstances of both, drugs the mind, and makes us forget the improbabilities of their general design.

An awakened ambition and the healthful influence of a conviction that his works were appreciated, and that his fame was increasing, led him for a while to cheerful views of life, and to regular habits of conduct. He wrote to a friend, the author of "Edge Hill," in Richmond, that he had quite overcome "the seductive and dangerous besetment" by which he had so often been prostrated, and to another friend that, incredible as it might seem, he had become a "model of temperance," and of "other virtues," which it had sometimes been difficult for him to practise. Before the close of the summer, however, he relapsed into his former courses, and for weeks was regardless of everything but a morbid and insatiable appetite for the means of intoxication.

In the autumn he published all the prose stories he had then written, in two volumes, under the title of "Tales of the Grotesque and Arabesque." The work was not saleable, perhaps because its contents were too familiar from recent separate publication in magazines; and it was not so warmly praised, generally, as I think it should have been, though in point of style the pieces which it embraced are much less perfect than they were made subsequently.

He was with Mr. Burton until June, 1840—more than a year. Mr. Burton appreciated his abilities and would gladly have continued the connexion; but Poe was so unsteady of purpose and so unreliable that the actor was never sure when he left the city that his business would be cared for. On one occasion, returning after the regular day of publication, he found the number unfinished, and Poe incapable of duty. He prepared the necessary copy himself, published the magazine, and was proceeding with arrangements for another month, when he received a letter from his assistant, of which the tone may be inferred from this answer:

"I am sorry you have thought it necessary to send me such a letter. Your troubles have given a morbid tone to your feelings which it is your duty to discourage. I myself have been as severely handled by the world as you can possibly have been, but my sufferings have not tinged my mind with melancholy, nor jaundiced my views of society. You must rouse your energies, and if care assail you, conquer it. I will gladly overlook the past. I hope you will as easily fulfil your pledges for the future. We shall agree very well, though I cannot permit the magazine to be made a vehicle for that sort of severity which you think is so 'successful with the mob.' I am truly much less anxious about making a monthly 'sensation' than I am upon the point of fairness. You must, my dear sir, get rid of your avowed ill-feelings toward your brother authors. You see I speak plainly: I cannot do otherwise upon such a subject. You say the people love havoc. I think they love justice. I think you yourself would not have written the article on Dawes, in a more healthy state of mind. I am not trammelled by any vulgar consideration of expediency; I would rather lose money than by such undue severity wound the feelings of a kind-hearted and honorable man. And I am satisfied that Dawes has something of the true fire in him. I regretted your word-catching spirit. But I wander from my design. I accept your proposition to recommence your interrupted avocations upon the *Maga*. Let us meet as if we had not exchanged letters. Use more exercise, write when feelings prompt, and be assured of my friendship. You will soon regain a healthy activity of mind, and laugh at your past vagaries."

This letter was kind and judicious. It gives us a glimpse of Poe's theory of criticism, and displays the temper and principles of the literary comedian in an honorable light. Two or three months afterward Burton went out of town to fulfil a professional engagement, leaving material and directions for completing the next number of the magazine in four days. He was absent nearly a fortnight, and on returning he found that his printers in the meanwhile had not received a line of copy; but that Poe had prepared the prospectus of a new monthly, and obtained transcripts of his subscription and account books, to be used in a scheme for supplanting him. He encountered his associate late in the evening at one of his accustomed haunts, and said, "Mr. Poe, I am astonished: Give me my manuscripts so that I can attend to the duties you have so shamefully neglected, and when you are sober we will settle." Poe interrupted him with "Who are you that presume to address me in this manner? Burton, I am—*the editor*—*of the Penn Magazine*—and you are—hiccup—*a fool*." Of course this ended his relations with the "Gentleman's."

In November, 1840, Burton's miscellany was merged in "The Casket," owned by Mr. George R. Graham, and the new series received the name of its proprietor, who engaged Poe in its editorship. His connexion with "Graham's Magazine" lasted about a year and a half, and this was one of the most active and brilliant periods of his literary life. He wrote in it several of his finest tales and most trenchant criticisms, and challenged attention by his papers entitled "Autography," and those on cryptology and cyphers. In the first, adopting a suggestion of Lavater, he attempted the illustration of character from handwriting; and in the second, he assumed that human ingenuity could construct no secret writing which human ingenuity could not resolve: a not very dangerous proposition, since it implied no capacity in himself to discover every riddle of this kind that should be invented. He however succeeded with several difficult cryptographs that were sent to him, and the direction of his mind to the subject led to the composition of some of the tales of ratiocination which so largely increased his reputation. The infirmities which induced his separation from Mr. White and from Mr. Burton at length compelled Mr. Graham to seek for another editor; but Poe still remained in Philadelphia, engaged from time to time in various literary occupations, and in the vain effort to establish a journal of his own to be called "The Stylus." Although it requires considerable capital to carry on a monthly of the description he proposed, I think it would not have been difficult, with his well-earned fame as a magazinist, for him to have found a competent and suitable publisher, but for the unfortunate notoriety of his habits, and the failure in succession of three persons who had admired him for his genius and pitied him for his misfortunes, by every means that tact or friendship could suggest, to induce the consistency and steadiness of application indispensable to success in such pursuits. It was in the spring of 1843—more than a year after his dissociation from Graham—that he wrote the story of "The Gold Bug," for which he was paid a prize of one hundred dollars. It has relation to Captain Kyd's treasure, and is one of the most remarkable illustrations of his ingenuity of construction and apparent subtlety of reasoning. The interest depends upon the solution of an intricate cypher. In the autumn of 1844 Poe removed to New-York.

It was while he resided in Philadelphia that I became acquainted with him. His manner, except during his fits of intoxication, was very quiet and gentlemanly; he was usually dressed with simplicity and elegance; and when once he sent for me to visit him, during a period of illness caused by protracted and anxious watching at the side of his sick wife, I was impressed by the singular neatness of the air of refinement in his home. It was in a small house, in one of the pleasant and silent neighborhoods far from the centre of the town, and though slightly and cheaply furnished, everything in it was so tasteful and so fitly disposed that it seemed altogether suitable for a man of genius. For this and for most of the comforts he enjoyed in his brightest as in his darkest years, he was chiefly indebted to his mother-in-law, who loved him with more than maternal devotion and constancy.

He had now written his most acute criticisms and his most admirable tales. Of tales, besides those to which I have referred, he had produced "The Descent into the Mælström," "The Premature Burial," "The Purloined Letter," "The Murders of the Rue Morgue," and its sequel, "The Mystery of Marie Roget." The scenes of the last three are in Paris, where the author's friend, the Chevalier Auguste Dupin, is supposed to reveal to him the curiosities of his experience and observation in matters of police. "The Mystery of Marie Roget" was first published in the autumn of 1842, before an extraordinary excitement, occasioned by the murder of a young girl named Marie Rogers, in the vicinity of New-York, had quite subsided, though several months after the tragedy. Under pretense of relating the fate of a Parisian *grisette*, Mr. Poe followed in minute detail the essential while merely paralleling the inessential facts of the real murder. His object appears to have been to reinvestigate the case and to settle his own conclusions as to the probable culprit. There is a great deal of hair-splitting in the incidental discussions by Dupin, throughout all these stories, but it is made effective. Much of their popularity, as well as that of other tales of ratiocination by Poe, arose from their being in a new key. I do not mean to say that they are not ingenious; but they have been thought more ingenious than they are, on account of their method and air of method. In "The Murders of the Rue Morgue," for instance, what ingenuity is displayed in unravelling a web which has been woven for the express purpose of unravelling? The reader is made to confound the ingenuity of the supposititious Dupin with that of the writer of the story. These works brought the name of Poe himself somewhat conspicuously before the law courts of Paris. The journal, *La Commerce*, gave a *feuilleton* in which "The Murders of the Rue Morgue" appeared in translation. Afterward a writer for *La Quotidienne* served it for that paper under the title of "*L'Orang-Otang.*" A third party accused *La Quotidienne* of plagiary from *La Commerce*, and in the course of the legal investigation which ensued, the *feuilletoniste* of *La Commerce* proved to the satisfaction of the tribunal that he had stolen the tale entirely from Mr. Poe,[4] whose merits were soon after canvassed in the "*Revue des Deux Mondes*," and whose best tales were upon this impulse translated by Mme. Isabelle Meunier for the *Democratie Pacifique* and other French gazettes.

In New-York Poe entered upon a new sort of life. Heretofore, from the commencement of his literary career, he had resided in provincial towns. Now he was in a metropolis, and with a reputation which might have served as a passport to any society he could desire. For the first time he was received into circles capable of both the appreciation and the production of literature. He added to his fame soon after he came to the city by the publication of that remarkable composition "The Raven," of which Mr. Willis has observed that in his opinion "it is the most effective single example of fugitive poetry ever published in this country, and is unsurpassed in English poetry for subtle conception, masterly ingenuity of versification, and consistent sustaining of imaginative lift;" and by that of one of the most extraordinary instances of the naturalness of detail—the verisimilitude of minute narrative—for which he was preeminently distinguished, his "Mesmeric Revelation," purporting to be the last conversation of a somnambule, held just before death with his magnetizer; which was followed by the yet more striking exhibition of abilities in the same way, entitled "The Facts in the Case of M. Valdemar," in which the subject is represented as having been mesmerized in *articulo mortis*. These pieces were reprinted throughout the literary and philosophical world, in nearly all languages, everywhere causing sharp and curious speculation, and when readers could be persuaded that they were fables, challenging a reluctant but genuine admiration.

He had not been long in New-York before he was engaged by Mr. Willis and General Morris as critic and assistant editor of "The Mirror." He remained in this situation about six months, when he became associated with Mr. Briggs in the conduct of the "Broadway Journal," which in October, 1845, passed entirely into his possession. He had now the long-sought but never before enjoyed absolute control of a literary gazette, and, with much friendly assistance, he maintained it long enough to show that whatever his genius, he had not the kind or degree of talent necessary to such a position. His chief critical writings in the "Broadway Journal," were a paper on Miss Barrett's Poems and a long discussion of the subject of plagiarism, with especial reference to Mr. Longfellow. In March, 1845, he had given a lecture at the Society Library upon the American poets, composed, for the most part, of fragments of his previously published reviewals; and in the autumn he accepted an invitation to read a poem before the Boston Lyceum. A week after the event, he printed in the "Broadway Journal" the following account of it, in reply to a paragraph in one of the city papers, founded upon a statement in the Boston "Transcript."

"Our excellent friend, Major Noah, has suffered himself to be cajoled by that most beguiling of all beguiling little divinities, Miss Walter, of 'The Transcript.' We have been looking all over her article with the aid of a taper, to see if we could discover a single syllable of truth in it—and really blush to acknowledge that we cannot. The adorable creature has been telling a parcel of fibs about us, by way of revenge for something that we did to Mr. Longfellow (who admires her very much) and for calling her 'a pretty little witch' into the bargain. The facts of the case seem to be these: We *were* invited to 'deliver' (stand and deliver) a poem before the Boston Lyceum. As a matter of course, we accepted the invitation. The audience *was* 'large and distinguished.' Mr. Cushing[5] preceded us with a very capital discourse: he was much applauded. On arising, we were most cordially received. We occupied some fifteen minutes with an apology for not 'delivering,' as is usual in such cases, a didactic poem: a didactic poem, in our opinion, being precisely no poem at all. After some farther words—still of apology—for the 'indefinitiveness' and 'general imbecility' of what we had to offer—all so unworthy a *Bostonian* audience—we commenced, and, with many interruptions of applause, concluded. Upon the whole the approbation was considerably more (the more the pity too) than that bestowed upon Mr. Cushing. When we had made an end, the audience, of course, arose to depart; and about one-tenth of them, probably, had really departed, when Mr. Coffin, one of the managing committee, arrested those who remained, by the announcement that we had been requested to deliver 'The Raven.' We delivered 'The Raven' forthwith—(without taking a receipt)—were very cordially applauded again—and this was the end of it—with the exception of the sad tale invented to suit her own purposes, by that amiable little enemy of ours, Miss. Walter. We shall never call a woman 'a pretty little witch' again, as long as we live.

"We like Boston. We were born there—and perhaps it is just as well not to mention that we are heartily ashamed of the fact. The Bostonians are very well in their way. Their hotels are bad. Their pumpkin pies are delicious. Their poetry is not so good. Their common is no common thing—and the duck-pond might answer—if its answer could be heard for the frogs. But with all these good qualities the Bostonians have no soul. They have always evinced towards us, individually, the basest ingratitude for the services we rendered them in enlightening them about the originality of Mr. Longfellow. When we accepted, therefore, an invitation to 'deliver' a poem in Boston—we accepted it simply and solely, because we had a curiosity to know how it felt to be publicly hissed—and because we wished to see what effect we could produce by a neat little *impromptu* speech in reply. Perhaps, however, we overrated our own importance, or the Bostonian want of common civility—which is not quite so manifest as one or two of their editors would wish the public to believe. We assure Major Noah that he is wrong. The Bostonians are well-bred—as *very* dull persons generally are. Still, with their vile ingratitude staring us in the eyes, it could scarcely be supposed that we would put ourselves to the trouble of composing for the Bostonians anything in the shape of an *original* poem. We did not. We had a poem (of about 500 lines) lying by us—one quite as good as new—one, at all events, that we considered would answer sufficiently well for an audience of Transcendentalists. *That* we gave them—it was the best that we had—for the price—and it *did* answer remarkably well. Its name was *not* 'The Messenger-Star'—who but Miss Walter would ever think of so delicious a little bit of invention as that? We had no name for it at all. The poem is what is occasionally called a 'juvenile poem'—but the fact is, it is anything but juvenile now, for we wrote it, printed it, and published it, in book form, before we had fairly completed our tenth year. We read it *verbatim*, from a copy now in our possession, and which we shall be happy to show at any moment to any of our inquisitive friends. We do not, ourselves, think the poem a remarkably good one:—it is not sufficiently transcendental. Still it did well enough for the Boston audience—who evinced characteristic discrimination in understanding, and especially applauding, all those knotty passages which we ourselves have not yet been able to understand.

"As regards the anger of the 'Boston Times' and one or two other absurdities—as regards, we say, the wrath of Achilles—we incurred it—or rather its manifestation—by letting some of our cat out of the bag a few hours sooner than we had intended. Over a bottle of champagne, that night, we confessed to Messrs. Cushing, Whipple, Hudson, Fields, and a few other natives who swear not altogether by the frog-pond—we confessed, we say, the soft impeachment of the hoax. *Et hinc illae irae.* We should have waited a couple of days."

It is scarcely necessary to suggest that this must have been written before he had quite recovered from the long intoxication which maddened him at the time to which it refers—that he was not born in Boston, that the poem was not published in his tenth year, and that the "hoax" was all an after-thought. Two weeks later he renewed the discussion of the subject in the "Broadway Journal," commenting as follows upon allusions to it by other parties:

"Were the question demanded of us—'What is the most exquisite of sub-lunary pleasures?' we should reply, without hesitation, the making of a fuss, or, in the classical words of a western friend, the 'kicking up a bobbery.' Never was a 'bobbery' more delightful than which we have just succeeded in 'kicking up' all around about Boston Common. We never saw the Frog-pondians so lively in our lives. They seem absolutely to be upon the point of waking up. In about nine days the puppies may get open their eyes. That is to say they may get open their eyes to certain facts which have long been obvious to all the world except themselves—the facts that there exist other cities than Boston—other men of letters than Professor Longfellow—other vehicles of literary information than the 'Down-East Review.'

"We had *tact* enough not to be 'taken in and done for' by the Bosto-nians. *Timeo Danaos et dona ferentes*—(*for timeo* substitute *contemno* or *turn-up-our-nose-o*). We knew very well that among a certain *clique* of the Frogpondians, there existed a predetermination to abuse us under *any* circumstances. We knew that, write what we would, they would swear it to be worthless. We knew that were we to compose for them a 'Paradise Lost,' they would pronounce it an indifferent poem. It would have been very weak in us, then, to put ourselves to the trouble of attempting to please these people. We preferred pleasing ourselves. We read before them a 'juvenile'—a *very* 'juvenile' poem—and thus the Frogpondians were *had*—were delivered up to the enemy bound hand and foot. Never were a set of people more completely demolished. They have blustered and flustered—but what have they done or said that had not made them more thoroughly ridiculous?—what, in the name of Momus, is it *possible* for them to do or to say? We 'delivered' them the 'juvenile poem' and they received it with applause. This is accounted for by the fact that the *clique* (contemptible in numbers as in everything else) were overruled by the rest of the assembly. These malignants did not *dare* to interrupt by their preconcerted hisses, the respectful and profound attention of the majority. We have been told, indeed, that as many as three or four of the personal friends of the little old lady entitled Miss Walter, did actually leave the hall during the recitation—but, upon the whole, this was the very best thing they could do. We have been told this, we say—we did not *see* them take their departure:—the fact is they belong to a class of people that we make it a point *never to see*. The poem being thus well received, in spite of this ridiculous little cabal— the next thing to be done was to abuse it in the papers. Here, they imagined, they were sure of their game. But what have they accomplished? The poem, they say, is bad. We admit it. We insisted upon this fact in our prefatory remarks, and we insist upon it now, over and over again. It *is* bad—it is wretched—and what then? We wrote it at ten years of age—had it been worth even a pumpkin-pie undoubtedly we should not have 'delivered' it to *them*. To demonstrate its utter worthlessness, 'The Boston Star' has copied the poem in full, with two or three columns of criticism (we suppose) by way of explaining that we should have been hanged for its perpetration. There is no doubt of it whatever—we should. 'The Star,' however, (a dull luminary) has done us more honor than it intended; it has copied our *third* edition of the poem, revised and improved. We considered this too good for the occasion by one-half, and so 'delivered' the *first* edition with all its imperfections on its head. It is the first—the original edition—the *delivered* edition—which we now republish in our collection of Poems."

When he accepted the invitation of the Lyceum he intended to write an original poem, upon a subject which he said had haunted his imagination for years; but cares, anxieties, and feebleness of will, prevented; and a week before the appointed night he wrote to a friend, imploring assistance. "You compose with such astonishing facility," he urged in his letter, "that you can easily furnish me, quite soon enough, a poem that shall be equal to my reputation. For the love of God I beseech you to help me in this extremity." The lady wrote him kindly, advising him judiciously, but promising to attempt the fulfilment of his wishes. She was, however, an invalid, and so failed.[6] At last, instead of pleading illness himself, as he had previously done on a similar occasion, he determined to read his poem of "Al Aaraaf," the original publication of which, in 1829, has already been stated.

The last number of the "Broadway Journal" was published on the third of January, 1846, and Poe soon after commenced the series of papers entitled "The Literati of New-York City," which were published in "The Lady's Book" in six numbers, from May to October. Their spirit, boldness, and occasional causticity, caused them to be much talked about, and three editions were necessary to supply the demand for some numbers of the magazine containing them. They however led to a disgraceful quarrel, and this to their premature conclusion. Dr. Thomas Dunn English, who had at one time sustained the most intimate relations with Poe, chose to evince his resentment of the critic's unfairness by the publication of a card in which he painted strongly the infirmities of Poe's life and character, and alleged that he had on several occasions inflicted upon him personal chastisement. This was not a wise confession, for a gentleman never appeals to his physical abilities except for defence. But the entire publication, even if every word of it were true, was unworthy of Dr. English, unnecessary, and not called for by Poe's article, though that, as every one acquainted with the parties might have seen, was entirely false in what purported to be its facts. The statement of Dr. English appeared in the New-York "Mirror" of the twenty-third of June, and on the twenty-seventh Mr. Poe sent to Mr. Godey for publication in the "Lady's Book" his rejoinder, which would have made about five of the large pages of that miscellany. Mr. Godey very properly declined to print it, and observed, in the communication of his decision, that the tone of the article was regarded as unsuitable for his work and as altogether wrong. In compliance with the author's wishes, however, he had caused its appearance in a daily paper. Poe then wrote to him:

"The man or men who told you that there was anything wrong in *the tone* of my reply were either my enemies, or your enemies, or asses. When you see them, tell them so, from me. I have never written an article upon which I more confidently depend for *literary* reputation than that Reply. Its merit lay in its being precisely adapted to its purpose. In this city I have had upon it the favorable judgments of the best men. All the error about it was yours. You should have done as I requested—published it in the 'Book.' It is of no use to conceive a plan if you have to depend upon another for its execution."

Nevertheless, I agree with Mr. Godey. Poe's article was as bad as that of English. Yet a part of one its paragraphs is interesting, and it is here transcribed:

—"Let me not permit any profundity of disgust to induce, even for an instant, a violation of the dignity of truth. What is *not false*, amid the scurrility of this man's statements, it is not in my nature to brand as false, although oozing from the filthy lips of which a lie is the only natural language. The errors and frailties which I deplore, it cannot at least be asserted that I have been the coward to deny. Never, even, have I made attempt at *extenuating* a weakness which is (or, by the blessing of God, *was*) a calamity, although those who did not know me intimately had little reason to regard otherwise than as a crime. For, indeed, had my pride, or that of my family permitted, there was much—very much—there was everything—to be offered in extenuation. Perhaps, even, there was an epoch at which it might not have been wrong in me to hint—what by the testimony of Dr. Francis and other medical men I might have demonstrated, had the public, indeed, cared for the demonstration—that the irregularities so profoundly lamented were the *effect* of a terrible evil rather than its cause.—And now let me thank God that in redemption from the physical ill I have forever got rid of the moral."

Dr. Francis never gave any such testimony. On one occasion Poe borrowed fifty dollars from a distinguished literary woman of South Carolina, promising to return it in a few days, and when he failed to do so, and was asked for a written acknowledgement of the debt that might be exhibited to the husband of the friend who had thus served him, he denied all knowledge of it, and threatened to exhibit a correspondence which he said would make the woman infamous, if she said any more on the subject. Of course there had never been any such correspondence, but when Poe heard that a brother of the slandered party was in quest of him for the purpose of taking the satisfaction supposed to be due in such cases, he sent for Dr. Francis and induced him to carry to the gentleman his retraction and apology, with a statement which seemed true enough at the moment, that Poe was "out of his head." It is an ungracious duty to describe such conduct in a person of Poe's unquestionable genius and capacities of greatness, but those who are familiar with the career of this extraordinary creature can recall but too many similar anecdotes; and as to his intemperance, they perfectly well understand that its pathology was like that of ninety-nine of every hundred cases of the disease.

As the autumn of 1846 wore on Poe's habits of frequent intoxication and his inattention to the means of support reduced him to much more than common destitution. He was now living at Fordham, several miles from the city, so that his necessities were not generally known even among his acquaintances; but when the dangerous illness of his wife was added to his misfortunes, and his dissipation and accumulated causes of anxiety had prostrated all his own energies, the subject was introduced into the journals. The "Express" said:

"We regret to learn that Edgar A. Poe and his wife are both dangerously ill with the consumption, and that the hand of misfortune lies heavy upon their temporal affairs. We are sorry to mention the fact that they are so far reduced as to be barely able to obtain the necessaries of life. This is indeed a hard lot, and we hope that the friends and admirers of Mr. Poe will come promptly to his assistance in his bitterest hour of need."

Mr. Willis, in an article in the "Home Journal" suggesting a hospital for disabled laborers with the brain, said—

"The feeling we have long entertained on this subject, has been freshened by a recent paragraph in the 'Express,' announcing that Mr. Edgar A. Poe and his wife were both dangerously ill, and suffering for want of the common necessaries of life. Here is one of the finest scholars, one of the most original men of genius, and one of the most industrious of the literary profession of our country, whose temporary suspension of labor, from bodily illness, drops him immediately to a level with the common objects of public charity. There was no intermediate stopping-place—no respectful shelter where, with the delicacy due to genius and culture, he might secure aid, unadvertised, till, with returning health, he could resume his labors and his unmortified sense of independence. He must either apply to individual friends—(a resource to which death is sometimes almost preferable)—or *suffer down* to the level where Charity receives claimants, but where Rags and Humiliation are the only recognized Ushers to her presence. Is this right? Should there not be, in all highly civilized communities, an Institution designed expressly for educated and refined objects of charity—a hospital, a retreat, a home of seclusion and comfort, the sufficient claims to which would be such susceptibilities as are violated by the above mentioned appeal in a daily newspaper."

The entire article from which this paragraph is taken, was an ingenious apology for Mr. Poe's infirmities; but it was conceived and executed in a generous spirit, and it had a quick effect in various contributions, which relieved the poet from pecuniary embarrassments. The next week he published the following letter:

"*My Dear Willis*:—The paragraph which has been put in circulation respecting my wife's illness, my own, my poverty, etc., is now lying before me; together

[131]

with the beautiful lines by Mrs. Locke and those by Mrs. ———, to which the paragraph has given rise, as well as your kind and manly comments in 'The Home Journal.' The motive of the paragraph I leave to the conscience of him or her who wrote it or suggested it. Since the thing is done, however, and since the concerns of my family are thus pitilessly thrust before the public, I perceive no mode of escape from a public statement of what is true and what erroneous in the report alluded to. That my wife is ill, then, is true; and you may imagine with what feelings I add that this illness, hopeless from the first, has been heightened and precipitated by her reception at two different periods, of anonymous letters,—one enclosing the paragraph now in question; the other, those published calumnies of Messrs. ———, for which I yet hope to find redress in a court of justice.

"Of the facts, that I myself have been long and dangerously ill, and that my illness has been a well understood thing among my brethren of the press, the best evidence is afforded by the innumerable paragraphs of personal and of literary abuse with which I have been latterly assailed. This matter, however, will remedy itself. At the very first blush of my new prosperity, the gentlemen who toadied me in the old, will recollect themselves and toady me again. You, who know me, will comprehend that I speak of these things only as having served, in a measure, to lighten the gloom of unhappiness by a gentle and not unpleasant sentiment of mingled pity, merriment and contempt. That, as the inevitable consequence of so long an illness, I have been in want of money, it would be folly in me to deny—but that I have ever materially suffered from privation, beyond the extent of my capacity for suffering, is not altogether true. That I am 'without friends' is a gross calumny, which I am sure *you* never could have believed, and which a thousand noble-hearted men would have good right never to forgive me for permitting to pass unnoticed and undenied. Even in the city of New York I could have no difficulty in naming a hundred persons, to each of whom—when the hour for speaking had arrived—I could and would have applied for aid with unbounded confidence, and with absolutely *no* sense of humiliation. I do not think, my dear Willis, that there is any need of my saying more. I am getting better, and may add—if it be any comfort to my enemies—that I have little fear of getting worse. The truth is, I have a great deal to do; and I have made up my mind not to die till it is done.

"December 30th, 1846. Sincerely yours, Edgar A. Poe."

This was written for effect. He had not been ill a great while, nor dangerously at all; there was no literary or personal abuse of him in the journals; and his friends in town had been applied to for money until their patience was nearly exhausted. His wife, however, was very sick, and in a few weeks she died. In a letter to a lady in Massachusetts, who, upon the appearance of the newspaper articles above quoted, had sent him money and expressions of sympathy, he wrote, under date of March 10, 1847:

"In answering your kind letter permit me in the very first place to absolve myself from a suspicion which, under the circumstances, you could scarcely have failed to entertain—a suspicion of discourtesy toward yourself, in not having more promptly replied to you . . . I could not help fearing that should you see my letter to Mr. Willis—in which a natural pride, which I feel you could not blame, impelled me to shrink from public charity, *even at the cost of truth, in denying those necessities which were but too real*—I could not help fearing that, should you see this letter, you would yourself feel pained at having caused me pain—at having been the means of giving further publicity to an unfounded report—at all events to the report of a wretchedness which I had thought it prudent (since the world regards wretchedness as a crime) so publicly to disavow. In a word, venturing to judge your noble nature by my own, I felt grieved lest my published denial might cause you to regret what you had done; and my first impulse was to write you, and assure you even at the risk of doing so too warmly, of the sweet emotion, made up of respect and gratitude alone, with which my heart was filled to overflowing. While I was hesitating, however, in regard to the propriety of this step, I was overwhelmed by a sorrow so poignant as to deprive me for several weeks of all thought or action. Your letter, now lying before me, tells me that I had not been mistaken in your nature, and that I should not have hesitated to address you; but believe me, my dear Mrs. L——, that I am already ceasing to regard those difficulties or misfortunes which have led me to even this partial correspondence with yourself."

For nearly a year Mr. Poe was not often before the public, but he was as industrious, perhaps, as he had been at any time, and early in 1848 advertisement was made of his intention to deliver several lectures, with a view to obtain an amount of money sufficient to establish his so-long-contemplated monthly magazine. His first lecture—and only one at this period—was given at the Society Library, in New-York, on the ninth of February, and was upon the Cosmogony of the Universe; it was attended by an eminently intellectual auditory, and the reading of it occupied about two hours and a half; it was what he afterwards published under the title of "Eureka, a Prose Poem."

To the composition of this work he brought his subtlest and highest capacities, in their most perfect development. Denying that the arcana of the universe can be explored by induction, but informing his imagination with the various results of science, he entered with unhesitating boldness, though with no guide but the divinest instinct,—that sense of beauty, in which our great Edwards recognises the flowering of all truth—into the sea of speculation, and there built up of according laws and their phenomena, as under the influence of a scientific inspiration, his theory of Nature. I will not attempt the difficult task of condensing his propositions; to be apprehended they must be studied in his own terse and simple language; but in this we have a summary of that which he regards as fundamental: "The law which we call *Gravity*," he says, "exists on account of matter having been radiated, at its origin, atomically, into a *limited* sphere of space, from one, individual, unconditional, irrelative, and absolute Particle Proper, by the sole process in which it was possible to satisfy, at the same time, the two conditions, radiation and equable distribution throughout the sphere— that is to say, by a force varying in *direct* proportion with the squares of the distances between the radiated atoms, respectively, and the particular centre of radiation."

Poe was thoroughly persuaded that he had discovered the great secret; that the propositions of "Eureka" were true; and he was wont to talk of the subject with a sublime and electrical enthusiasm which they cannot have forgotten who were familiar with him at the period of its publication. He felt that an author known solely by his adventures in the lighter literature, throwing down the gauntlet to professors of science, could not expect absolute fairness, and he had no hope but in discussions led by wisdom and candor. Meeting me, he said, "Have you read 'Eureka?'" I answered, "Not yet: I have just glanced at the notice of it by Willis, who thinks it contains no more fact than fantasy, and I am sorry to see—sorry if it be true—suggests that it corresponds in tone with that gathering of sham and obsolete hypotheses addressed to fanciful tyros, the 'Vestiges of Creation;' and our good and really wise friend Bush, whom you will admit to be of all the professors, in temper one of the most habitually just, thinks that while you may have guessed very shrewdly, it would not be difficult to suggest many difficulties in the way of your doctrine." "It is by no means ingenuous," he replied, "to hint that there are such difficulties, and yet to leave them unsuggested. I challenge the investigation of every point in the book.

I deny that there are any difficulties which I have not met and overthrown. Injustice is done me by the application of this word 'guess:' I have assumed *nothing* and proved *all*." In his preface he wrote: "To the few who love me and whom I love; to those who feel rather than to those who think; to the dreamers and those who put faith in dreams as in the only realities—I offer this book of truths, not in the character of Truth-Teller, but for the beauty that abounds in its truth: constituting it true. To these I present the composition as an Art-Product alone:—let us say as a Romance; or, if it be not urging too lofty a claim, as a Poem. What I here propound is true: therefore it cannot die: or if by any means it be now trodden down so that it die, it will rise again to the life everlasting."

When I read "Eureka" I could not help but think it immeasurably superior as an illustration of genius to the "Vestiges of Creation;" and as I admired the poem, (except the miserable attempt at humor in what purports to be a letter found in a bottle floating on the *Mare tenebrarum*,) so I regretted its pantheism, which is not necessary to its main design. To some of the objections to his work he made this answer in a letter to Mr. C. F. Hoffman, then editor of the "Literary World:"

"*Dear Sir*:—In your paper of July 29, I find some comments on 'Eureka,' a late book of my own; and I know you too well to suppose, for a moment, that you will refuse me the privilege of a few words in reply. I feel, even, that I might safely claim, from Mr. Hoffman, the right, which every author has, of replying to his critic *tone for tone*—that is to say, of answering your correspondent, flippancy by flippancy and sneer by sneer—but, in the first place, I do not wish to disgrace the 'World;' and, in the second, I feel that I never should be done sneering, in the present instance, were I once to begin. Lamartine blames Voltaire for the use which he made of (*ruse*) misrepresentation, in his attacks on the priesthood; but our young students of Theology do not seem to be aware that in defence, or what they fancy to be defence, of Christianity, there is anything wrong in such gentlemanly peccadillos as the deliberate perversion of an author's text—to say nothing of the minor *indecora* of reviewing a book without reading it and without having the faintest suspicion of what it is about.

"You will understand that it is merely the *misrepresentations* of the *critique* in question to which I claim the privilege of reply:—the mere *opinions* of the writer can be of no consequence to me—and I should imagine of very little to himself—that is to say if he knows himself, personally, as well as *I* have the honor of knowing him. The first misrepresentation is contained in this sentence:—'This letter is a keen burlesque on the Aristotelian or Baconian methods of ascertaining Truth, both of which the writer ridicules and despises, and pours forth his rhapsodical ecstasies in a glorification of the third mode—the noble art of *guessing*.' What I *really* say is this:—That there is no absolute *certainty* either in the Aristotelian or Baconian process—that, for this reason, neither Philosophy is so profound as it fancies itself—and that neither has a right to sneer at that *seemingly* imaginative process called Intuition (by which the great Kepler attained his laws;) since 'Intuition,' after all, 'is but the conviction arising from those *in*ductions or *de*ductions of which the processes are so shadowy as to escape our consciousness, elude our reason or defy our capacity of expression.' The second misrepresentation runs thus:—'The developments of electricity and the formation of stars and suns, luminous and non-luminous, moons and planets, with their rings, &c., is deduced, very much according to the nebular theory of Laplace, from the principle propounded above.' Now the impression intended to be made here upon the reader's mind, by the 'Student of Theology,' is, evidently, that my theory may all be very well in its way, but that it is nothing but Laplace all over again, with some modifications that he (the Student of Theology) cannot regard as at all important. I have only to say that no gentleman can accuse me of the disingenuousness here implied; inasmuch as, having proceeded with my theory up to that point at which Laplace's theory *meets* it, I then *give Laplace's theory in full*, with the expression of my firm conviction of its absolute truth *at all points*. The *ground* covered by the great French astronomer compares with that covered by my theory, as a bubble compares with the ocean on which it floats; nor has he the slightest allusion to the 'principle propounded above,' the principle of Unity being the source of all things—the principle of Gravity being merely the Reaction of the Divine Act which irradiated all things from Unity. In fact, *no* point of *my* theory has been even so much as alluded to by Laplace. I have not considered it necessary, here, to speak of the astronomical knowledge displayed in the 'stars *and* suns' of the Student of Theology, nor to hint that it would be better grammar to say that 'development and formation' *are*, than that development and formation *is*. The third misrepresentation lies in a foot-note, where the critic says:—'Further than this, Mr. Poe's claim that he can account for the existence of all organized beings—man included—merely from those principles on which the origin and present appearance of suns and worlds are explained, must be set down as mere bald assertion, without a particle of evidence. In other words we should term it *arrant fudge*.' The perversion at this point is involved in a wilful misapplication of the word 'principles.' I say 'wilful;' because, at page 63, I am *particularly* careful to distinguish between the principles proper, Attraction and Repulsion, and those merely resultant *sub*-principles which control the universe in detail. To these sub-principles, swayed by the immediate spiritual influence of Deity, I leave, without examination, *all that* which the Student of Theology so roundly asserts I account for on the *principles* which account for the constitution of suns, &c.

"In the third column of his 'review' the critic says:—'He asserts that each soul is its own God—its own Creator.' What I *do* assert is, that 'each soul is, *in part*, its own God—its own Creator.' Just below, the critic says:—'After all these contradictory propoundings concerning God we would remind him of what he lays down on page 28—'of this Godhead in itself he alone is not imbecile—he alone is not impious who propounds *nothing*. A man who thus conclusively convicts himself of imbecility and impiety needs no further refutation.' Now the sentence, *as I wrote it*, and as *I find it* printed on that very page which the critic refers to and which *must have been lying before him* while he quoted my words, runs thus:—'Of this Godhead, *in itself*, he alone is not imbecile, &c., who propounds nothing.' By the italics, as the critic well knew, I design to distinguish between the two possibilities—that of a knowledge of God through his works and that of a knowledge of Him in his *essential nature.* The Godhead, *in itself*, is distinguished from the Godhead observed *in its effects.* But our critic is zealous. Moreover, being a divine, he is honest—ingenuous. It is his *duty* to pervert my meaning by omitting my italics—just as, in the sentence previously quoted, it was his Christian duty to falsify my argument by leaving out the two words, 'in part,' upon which turns the whole force—indeed the whole intelligibility of my proposition.

"Were these 'misrepresentations' (*is* that the name for them?) made for any less serious a purpose than that of branding my book as 'impious' and myself as a 'pantheist,' a 'polytheist,' a Pagan, or a God knows what (and indeed I care very little so it be not a 'Student of Theology') I would have permitted their dishonesty to pass unnoticed, through pure contempt for the boyishness—for the *turn-down-shirt-collar-ness* of their tone:—but, as it is, you will pardon me, Mr. Editor, that I have been compelled to expose a 'critic' who, courageously preserving his own *anonymosity*, takes advantage of my absence from the city to misrepresent, and thus villify me, *by name.*

"*Fordham*, September 20, 1848."
"Edgar A. Poe."

From this time Poe did not write much; he had quarreled with the conductors of the chief magazines for which he had previously written, and they no longer sought his assistance. In a letter to a friend, he laments the improbabilities of an income from literary labor, saying:

"I have represented —— to you as merely an ambitious simpleton, anxious to get into society with the reputation for conducting a magazine which somebody behind the curtain always prevents him from quite damning with his stupidity; he is a knave and a beast. I cannot write any more for the Milliner's Book, where T——n prints his feeble and *very* quietly made dilutions of other people's reviews; and you know that —— can afford to pay but little, though I am glad to do anything for a good fellow like ——. In this emergency I sell articles to the vulgar and trashy —— —— —— ——, for $5 a piece. I enclose my last, cut out, lest you should see by my sending the paper in what company I am forced to appear."

His name was now frequently associated with that of one of the most brilliant women of New England, and it was publicly announced that they were to be married. He had first seen her on his way from Boston, when he visited that city to deliver a poem before the Lyceum there. Restless, near the midnight, he wandered from his hotel near where she lived, until he saw her walking in a garden. He related the incident afterward in one of his most exquisite poems, worthy of himself, of her, and of the most exalted passion [text of "To Helen" (1848) follows].

They were not married, and the breaking of the engagement affords a striking illustration of his character. He said to an acquaintance in New-York, who congratulated with him upon the prospect of his union with a person of so much genius and so many virtues—"It is a mistake: I am not going to be married." "Why Mr. Poe, I understand that the banns have been published." "I cannot help what you have heard, my dear Madam: but mark me, I shall not marry her." He left town the same evening, and the next day was reeling through the streets of the city which was the lady's home, and in the evening—that should have been the evening before his bridal—in his drunkenness he committed at her house such outrages as made necessary a summons of the police. Here was no insanity leading to indulgence: he went from New-York with a determination thus to induce an ending of the engagement; and he succeeded.

Sometime in August, 1849, Mr. Poe left New-York for Virginia. In Philadelphia he encountered persons who had been his associates in dissipations while he lived there, and for several days he abandoned himself entirely to the control of his worst appetites. When his money was all spent, and the disorder of his dress evinced the extremity of his recent intoxication, he asked in charity means for the prosecution of his journey to Richmond.

There, after a few days, he joined a temperance society, and his conduct showed the earnestness of his determination to reform his life. He delivered in some of the principal towns of Virginia two lectures, which were well attended, and renewing his acquaintance with a lady whom he had known in his youth, he was engaged to marry her, and wrote to his friends that he should pass the remainder of his days among the scenes endeared by all his pleasantest recollections of youth.

On Thursday, the fourth of October, he set out for New-York, to fulfill a literary engagement, and to prepare for his marriage. Arriving in Baltimore he gave his trunk to a porter, with directions to convey it to the cars which were to leave in an hour or two for Philadelphia, and went into a tavern to obtain some refreshment. Here he met acquaintances who invited him to drink; all his resolutions and duties were soon forgotten; in a few hours he was in such a state as is commonly induced only by long-continued intoxication; after a night of insanity and exposure, he was carried to a hospital; and there, on the evening of Sunday, the seventh of October, 1849, he died, at the age of thirty-eight years.

It is a melancholy history. No author of as much genius had ever in this country as much unhappiness; but Poe's unhappiness was in an unusual degree the result of infirmities of nature, or of voluntary faults in conduct. A writer who evidently knew him well, and who comes before us in the "Southern Literary Messenger" as his defender, is "compelled to admit that the blemishes in his life were effects of character rather than of circumstances."[7] How this character might have been modified by a judicious education of all his faculties I leave for the decision of others, but it will be evident to those who read this biography that the unchecked freedom of his earlier years was as unwise as its results were unfortunate.

It is contended that the higher intelligences, in the scrutiny to which they appeal, are not to be judged by the common laws; but I apprehend that this doctrine, as it is likely to be understood, is entirely wrong. All men are amenable to the same principles, to the extent of the parallelism of these principles with their experience; and the line of duty becomes only more severe as it extends into the clearer atmosphere of truth and beauty which is the life of genius. *De mortuis nil nisi bonum* is a common and an honorable sentiment, but its proper application would lead to the suppression of the histories of half of the most conspicuous of mankind; in this case it is impossible on account of the notoriety of Mr. Poe's faults; and it would be unjust to the living against whom his hands were always raised and who had no resort but in his outlawry from their sympathies. Moreover, his career is full of instruction and warning, and it has always been made a portion of the penalty of wrong that its anatomy should be displayed for the common study and advantage.

The character of Mr. Poe's genius has been so recently and so admirably discussed by Mr. Lowell, with whose opinions on the subject I for the most part agree, that I shall say but little of it here, having already extended this notice beyond the limits at first designed. There is a singular harmony between his personal and his literary qualities. St. Pierre, who seemed to be without any nobility in his own nature, in his writings appeared to be moved only by the finest and highest impulses. Poe exhibits scarcely any virtue in either his life or his writings. Probably there is not another instance in the literature of our language in which so much has been accomplished without a recognition or a manifestation of conscience. Seated behind the intelligence, and directing it, according to its capacities, Conscience is the parent of whatever is absolutely and unquestionably beautiful in art as well as in conduct. It touches the creations of the mind and they have life; without it they have never, in the range of its just action, the truth and naturalness which are approved by universal taste or in enduring reputation. In Poe's works there is constantly displayed the most touching melancholy, the most extreme and terrible despair, but never reverence or remorse.

His genius was peculiar, and not, as he himself thought, various. He remarks in one of his letters [to Philip Pendleton Cooke, 19 August 1846]:[8]

"There is one particular in which I have had wrong done me, and it may not be indecorous in me to call your attention to it. The last selection of my tales was made from about seventy by one of our great little cliquists and claquers, Wiley and Putnam's reader, Duyckinck. He has what he thinks a taste for ratiocination, and has accordingly made up the book mostly of analytic stories. But this is not *representing* my mind in its various phases—it is not giving me fair play. In writing these tales one by one, at long intervals, I have kept the book unity always in mind—that is, each has been composed with reference to its effect as part of *a whole*. In this view, one of my chief aims has been the wildest diversity of subject, thought, and especially *tone* and manner of handling. Were *all* my tales now before me in a large volume, and as the composition of another, the merit which would

[140]

principally arrest my attention would be their wide *diversity and variety*. You will be surprised to hear me say that, (omitting one or two of my first efforts,) I do not consider any one of my stories *better* than another. There is a vast variety of kinds, and, in degree of value, these kinds vary—but each tale is equally good *of its kind*. The loftiest kind is that of the highest imagination—and for this reason only 'Ligeia' may be called my best tale."

But it seems to me that this selection of his tales was altogether judicious. Had it been submitted to me I might indeed have changed it in one or two instances, but I should not have replaced any tale by one of a different tone. One of the qualities upon which Poe prided himself was his humor, and he has left us a large number of compositions in this department, but except a few paragraphs in his "Marginalia," scarcely anything which it would not have been injurious to his reputation to republish. His realm was on the shadowy confines of human experience, among the abodes of crime, gloom, and horror, and there he delighted to surround himself with images of beauty and terror, to raise his solemn palaces and towers and spires in a night upon which should rise no sun. His minuteness of detail, refinement of reasoning, and propriety and power of language—the perfect keeping (to borrow a phrase from another domain of art) and apparent good faith with which he managed the evocation and exhibition of his strange and spectral and revolting creations—gave him an astonishing mastery over his readers, so that his books were closed as one would lay aside the nightmare or the spells of opium. The analytical subtlety evinced in his works has frequently been overestimated, as I have before observed, because it has not been sufficiently considered that his mysteries were composed with the express design of being dissolved. When Poe attempted the illustration of the profounder operations of the mind, as displayed in written reason or in real action, he frequently failed entirely.

In poetry, as in prose, he was eminently successful in the metaphysical treatment of the passions. His poems are constructed with wonderful ingenuity, and finished with consummate art. They display a sombre and weird imagination, and a taste almost faultless in the apprehension of that sort of beauty which was most agreeable to his temper. But they evince little genuine feeling, and less of that spontaneous ecstasy which gives its freedom, smoothness and naturalness to immortal verse. His own account of the composition of "The Raven," discloses his methods—the absence of all impulse, and the absolute control of calculation and mechanism. That curious analysis of the processes by which he wrought would be incredible if from another hand.

He was not remarkably original in invention. Indeed some of his plagiarisms are scarcely paralleled for their audacity in all literary history: For instance, in his tale of "The Pit and the Pendulum," the complicate machinery upon which the interest depends is borrowed from a story entitled "Vivenzio, or Italian Vengeance," by the author of "The First and Last Dinner," in "Blackwood's Magazine." And I remember having been shown by Mr. Longfellow, several years ago, a series of papers which constitute a demonstration that Mr. Poe was indebted to him for the idea of "The Haunted Palace," one of the most admirable of his poems, which he so pertinaciously asserted had been used by Mr. Longfellow in the production of his "Beleaguered City." Mr. Longfellow's poem was written two or three years before the first publication of that by Poe, and it was during a portion of this time in Poe's possession; but it was not printed, I believe, until a few weeks after the appearance of "The Haunted Palace." "It would be absurd," as Poe himself said many times, "to believe the similarity of these pieces entirely accidental." This was the first cause of all that malignant criticism which for so many years he carried on against Mr. Longfellow. In his "Marginalia" he borrowed largely especially from Coleridge, and I have omitted in the republication of these papers, numerous paragraphs which were rather compiled than borrowed from one of the profoundest and wisest of our own scholars.[9]

In criticism, as Mr. Lowell justly remarks, Mr. Poe had "a scientific precision and coherence of logic;" he had remarkable dexterity in the dissection of sentences; but he rarely ascended from the particular to the general, from subjects to principles: he was familiar with the microscope but never looked through the telescope. His criticisms are of value to the degree in which they are demonstrative, but his unsupported assertions and opinions were so apt to be influenced by friendship or enmity, by the desire to please or the fear to offend, or by his constant ambition to surprise, or produce a sensation, that they should be received in all cases with distrust of their fairness. A volume might be filled with literary judgments by him as antagonistical and inconsistent as the sharpest antitheses. For example, when Mr. Laughton Osborn's romance, "The Confessions of a Poet," came out, he reviewed it in "The Southern Literary Messenger," saying:

"There is nothing of the *vates* about the author. He is no poet—and most positively he is no prophet. He avers upon his word of honor that in commencing this work he loads a pistol and places it upon the table. He further states that, upon coming to a conclusion, it is his intention to blow out what he supposes to be his brains. Now this is excellent. But, even with so rapid a writer as the poet must undoubtedly be, there would be some little difficulty in completing the book under thirty days or thereabouts. The best of powder is apt to sustain injury by lying so long 'in the load.' We sincerely hope the gentleman took the precaution to examine his priming before attempting the rash act. A flash in the pan—and in such a case—were a thing to be lamented. Indeed there would be no answering for the consequences. We might even have a second series of the 'Confessions.'"—*Southern Literary Messenger*, i. 459.

This review was attacked, particularly in the Richmond "Compiler," and Mr. Poe felt himself called upon to vindicate it to the proprietor of the magazine, to whom he wrote:

"There is no necessity of giving the 'Compiler' a reply. The book is *silly enough of itself*, without the aid of any controversy concerning it. I have read it, from beginning to end, and was very much amused at it. My opinion of it is pretty neatly the opinion of the press at large. I have heard no person offer one serious word in its defence."—*Letter to T. W. White.*

Afterwards Mr. Poe became personally acquainted with the author and he then wrote, in his account of "The Literati of New-York City," as follows:

"The Confessions of a Poet made much noise in the literary world, and no little curiosity was excited in regard to its author, who was generally supposed to be John Neal. . . . The 'Confessions,' however, far surpassed any production of Mr. Neal's. . . . *He* has done nothing which, as a whole, is *even respectable*, and 'The Confessions' are quite remarkable for their artistic unity and perfection. But on higher regards they are to be commended. *I do not think, indeed, that a better book of its kind has been written in America.* . . . Its scenes of passion are intensely wrought, its incidents are striking and original, its sentiments audacious and suggestive at least, if not at all times tenable. In a word, it is that rare thing, a fiction of *power* without rudeness."

I will adduce another example of the same kind. In a notice of the "Democratic Review," for September, 1845, Mr. Poe remarks of Mr. William A. Jones's paper on American Humor:

"There is only one really bad article in the number, and that is insufferable: nor do we think it the less a nuisance because it inflicts upon ourselves individually a passage of maudlin compliment about our being a most 'ingenious critic' and 'prose poet,' with some other things of a similar kind. We thank for his good word no man who gives palpable evidence, in other cases than our own, of his *incapacity* to distinguish the false from the true—the right from the wrong. If we *are* an ingenious critic, or a prose poet, it is not because Mr. William Jones says so. The truth is that this essay on 'American Humor' is contemptible both in a moral and literary sense—is the composition of an *imitator and a quack*—and disgraces the magazine in which it makes its appearance."—*Broadway Journal*, Vol. ii. No. 11.

In the following week he reconsidered this matter, opening his paper for a defence of Mr. Jones; but at the close of it said—

"If we have done Mr. Jones injustice, we beg his pardon: but we do not think we have."

Yet in a subsequent article in "Graham's Magazine," on "Critics and Criticism," he says of Mr. Jones—referring only to writings of his that had been for years before the public when he printed the above paragraphs:

"Our most analytic, *if not altogether our best critic*, (Mr. Whipple, perhaps, excepted,) is Mr. *William A. Jones*, author of 'The Analyst.' How he would write elaborate criticisms I cannot say; but his summary judgments of authors are, in general, discriminative and profound. In fact, his papers on *Emerson* and on *Macaulay*, published in 'Arcturus,' are better than merely 'profound,' if we take the word in its now desecrated sense; for they are at once pointed, lucid, and just:—as summaries, leaving nothing to be desired."

I will not continue the display of these inconsistencies. As I have already intimated, a volume might be filled with passages to show that his criticisms were guided by no sense of duty, and that his opinions were so variable and so liable to be influenced by unworthy considerations as to be really of no value whatever.

It was among his remarkable habits that he preserved with scrupulous care everything that was published respecting himself or his works, and everything that was written to him in letters that could be used in any way for the establishment or extension of his reputation. In Philadelphia, in 1843, he prepared with his own hands a sketch of his life for a paper called

"The Museum." Many parts of it are untrue, but I refer to it for the purpose of quoting a characteristic instance of perversion in the reproduction
of compliments:

"Of 'William Wilson,' Mr. Washington Irving says: 'It is managed in a
highly picturesque style, and its singular and mysterious interest is ably
sustained throughout. In point of mere style, it is, perhaps, even superior
to "The House of Usher." It is simpler. In the latter composition, he seems
to have been distrustful of his effects, or, rather, too solicitous of bringing
them forth fully to the eye, and thus, perhaps, has laid on too much coloring. He has erred, however, on the safe side, that of exuberance, and the
evil might easily be remedied, by relieving the style of some of its epithets:'
[since done.] 'There would be no fear of injuring the graphic effect, *which
is powerful.*' The italics are Mr. Irving's own."

Now Mr. Irving had said in a private letter that he thought the "House
of Usher" was clever, and that "a volume of similar stories would be well
received by the public." Poe sent him a magazine containing "William Wilson," asking his opinion of it, and Mr. Irving expressly declining to *publish*
a word upon the subject, remarked in the same manner, that "the singular and mysterious interest is well sustained," and that in point of style the
tale was "much better" than the "House of Usher," which, he says, "might
be improved by relieving the style from some of the epithets: there is no
danger of destroying the graphic effect, which is powerful." There is not a
word in *italics* in Mr. Irving's letter, the meaning of which is quite changed
by Mr. Poe's alterations. And this letter was not only published in the face
of an implied prohibition, but made to seem like a deliberately expressed
judgment in a public reviewal. In the same way Mr. Poe published the following sentence as an extract from a letter by Miss Barrett:

"Our great poet, Mr. Browning, author of Paracelsus, etc. is *enthusiastic
in his admiration* of the rhythm."

But on turning to Miss Barrett's letter I find that she wrote:

"Our great poet, Mr. Browning, the author of 'Paracelsus,' and 'Bell and
Pomegranates,' was struck much by the rhythm of that poem."

The piece alluded to is "The Raven."

It is not true, as has been frequently alleged since Mr. Poe's death, that
his writings were above the popular taste, and therefore without a suitable
market in this country. His poems were worth as much to magazines as
those of Bryant or Longfellow, (though none of the publishers paid him

[145]

half as large a price for them,) and his tales were as popular as those of Willis, who has been commonly regarded as the best magazinist of his time. He ceased to write for "The Lady's Book" in consequence of a quarrel induced by Mr. Godey's justifiable refusal to print in that miscellany his "Reply to Dr. English," and though in the poor fustian published under the signature of "George R. Graham," in answer to some remarks upon Poe's character in "The Tribune," that individual is made to assume a passionate friendship for the deceased author that would have become a Pythias, it is known that the personal ill-will on both sides was such that for some four or five years *not a line by Poe was purchased for "Graham's Magazine."* To quote again the "Defence of Mr. Poe" in the "Southern Literary Messenger:"

"His changeable humors, his irregularities, his caprices, his total disregard of everything and body, save the fancy in his head, prevented him from doing well in the world. The evils and sufferings that poverty brought upon him, soured his nature, and deprived him of faith in human beings. This was evident to the eye—he believed in nobody, and cared for nobody. Such a mental condition of course drove away all those who would otherwise have stood by him in his hours of trial. He became, and was, an Ishmaelite."

After having, in no ungenerous spirit, presented the chief facts in Mr. Poe's history, not designedly exaggerating his genius, which none held in higher admiration, not bringing into bolder relief than was just and necessary his infirmities, I am glad to offer a portraiture of some of his social qualities, equally beautiful, and—so changeable and inconsistent was the man—as far it goes, truthful. Speaking of him one day soon after his death, with the late Mrs. Osgood, the beauty of whose character had made upon Poe's mind that impression which it never failed to produce upon minds capable of the apprehension of the finest traits in human nature, she said she did not doubt that my view of Mr. Poe, which she knew indeed to be the common view, was perfectly just, as it regarded him in his relations with men; but to women he was different, and she would write for me some recollections of him to be placed beside my harsher judgments in any notice of his life that the acceptance of the appointment to be his literary executor might render it necessary for me to give to the world. She was an invalid—dying of that consumption by which in a few weeks she was removed to heaven, and calling for pillows to support her while she wrote, she drew this sketch:

"You ask me, my friend, to write for you my reminiscences of Edgar Poe. For you, who knew and understood my affectionate interest in him, and my frank acknowledgement of that interest to all who had a claim upon my confidence, for you, I will willingly do so. I think no one could know him—no one *has* known him personally—certainly no woman—without feeling the same interest. I can sincerely say, that although I have frequently *heard* of aberrations on his part from 'the straight and narrow path,' I have never *seen* him otherwise than gentle, generous, well-bred, and fastidiously refined. To a sensitive and delicately-nurtured woman, there was a peculiar and irresistible charm in the chivalric, graceful, and almost tender reverence with which he invariably approached all women who won his respect. It was this which first commanded and always retained my regard for him.

"I have been told that when his sorrows and pecuniary embarrassments had driven him to the use of stimulants, which a less delicate organization might have borne without injury, he was in the habit of speaking disrespectfully of the ladies of his acquaintance. It is difficult for me to believe this; for to *me*, to whom he came during the year of our acquaintance for counsel and kindness in all his many anxieties and griefs, he never spoke of any woman save one, and then only in *my* defence, and though I rebuked him for his momentary forgetfulness of the respect due to himself and to me, I could not but forgive the offence for the sake of the generous impulse which prompted it. Yet even were these sad rumors true of him, the wise and well-informed knew how to regard, as they would the impetuous anger of a spoiled infant, balked of its capricious will, the equally harmless and unmeaning phrenzy of that stray child of Poetry and Passion. For the few unwomanly and slander-loving gossips who have injured *him* and *themselves* only by *repeating* his ravings, when in such moods they have accepted his society, I have only to vouchsafe my wonder and my pity. They cannot surely harm the true and pure, who, reverencing his genius and pitying his misfortunes and his errors, endeavored, by their timely kindness and sympathy, to soothe his sad career.

"It was in his own simple yet poetical home that, to me the character of Edgar Poe appeared in its most beautiful light. Playful, affectionate, witty, alternately docile and wayward as a petted child—for his young, gentle and idolized wife, and for all who came, he had even in the midst of his most harassing literary duties, a kind word, a pleasant smile, a graceful and courteous attention. At his desk beneath the romantic picture of his loved

and lost Lenore, he would sit, hour after hour, patient, assiduous and un-
complaining, tracing, in an exquisitely clear chirography and with almost
superhuman swiftness, the lightning thoughts—the 'rare and radiant' fancies as they flashed through his wonderful and ever wakeful brain. I recollect, one morning, towards the close of his residence in this city, when
he seemed unusually gay and light-hearted. Virginia, his sweet wife, had
written me a pressing invitation to come to them; and I, who never could
resist her affectionate summons, and who enjoyed his society far more in
his own home than elsewhere, hastened to Amity-street. I found him just
completing his series of papers entitled, 'The Literati of New-York.' 'See,'
said he, displaying, in laughing triumph, several little rolls of narrow paper, (he always wrote thus for the press,) 'I am going to show you, by the
difference of length in these, the different degrees of estimation in which
I hold all you literary people. In each of these, one of you is rolled up and
fully discussed. Come, Virginia, help me!' And one by one they unfolded
them. At last they came to one which seemed interminable. Virginia laugh-
ingly ran to one corner of the room with one end, and her husband to the
opposite with the other. 'And whose lengthened sweetness long drawn out
is that?' said I. 'Hear her!' he cried, 'just as if her vain little heart didn't tell
her it's herself!'

"My first meeting with the poet was at the Astor house. A few days previous, Mr. Willis had handed me, at the *table d'hote*, that strange and thrilling
poem entitled 'The Raven,' saying that the author wanted my opinion of it.
Its effect upon me was so singular, so like that of 'weird, unearthly music,'
that it was with a feeling almost of dread, I heard he desired an introduction. Yet I could not refuse without seeming ungrateful, because I had just
heard of his enthusiastic and partial eulogy of my writings, in his lecture
on American Literature. I shall never forget the morning when I was summoned to the drawing-room by Mr. Willis to receive him. With his proud
and beautiful head erect, his dark eyes flashing with the elective light of
feeling and of thought, a peculiar, an inimitable blending of sweetness and
hauteur in his expression and manner, he greeted me, calmly, gravely, almost coldly; yet with so marked an earnestness that I could not help being
deeply impressed by it. From that moment until his death we were friends;
although we met only during the first year of our acquaintance. And in his
last words, ere reason had forever left her impartial throne in that overtasked
brain, I have a touching memento of his undying faith and friendship.

"During that year, while traveling for my health, I maintained a correspondence with Mr. Poe, in accordance with the earnest entreaties of his wife, who imagined that my influence over him had a restraining and beneficial effect. It *had*, as far as this—that having solemnly promised me to give up the use of stimulants, he so firmly respected his promise and me, as never once, during our whole acquaintance, to appear in my presence when in the slightest degree affected by them. Of the charming love and confidence that existed between his wife and himself, always delightfully apparent to me, in spite of the many little poetical episodes, in which the impassioned romance of his temperament impelled him to indulge; of this I cannot speak too earnestly—too warmly. I believe she was the only woman whom he ever truly loved; and this is evidenced by the exquisite pathos of the little poem lately written, called Annabel Lee, of which she was the subject, and which is by far the most natural, simple, tender and touchingly beautiful of all his songs. I have heard it said that it was intended to illustrate a late love affair of the author; but they who believe this, have in their dullness, evidently misunderstood or missed the beautiful meaning latent in the most lovely of all of its verses—where he says,

> 'A wind blew out of a cloud, chilling
> My beautiful Annabel Lee,
> So that her *high-born kinsman* came,
> And bore her away from me.'

"There seems a strange and almost profane disregard of the sacred purity and spiritual tenderness of this delicious ballad, in this overlooking the allusion to the *kindred angels* and the heavenly *Father* of the lost and loved and unforgotten wife.

"But it was in his conversations and his letters, far more than in his published poetry and prose writings, that the genius of Poe was most gloriously revealed. His letters were divinely beautiful, and for hours I have listened to him, entranced by strains of such pure and almost celestial eloquence as I have never read nor heard elsewhere. Alas! in the thrilling words of Stoddard,

> " 'He might have soared in the morning light,
> But he built his nest with the birds of night!
> But he lies in dust, and the stone is rolled
> Over the sepulchre dim and cold;

He has cancelled all he has done or said,
And gone to the dear and holy dead.
Let us forget the path he trod,
And leave him now, to his Maker, God.'"

The influence of Mr. Poe's aims and vicissitudes upon his literature, was more conspicuous in his later than in his earlier writings. Nearly all that he wrote in the last two or three years—including much of his best poetry,—was in some sense biographical; in draperies of his imagination, those who take the trouble to trace his steps, will perceive, but slightly concealed, the figure of himself. The lineaments here disclosed, I think, are not different from those displayed in this biography, which is but a filling up of the picture. Thus far the few criticisms of his life or works that I have ventured have been suggested by the immediate examination of the points to which they referred. I add but a few words, of more general description.

In person he was below the middle height, slenderly but compactly formed, and in his better moments he had in an eminent degree that air of gentlemanliness which men of a lower order seldom succeed in acquiring.

His conversation was at times almost supra-mortal in its eloquence. His voice was modulated with astonishing skill, and his large and variably expressive eyes looked repose or shot fiery tumult into theirs who listened, while his own face glowed, or was changeless in pallor, as his imagination quickened his blood or drew it back frozen to his heart. His imagery was from the worlds which no mortals can see but with the vision of genius. Suddenly starting from a proposition, exactly and sharply defined, in terms of utmost simplicity and clearness, he rejected the forms of customary logic, and by a crystalline process of accretion, built up his ocular demonstrations in forms of gloomiest and ghastliest grandeur, or in those of the most airy and delicious beauty—so minutely and distinctly, yet so rapidly, that the attention which was yielded to him was chained till it stood among his wonderful creations—till he himself dissolved the spell, and brought his hearers back to common and base existence, by vulgar fancies or exhibitions of the ignoblest passion.

He was at all times a dreamer—dwelling in ideal realms—in heaven or hell—peopled with the creatures and the accidents of his brain. He walked the streets, in madness or melancholy, with lips moving in indistinct curses, or with eyes upturned in passionate prayer, (never for himself, for he felt, or professed to feel, that he was already damned, but) for their happiness who at the moment were objects of his idolatry;—or, with his glances introverted to a heart gnawed with anguish, and with a face shrouded in gloom, he would brave the wildest storms; and all night, with drenched garments and arms beating the winds and rains, would speak as if to spirits that at such times could only be evoked by him from the Aidenn, close by whose portals his disturbed soul sought to forget the ills to which his constitution subjected him—close by the Aidenn where were those he loved—the Aidenn which he might never see, but in fitful glimpses, as its gates opened to receive the less fiery and more happy natures whose destiny to sin did not involve the doom of death.

He seemed, except when some fitful pursuit subjugated his will and engrossed his faculties, always to bear the memory of some controlling sorrow. The remarkable poem of "The Raven" was probably much more nearly than has been supposed, even by those who were very intimate with him, a reflection and an echo of his own history. *He* was that bird's

> "— unhappy master whom unmerciful Disaster
> Followed fast and followed faster till his songs one burden bore—
> Till the dirges of his Hope that melancholy burden bore
> Of 'Never—nevermore.'"

Every genuine author, in a greater or less degree, leaves in his works, whatever their design, traces of his personal character: elements of his immortal being, in which the individual survives the person. While we read the pages of the "Fall of the House of Usher," or of "Mesmeric Revelations," we see in the solemn and stately gloom which invests one, and in the subtle metaphysical analysis of both, indications of the idiosyncracies—of what was most remarkable and peculiar—in the author's intellectual nature. But we see here only the better phases of his nature, only the symbols of his juster action, for his harsh experience had deprived him of all faith, in man or woman. He had made up his mind upon the numberless complexities of the social world, and the whole system with him was an imposture. This conviction gave a direction to his shrewd and naturally unamiable character. Still, though he regarded society as composed altogether of villains, the sharpness of his intellect was not of that kind which enabled him to cope with villainy, while it continually caused him by overshots to fail of the success of honesty. He was in many respects like Francis Vivian in Bulwer's

[151]

novel of "The Caxtons." Passion, in him, comprehended many of the worst emotions which militate against human happiness. You could not contradict him, but you raised quick choler; you could not speak of wealth, but his cheek paled with gnawing envy. The astonishing natural advantages of this poor boy—his beauty, his readiness, the daring spirit that breathed around him like a fiery atmosphere—had raised his constitutional self-confidence into an arrogance that turned his very claims to admiration into prejudices against him. Irascible, envious—bad enough, but not the worst, for these salient angles were all varnished over with a cold repellent synicism, his passions vented themselves in sneers. There seemed to him no moral susceptibility; and, what was more remarkable in a proud nature, little or nothing of the true point of honor. He had, to a morbid excess, that desire to rise which is vulgarly called ambition, but no wish for the esteem of the love of his species; only the hard wish to succeed—not shine, not serve—succeed, that he might have the right to despise a world which galled his self-conceit.

Notes

1. This statement was first printed during Mr. Poe's life-time, and its truth being questioned in some of the journals, the following certificate was published by a distinguished gentleman of Virginia: "I was one several who witnessed this swimming feat. We accompanied Mr. Poe in boats. Messrs. Robert Stannard, John Lyle, (since dead) Robert Saunders, John Munford, I think, and one or two others, were also of the party. Mr. P. did not seem at all fatigued, and *walked* back to Richmond immediately after the feat—which was undertaken for a wager. Robert G. Cabell." [note in original]

2. The writer of a eulogium upon the life and genius of Mr. Poe, in the *Southern Literary Messenger*, for March, 1850, thus refers to this point in his history:

"The story of the other side is different; and if true, throws a dark shade upon the quarrel, and a very ugly light upon Poe's character. We shall not insert it, because it is one of those relations which we think with Sir Thomas Browne, should never be recorded,—being 'verities whose truth we fear and heartily wish there were no truth therein . . . whose relations honest minds do deprecate. For of sins heteroclital, and such as want name or precedent, there is oft-times a sin even in their history. We desire no record of enormities: sins should be accounted new. They omit of their monstrosity as they fall from their rarity; for men count it venial to err with their forefathers, and foolishly conceive they divide a sin in its society. . . . In things of this nature, silence commendeth history: 'tis the veniable part of things lost; wherein there must never arise a Pancirollus, nor remain any register but that of hell.'" [from original]

3. The Narrative of Arthur Gordon Pym, of Nantucket: comprising the Details of a Mutiny and Atrocious Butchery on board the American Brig Grampus, on her way to

the South Seas—with an Account of the Re-capture of the Vessel by the Survivors; their Shipwreck, and subsequent Horrible Sufferings from Famine; their Deliverance by means of the British schooner Jane Gray; the brief Cruise of this latter Vessel in the Antarctic Ocean; her Capture, and the Massacre of her Crew among a Group of Islands in the 84th parallel of southern latitude; together with the incredible Adventures and Discoveries still further South, to which that distressing Calamity gave rise.—1 vol. 12mo. pp. 198. New-York, Harper & Brothers. 1838. [from original]

4. The controversy is wittily described in the following extract from a Parisian journal, *L'Entr Acte*, of the twentieth of October, 1846. [Note from original. The argument, in French, is a commentary on the supposed plagiarism, which essentially repeats, at greater length, what appears in the text above.]

5. Hon. Caleb Cushing, then recently returned from his mission to China. [from original]

6. This lady was the late Mrs. Osgood, and a fragment of what she wrote under these circumstances may be found in the last edition of her works under the title of "Lulin, or the Diamond Fay." [from original]

7. *Southern Literary Messenger*, March, 1850, p. 179. [from original]

8. [The text of the original letter may be seen in the Berg Collection, New York Public Library.]

9. I have neither space, time, nor inclination for a continuation of this subject, and I add but one other instance, in the words of the Philadelphia "Saturday Evening Post,"—published while Mr. Poe was living [Note from original. Treatment of Poe's supposed plagiarism of Thomas Wyatt's *The Conchologist's First Book* follows].

Rufus Wilmot Griswold, "Memoir of the Author." From *The Works of the Late Edgar Allan Poe*, I: xxi–lv.

"Edgar Allan Poe" in
McMakin's Model American Courier (1849)

Henry B. Hirst

Poe and Henry B. Hirst, a Philadelphia attorney, became friends when Poe established himself in Philadelphia in the early 1840s, assuming editorial duties for *Graham's Magazine*. Also a poet whose work attracted attention in his day, Hirst had earlier published a long article on Poe in the *Philadelphia Saturday Museum*, from information supplied by Poe. Both that article and this one are rife with factual errors, for example, that Poe's father died from consumption shortly before Poe's birth, or that his foster father is named Richard, instead of the correct John, Allan. Hirst's opinions are nonetheless valuable as outlooks of one who had been close to Poe, and he is by no means the only one, among writers about Poe, to commit factual mistakes in regard to Poe's life and work.

The first paragraph of the following was apparently written by the editor of *McMakin's Model American Courier*, where Hirst's short biographical sketch was published.

Memoir of Edgar A. Poe.

We had just sat down to pen a notice of Edgar Allan Poe, when we received the following communication from one who knew the Poet better than ourself. The initials at the foot mark the writer as the successful author of "Endymion," "Penance of Roland," &c., &c. We gladly present our readers with *Mr. Hirst's* recollections of poor Poe, whose brilliant but erratic genius always commanded our admiration. He knew him well, and in those things in which he was little known by the world. Such a tribute to the deceased, from such a man and such a pen, has something in it which speaks volumes in favor of the "mystic tie" which unites the brotherhood of song.

Edgar Allan Poe.

Edgar A. Poe is no more. We knew him well, perhaps better than any other man living; and loved him, despite his infirmities. He was a man of great and original genius, but the sublime *afflatus*, which lifted him above his fellows, made him a shining mark for the covert as well as open attacks of literary rivals, and, alas! That it should be so, eventually proved his ruin. So much we gather from the unwritten history of his latter years. His was a life of strange vicissitudes. His father and mother, while he was yet an infant, died within a few weeks of each other, of consumption. He was adopted by Mr. Richard Allan, a wealthy gentleman, almost a millionaire, of Richmond, Virginia, who at once announced his intention of educating him as his heir. Mr. Allan took him with him to England, and he received his first rudiments of his fine classical education at Stoke Newington, near London. The Rev. Dr. Bransby was his tutor. Dr. Bransby's school is very forcibly described in "William Wilson," one of Mr. Poe's most powerful stories. He subsequently returned to America, and passed some time at the Jefferson University, in Virginia. He graduated, although a careless student, with the first honors. His life, at that institution, was full of romance. At even-fall he wandered away among the mountains, seeking inspiration:

"In silence, desolation and dim night."

During the day, frequently for weeks together, he passed his hours in studies which were only pursued in chambers litten with sepulchral lamps, of various-colored chemical fires, which he afterward described in that spirit-haunted apartment of the Lady Rowna of Tremaine, in his terribly imaginative tale of "Ligeia." He was a poet at the age of twelve, and some of his finest still-existing poems were written at that time.

Shortly after he left college, owing to some pecuniary difficulties with Mr. Allan, he ran off on an expedition to join the Greeks, who were then struggling for their liberty, and actually made his way as far as St. Petersburg, in which place he again became involved in difficulties. He was sent back by the American Consul. On his return home, he found Mr. Allan married to a young wife. The old gentleman was then 65 years of age. Much against his inclination he went to West Point, to which place he was recommended by General Scott. Mr. Allan became the father of a son. Young Poe at once saw that all his hope of fortune had fallen to the ground, and

[155]

wrote for leave to resign. It was refused. He applied to General Scott, who seconded Mr. Allan. Poe then refused to perform any duty, and covered the walls of the institution with pasquinades on the professors. One, Mr. Joe Locke, was particularly obnoxious to the students, and he became the principal victim. Mr. Locke was rather a Martinet; he never failed to appear on the parade ground, and he invariably reported a delinquent. A report, at West Point, is a matter of no small moment, for whenever the bad marks amount to a certain number, we forget what it is, charges are preferred against the cadet, the consequences of which are expulsion. We quote one of these satires from memory:

> "John Locke is a notable name,
>   Joe Locke is a greater in short,
> The former was well known to fame,
>   But the latter's well known to 'report.'"

Another:

> "As for Locke—he is 'all in my eye,'
>   May the devil right soon for his soul call,
> He never was known to *lie*—
>   In bed, at a reveille roll call."

Ridicule is a weapon few can withstand, and the affair ended in the way Mr. Poe wished. Charges were preferred against him, the specifications amounting to 152 in number. He at once pleaded guilty, and left the Institution. Mr. Allan instantly abandoned his protégé, and Poe was left penniless. Mr. A. soon after died, and without a reconciliation.

Mr. Poe, bankrupt in every thing except genius, entered the arena of authorship. Some time after, in 1831, the proprietor of a literary weekly paper, in Baltimore, offered two premiums, the one for the best prose story, the other for the best poem. Poe entered into the competition, and took both prizes. His "MS. Found in a Bottle,"—such is our recollection—was the tale; the "Coliseum," the poem. John P. Kennedy, Esq., Author of "Horse Shoe Robinson," was one of the committee, who unanimously united in publishing a card in the Gazette, expressive of the high sense they entertained of his literary abilities. But Mr. Kennedy did not stop here; he applied to the late Thomas W. White, who was then engaged in publishing the "Southern Literary Messenger," and Mr. W. immediately wrote to

Poe, offering him the editorship of that periodical. Poe accepted, and the Messenger, under his care, took the first rank in American literature. He subsequently left Richmond, and came to Philadelphia to take charge of the "Gentleman's Magazine," afterwards "Graham's." On its being merged with Graham, he assumed the editorship of the latter Monthly, which attained its present unequalled reputation under his care. When his engagement with "Graham's Magazine" terminated he removed to New York, where he edited, during its brief but brilliant existence, the "Broadway Journal." Since that time, some two or three years, he has remained unconnected with the press.

Shortly after the decease of his young and beautiful wife, the "Lenore" of his muse, Mr. Poe removed to a little cottage on the banks of the romantic Bronx, in the vicinity of New York, where he supported himself, and his aged mother-in-law, by the occasional use of his brilliant pen. The death of his wife, who was his cousin, and whom he loved from youth, clouded his fine intellect, and he almost sunk under the blow. Adversity hung like a lean and hungry blood-hound on his trail, and he yielded. On a visit to the South, while on his return home, in Baltimore, he succumbed to the destroying angel, and descended into the charnel, there to become prey to the "Conqueror Worm."

Poe had his faults—who has not his errors? We are none of us infallible, but had his opportunities equaled his genius and his ambition, he would have died an universally esteemed great man. As it is, the world of authors and author-lovers, with some few pitiful exceptions, will mourn a departed brother. His name, under any circumstances, cannot be forgotten. His tales are without existing equals in English literature, and his "Raven," the personification of his own despair at the loss of his wife, had made him immortal.

Poor Poe! Hour by hour we have listened to his delightful abstractions, poured forth in a voice so remarkable in the peculiarity of the intonation as to incline to the extraordinary in tone. He was unfortunate in every sense of the word. When miserable authors of still more miserable love stories and puling love poems, were winning gold from the Magazines of the day, he was rarely able to "sell an article," and was always suffering in the iron grasp of penury, and that, too, when the brilliant coruscations of his genius were eagerly sought for by the public *in vain*. Poe wielded too formidable a pen; he was no time-server, and as a critic he could not, and would not *lie*.

What he thought he wrote, and, as a consequence, he made enemies,—little carping muck worms in the barnyards of literature, whose very odors offended the nostrils of his genius. But their number was legion—and he was only one. Gulliver was in the hands of the Lilliputians; they triumphed— he fell. Few would imagine his occasional suffering under the awful wrong of undeserved poverty, for Poe was an industrious man, who would and did toil, delving, when his labors were demanded, imperishable gold from the California of his heart—gold which was exchanged for copper in the Jewry of American literature. And with all his talent how little was he understood. We saw him twice and thrice a day, for two years. We sat night by night, a welcome guest at the often meager, but, when fortune smiled on him, the well-filled board: In all that time, in all our acquaintance, we never heard him express the single word of personal ill-feeling against any man, not even in his blackest hours of poverty.

His criticisms of individuals, and they were nervous enough, referred only to their literary merits, and he was always just and *always right*. Unamiable he was not; he was otherwise to a fault; and always ready to forget and forgive. But his philippics against pretenders in literature, which he loved as an art, and for its own sweet sake, have been misunderstood; they were the expression of the artist, not the man; the object of them would have found a brother in the individual who, as a critic, would have weeded him from the garden of song with joy that he had done so much toward piercing its parterres. Poor Poe!

H. B. H.

Since the receipt of the above notice, a brilliant, but not altogether just review, of the late Mr. Poe, appeared in the New York Tribune. It contains his last poem, written just before his departure from New York. It was presented in manuscript to the author of the review. It embodies in an eminent degree Mr. Poe's peculiarities of style. We have italicized one or two very happy lifts of thought. The whole force of the poem depends, it will be seen, upon the refrain [text of "Annabel Lee" follows].

Henry B. Hirst, "Edgar Allan Poe," *McMakin's Model American Courier,* 20 October 1849: 2.

From "Edgar Allan Poe"
in *Southern Literary Messenger* (1850)

John M. Daniel

> Although the following item is not placed in the otherwise chronological or-
> der of the selections in this book, it concerns Poe's last lecture in the South,
> and thus may more properly appear here even if the larger article of which it
> is part appeared after Poe's death. John M. Daniel is remembered mainly as
> the editor of the Richmond *Semi-Weekly Examiner*, who lent columns of his
> newspaper for publication of Poe's latest revisions of several of his poems.
> Daniel's lengthy sketch, published five months after Poe's death, overflows
> with hostility, though this excerpt, which addresses Poe as lecturer, is far
> more objective than much else in the article. Here John M. Daniel provides
> mixed opinions concerning Poe's effective speaking contrasted with his inef-
> fective recitation of poetry.

. . . FOR THE LAST two years he has been seen now and then about Richmond, generally in a state of intoxication very unbecoming to a man of
genius. But during his last visit of nearly two month's duration, he was
perfectly himself, neatly dressed, and exceedingly agreeable in his deportment. He delivered two lectures during this visit to Richmond, which were
worthy of his genius in its best moods.

These lectures are not to be found in this edition of his works [Griswold's
first two volumes], and have never been published. They were delivered in
the Exchange Concert Room, and their subject was the "Poetic Principle."
He treated this congenial theme with even more acuteness and discrimination than we had expected. His chief object was the refutation of what he
very properly denominated the "poetical heresy of modern times," to wit:
that poetry should have a purpose, and end to accomplish beyond that of
ministering to our sense of the beautiful. We have in these days poets of humanity and poets of universal suffrage, poets whose mission it is to break
down corn-laws and poets to build up workhouses. The idea infects half

the criticism and all the poetry of this utilitarian country. But no idea can be more false. As we have elementary faculties in our minds, whose end is to reason, others to perceive colors and forms, and others to construct; and as logic, painting and mechanics are the products of those faculties and are adapted only to them; as we have nerves to be pleased with perfumes; others with gay colors, and others with the contact of soft bodies;—so have we an elementary faculty for perceiving beauty, with an end of its own and means of its own. Poetry is the product of this faculty and of no other; and it is addressed to the sense of the beautiful and to no other sense. It is ever injured when subjected to the criterion of other faculties, and was never intended to fulfill any other objects than those peculiar to the organ of the mind from which it received its birth. Mr. Poe made good the distinction with a great deal of acuteness and in a very clear manner. He illustrated his general subject by various pieces of criticism upon the popular poets of this country, and by many long recitations of English verse. The critiques were for the most part just and were all entertaining. But we were disappointed in his recitations. His voice was soft and distinct, but neither clear nor sonorous. He did not make rhyme effective; he read all verse like blank verse; yet he gave it a sing-song of his own, more monotonous than the most marked cadence of versification. On the two last syllables of every sentence he fell invariably the fifth of an octave. He did not make his own "Raven" an effective piece of reading. At this we would not be surprised were any other than the author its reader. The chief charm perhaps of that extraordinary composition is the strange and subtle music of the versification. As in Mr. Longfellow's rhythm, we can hear it with our mind's ear while we read it to ourselves, but no human organs are sufficiently delicate to weave it into articulate sounds. For this reason we are not surprised at ordinary failures in reading the piece. But we had anticipated some peculiar charm in its utterance by the lips of him who had created the verse, and in this case we were disappointed.

A large audience, we recollect, attended these lectures. Those who had not seen Edgar Poe since the days of his obscurity, came in crowds to behold their townsman then so famous. The treatment which he received thereafter seems to have pleased him much;—and he became anxious to make Richmond his permanent home. . . .

From John M. Daniel, "Edgar Allan Poe," *Southern Literary Messenger* 16 (March 1850): 177–178 [entire article: 172–187].

"The Late Edgar A. Poe" in
Southern Literary Messenger (1849)

JOHN R. THOMPSON

> Several comments about Poe by the same writer are set forth here. John R.
> Thompson, editor of the *Southern Literary Messenger* in the late 1840s,
> had known Poe slightly, but had formed a sensible impression of the man.
> Thompson was also well informed about the national literary scene of the
> times. His obituary notice offers a far less partisan viewpoint than is evident
> in many other estimates of Poe. Thus it provides a good corrective to some
> of the more effusive commentaries that circulated after Poe's death.

SO MUCH HAS BEEN said by the newspaper press of the country concerning this gifted child of genius, since his recent death, that our readers are already in possession of the leading incidents of his short, brilliant, erratic and unhappy career. It is quite unnecessary that we should recount them in this place. We feel it due to the dead, however, as editor of a magazine which owes its earliest celebrity to his efforts, that some recognition of his talent, on the part of the Messenger, should mingle with the general apotheosis which just now enrols him on the list of "heroes in history and gods in song."

Mr. Poe became connected with the Messenger during the first year of its existence. He was commended to the favorable consideration of the proprietor, the late T. W. White, by the Honorable John P. Kennedy who, as Chairman of a Committee, had just awarded to Poe the prize for the successful tale in a literary competition at Baltimore. Under his editorial management the work soon became well-known every where. Perhaps no similar enterprise ever prospered so largely in its inception, and we doubt if any, in the same length of time—even Blackwood in the days of Dr. Maginn, whom Poe in some respects closely resembled—ever published so many shining articles from the same pen. Those who will turn to the first two volumes of the Messenger will be struck with the number and variety of his contributions. On one page may be found some lyric cadence, plaintive and inexpressibly sweet, the earliest vibrations of those chords which have since thrilled with so many wild and wondrous harmonies. On another some strange story of the German school, akin to the most fanciful legends of the Rhine, fascinates and astonishes the reader with the verisimilitude of its improbabilities. But it was in the editorial department of the magazine that his power was most conspicuously displayed. There he appeared as the critic, not always impartial, it may be, in the distribution of his praises, or correct in the positions he assumed, but ever merciless to the unlucky author who offended by a dull book. A blunder in this respect he considered worse than a crime, and visited it with corresponding rigor. Among the nascent novelists and newly fledged poetasters of fifteen years ago he came down "like a Visigoth marching on Rome." No elegant imbecile or conceited pedant, no matter whether he made his avatar under the auspices of a Society, or with the *prestige* of a degree, but felt the lash of his severity. *Baccalaurei baculo potius quain laureo digni* was the principle of his action in such cases, and to the last he continued to castigate impudent aspirants for the bays. Now that he is gone, the vast multitude of blockheads may breathe again, and we can imagine that we hear the shade of the departed crying out to them, in the epitaph designed for Robespierre,

> Passant! ne plains point mon sort,
> Si je vivais, tu serais mort![1]

It will readily occur to the reader that such a course, while it gained subscribers to the review, was not well calculated to gain friends for the reviewer. And so Mr. Poe found it, for during the two years of his connection with the Messenger, he contrived to attach to himself animosities of the most enduring kind. It was the fashion with a large class to decry his literary pretensions, as poet and romancer and scholar, to represent him as one who possessed little else than

> th' extravagancy
> And crazy ribaldry of fancy—

and to challenge his finest efforts with a chilling *cui bono*; while the critics of other lands and other tongues, the Athenaeum and the *Revue des deux Mondes*, were warmly recognizing his high claims. They did not appreciate him. To the envious obscure, he might not indeed seem entitled to the first literary honors, for he was versed in a more profound learning and skilled in a more lofty minstrelsy, scholar by virtue of a larger erudition and poet by the transmission of a diviner spark.

Unquestionably he was a man of great genius. Among the *litterateurs* of his day he stands out distinctively as an original writer and thinker. In nothing did he conform to established custom. Conventionality he contemned. Thus his writings admit of no classification. And yet in his most eccentric vagaries he was always correct. The fastidious reader may look in vain, even among his earlier poems—where "wild words wander here and there"—for an offence against rhetorical propriety. He did not easily pardon solecisms in others; he committed none himself. It is remarkable too that a mind so prone to unrestrained imaginings should be capable of analytic investigation or studious research. Yet few excelled Mr. Poe in power of analysis or patient application. Such are the contradictions of the human intellect. He was an impersonated antithesis.

The regret has been often expressed that Mr. Poe did not bring his singular capacity to bear on subjects nearer ordinary life and of a more cheerful nature than the gloomy incidents of his tales and sketches. P. P. Cooke, (the accomplished author of the Froissart Ballads, who, we predict, will one day take, by common consent, his rightful high position in American letters,) in a discriminating essay on the genius of Poe, published in this magazine for January, 1848, remarks upon this point,

"For my individual part, having the seventy or more tales, analytic, mystic, grotesque, arabesque, always wonderful, often great, which his industry and fertility have already given us, I would like to read one cheerful book made by his *invention*, with little or no aid from its twin brother *imagination*—a book in his admirable style of full, minute, never tedious narrative—a book full of homely doings, of successful toils, of ingenious shifts and contrivances, of ruddy firesides—a book happy and healthy throughout, and with no poetry in it at all anywhere, except a good old English 'poetic justice' in the end."

That such a work would have greatly enhanced Mr. Poe's reputation with the million, we think, will scarcely be disputed. But it could not be. Mr. Poe was not the man to have produced a *home-book*. He had little of the domestic feeling and his thoughts were ever wandering. He was either in criticism or in the clouds, by turns a disciplinarian and a dreamer. And in his dreams, what visions came to him, may be gathered to some extent from the revealings he has given—visions wherein his fancy would stray off upon some new Walpurgis, or descend into the dark realms of the Inferno, and where occasionally, through the impenetrable gloom, the supernal beauty of Lenore would burst upon his sight, as did the glorified Beatrice on the rapt gaze of the Italian master.

The poems of Mr. Poe are remarkable above all other characteristics, for the exceeding melody of the versification. "Ulalume" might be cited as a happy instance of this quality, but we prefer to quote "The Bells" from the last number of the Union Magazine. It was the design of the author, as he himself told us, to express in language the exact sounds of bells to the ear. He has succeeded, we think, far better than Southey, who attempted a similar feat, to tell us "how the waters come down at Lodore" [text of "The Bells" follows].

The untimely death of Mr. Poe occasioned a very general feeling of regret, although little genuine sorrow was called forth by it, out of the narrow circle of his relatives. We have received, in our private correspondence, from various quarters of the Union, warm tributes to his talent, some of which we take the liberty of quoting, though not designed for publication. A friend in the country writes—

"Many who deem themselves perfect critics talk of the want of *moral* in the writings and particularly the poetry of Poe. They would have every one to write like Æsop, with the moral distinctly drawn at the end to prevent mistake. Such men would object to the meteor, or the lightning's flash, because it lasts only for the moment—and yet they speak the power of God, and fill our minds with the sublime more readily than does the enduring sunlight. It is thus with the writings of Poe. Every moment there comes across the darkness of his style a flash of that spirit which is not of earth. You cannot analyze the feeling—you cannot tell in what the beauty of a particular passage consists; and yet you feel that deep pathos which only genius can incite—you feel the trembling of that melancholy chord which fills the soul with pleasant mournfulness—you feel that deep yearning for something brighter and better than this world can give—that unutterable gushing of the heart which springs up at the touch of the enchanter, as poured the stream from

'Horeb's rock, beneath the prophet's hand.'

I wish I could convey to you the impression which the 'Raven' has made upon me. I had read it hastily in times gone by without appreciation; but now it is a study to me—as I go along like Sinbad in the Valley of Diamonds, I find a new jewel at every step. The beautiful rhythm, the mournful cadence, still ring in the ear for hours after a perusal—whilst the heart is bowed down by the outpourings of a soul made desolate not alone by disappointed love, but by the crushing of every hope, and every aspiration."

In a recent letter the following noble acknowledgement is made by the first of American poets—Henry W. Longfellow—towards whom, it must be said, Mr. Poe did not always act with justice. Mr. Longfellow will pardon us, we trust, for publishing what was intended as a private communication. The passage evidences a magnanimity which belongs only to great minds.

"What a melancholy death," says Mr. Longfellow, "is that of Mr. Poe—a man so richly endowed with genius! I never knew him personally, but have always entertained a high appreciation of his powers as a prose-writer and a poet. His prose is remarkably vigorous, direct and yet affluent; and his verse has a particular charm of melody, an atmosphere of true poetry about it, which is very winning. The harshness of his criticisms, I have never attributed to anything but the irritation of a sensitive nature, chafed by some indefinite sense of wrong."

It was not until within two years past that we ever met Mr. Poe, but during that time, and especially for two or three months previous to his death, we saw him very often. When in Richmond, he made the office of the Messenger a place of frequent resort. His conversation was always attractive, and at times very brilliant. Among modern authors his favorite was Tennyson, and he delighted to recite from "The Princess" the song "Tears, idle tears;" a fragment of which—

—when unto dying eyes
The casement slowly grows a glimmering square,—

he pronounced unsurpassed by any image expressed in writing. The day before he left Richmond, he placed in our hands for publication in the Messenger, the MS. of his last poem, which has since found its way (through a correspondent of a northern paper with whom Mr. Poe had left a copy) into the newspaper press, and been extensively circulated. As it was designed for this magazine, however, we publish it, even though all of our readers may have seen it before [text of "Annabel Lee" follows].

In what we have said of Mr. Poe, we have been considering only the brighter side of the picture. That he had many and sad infirmities cannot be questioned. Over these we would throw in charity the mantle of forget-fulness. The grave has come between our perception and his errors, and we pass them over in silence. They found indeed a mournful expiation in his alienated friendships and his early death.

J. R. T.

Note

1. We translate it freely,

> Traveller! forbear to mourn my lot,
> Thou would'st have died, if I had not. [Thompson's note]

John R. Thompson, "The Late Edgar A. Poe," *Southern Literary Messenger*, November 1849: 694–697.

From "Editor's Table" (1850)

JOHN R. THOMPSON

> In this extract Thompson offers some additional kind words regarding Poe. These are worth remembering because they appeared during a time when many who knew Poe had disliked him.

COMMENTING IN laudatory terms regarding the late Philip Pendleton Cooke's unfinished novel, "The Chevalier Merlin," serialized in the *Messenger* (Chs. 17–21, the latest installment, had appeared in the January number), Thompson concludes: "The late Edgar A. Poe expressed himself to us in terms of the warmest eulogy of the first three parts of this remarkable production, which he declared to be without a counterpart in American letters."

From John R. Thompson, "Editor's Table," *Southern Literary Messenger*, February 1850: 126.

Editorial Note to "Poe on
Headley and Channing" (1850)

[JOHN R. THOMPSON]

This comment from Thompson resembles much popular opinion as regards Poe the critic, particularly on Poe's semi-satiric portraits of contemporary authors in "Literati."

From advance sheets of "The Literati," a work in press [Griswold's edition], by the late Edgar A. Poe, we take the following sketches of Headley and Channing—as good specimens of that tomahawk-style of criticism of which the author was so great a master. In the present instances the satire is well-deserved. Neither of these sketches we believe have been in print before.

[John R. Thompson.] Editorial note to "Poe on Headley and Channing," *Southern Literary Messenger*, October 1850: 607.

"Estimates of Edgar A. Poe"
in *Home Journal* (1850)

Nathaniel P. Willis

Nathaniel Parker Willis inevitably championed Poe the man and writer. An irony connects with Willis's advocacy because Poe had burlesqued his work on several occasions. Here we read a defense of Poe from someone who knew him and wanted to refute John M. Daniel's hostility evinced in the *Southern Literary Messenger*. The piece was introduced by an editorial head-note in the original, which comprises the first paragraph below.

THE CERTAINTY WITH which you hear from a mustard plaster, is nothing to the certainty with which rejected articles drew out a purulent discharged on the rejecting Editor; and we silently throw aside the abusive articles which come to us from various parts of the country, and which indicate the residences of contributors, we have declined—submitting thus to one of the penalties necessarily incurred in throwing off rubbish that would also overwhelm us. On the last page of a late number of the *Southern Literary Messenger*, edited by our friend, John R. Thompson, we find a regret expressed that an article printed in the first sheets of that number should have been found irrevocable, inserted, as it was, accidentally, during his absence in New-York. The abuse of one of the Editors of the Home Journal, however, (whom the writer elegantly calls one of the "dirty little fleas and flies embalmed in the Memoir of Edgar A. Poe") is unimportant in comparison with the misrepresentation inflicted on the character of the dead poet; and to this a Southern gentleman has replied in the following well-written communication.—Eds.

To the Editors of The Home Journal:

Gentlemen,—In the absence of the Editor of the Southern Literary Messenger, there appeared in the number for March 1850, an article upon the late edition of the works of Edgar Allan Poe, which I am sure would never have found admission into its pages with his knowledge and consent. He speaks of the author as a contributor: but he must certainly have recommended himself by offerings of a very different kind. Of the present one it is difficult to say, whether it is most deficient in judgment, modesty, taste, or feeling. I knew something of the individual to whom it relates, both in his boyhood and towards the close of his life. I know something of the opinion generally entertained of him, by those who were best qualified to judge; and I think I may safely say that few will recognize the fidelity of this portraiture. The whole tone of it is exaggerated. The picture is a frightful caricature.

In the first place, his idea of Poe's intellectual character is mistaken. There was nothing of the philosopher about him. To compare him with Copernicus and Kepler, is simply absurd. To talk of the "Eureka" as a stupendous discovery, outstripping by three centuries the progress of human science—to laud it in such phrases as "demonstrating the law by which the universe was formed, and is to be again reduced into chaos," or "the logical concatenation of self-evident ideas"—is an abuse of words. There is nothing really original in the book, save the ingenuity with which vague hypotheses, set afloat by other dreamers, have been combined into shape.

"If shape that may be called, which shape had none."

It certainly does exhibit that extraordinary command of language which the critic justly attributes to the author, and which often in the music and force of its cadences, *seems* to be fraught with a meaning, that melts away as it is repeated to the ear. Poe himself called it a poem: and it is not clear to my mind that he meant it for anything else: or that the lofty tone in which he commits it to posterity is more than one of the artifices which he sometimes employed (as in his mesmeric story) to heighten the effect of an elaborate and mystical hoax. Be that as it may, it is plain to any sober vision, that it is full of Poe's leading characteristic imagination: imaginations wild, reckless, metaphysical, delighting in paradox, reveling in the marvellous, but preserving in its most erratic flights, a singular aspect of earnestness that gave "a method to his madness," unlike that of other men. This is the peculiar feature of his mind. In his prose works it is united with an extraordinary power of analysis and re-combination of minute circumstances. In his poems the images, sometimes gorgeous, oftener gloomy, are invested with a mysterious sadness, and a pathos that sinks into the very heart. But I do not mean to attempt a regular criticism. Let us proceed.

We are told by the reviewer that about *one person in two hundred* is competent to form an opinion of these productions: and in relation to the Eureka, he goes on to say—"The plan of the work is one which, in him who would thread its labyrinth, *requires an extensive knowledge of the entire cycle of material and metaphysical knowledge, etc.*" Now, inasmuch as the critic is evidently the *one man* of the two hundred, and as he has *threaded the labyrinth*, it must follow, "by a logical concatenation of self-evident ideas," that he is possessed of that extensive *knowledge* of the entire cycle of *knowledge*, vouchsafed only to men who are three centuries ahead of their contemporaries! A modest claim, truly, and one less likely to be admitted by the blind multitude than the supposed merits of "Eureka" itself.

The taste of the article is manifested in the profuse abundance of certain flowers of rhetoric, which seem transplanted from Billingsgate, and which, I trust, will never become acclimated in the *Messenger*. It is impossible to see, without disgust, such epithets as "dirty little fleas and flies,"—"the newest, the boldest, the most offensive, and the most impudent humbug,"—"swindle on the purchases,"—"counterfeit shinplaster, ragged, dirty, ancient, and worn"—"honey-eyed dunces," and other like expressions, which join the coarseness of Peter Porcupine to the spurious sign of Grub-street. But this is an unpleasant theme. May such a style not be mistaken for a sample of the sense and courtesy of Southern literature.

I come now to the feeling of this performance. In proportion as the ire of the critic was provoked by the supposed wrongs of the author, and misdeeds of his editors, I had looked for some touches of sympathy and tenderness for his reputation. But, excepting the ill-judged attempt to class him with the great astronomers, and a panegyric on his conversational talent, all that is said is calculated to sink him to a very low place in the public esteem. His intellectual excellence is the only thing praised. His moral character is absolutely blackened. His infirmities and vices are thrust upon our notice over and over, and in the grossest terms of description. We are told that he had "no conception or perception of the claims of civilized society,"—that he cared not what company he kept—that he believed in nobody, and cared for nobody—and that nothing prevented him from being a mocker and sneerer at religion, but an incapacity to perceive reverential things, so as to give them sufficient importance to be mocked. And this delineation, which could only be true of an outcast from society, an enemy to his kind, is prefaced by a declaration that his blemishes were the result of character, rather than of circumstance! Verily, the defence of the dead poet hath fallen into unfortunate hands. I venture little in saying, that this barbarous desecration of his remains will shock the least friendly of those who have survived him. I am sure that, among those who suffered most from his critical severity, not one could be found who would have lent his hand to such work as this. The indictment (for it deserves no other name) is not true. It is full of cruel misrepresentations. It deepens the shallows into unnatural darkness, and shuts out the rays of sunshine that ought to relieve them. I do not deny that there were shadows. The wayward disposition and the checkered life, which are too often the heritage of genius, did indeed fall to the lot of this gifted man. But it is not true that he lived and died the wretch that he is painted; nor is it true that the unhappy results were those of character alone. Those who remember the admiration and flattery which sounded in his boyish ears—the mistaken fondness which indulged him in every caprice and nourished his pride and willfulness into a pernicious growth—cannot but know that education and circumstance had much to do with his career. And with the evidence before us of the devotion to him displayed by his wife's mother, and the fact that even to the last, the hearts of his nearest kindred and friends still beat warmly for him, it is impossible to believe him so bad as he is here represented.

But, whatever he was, why this wanton exposure of the darker traits of his character? It is unnecessary, and it is unfeeling:—it seems as though the writer were reckless of the memory of the dead, or the sufferings of the living. One might imagine that he had dipped his pen in gall, and could not divest it of the bitter venom. It seems to overflow with angry and malignant feeling, with an Ishmaelitish spite such as is imputed to Poe himself, raising the hand against every man, without distinction of friend or foe. Has the critic unconsciously caught the spirit of that which he was describing? Or has he transferred to the subject of his sketch the feelings that corrode his own bosom? At all events, may he not find imitators anywhere in respectable journals, North or South: and may he himself, when he resumes his pen, do so in better temper, and with better manners.

Richmond.

Nathaniel P. Willis, "Estimates of Edgar A. Poe," *Home Journal*, 30 March 1850: [2].

From *Athenaeum* (1852)

ANONYMOUS

> Poe gained reputation in Great Britain from the time that *Pym* appeared
> under British imprint. *Bentley's Miscellany* pirated several tales. "Mesmeric
> Revelation," in modified form, created a sensation among British readers.
> The item below provides a sample of negative, but nevertheless widespread,
> opinion of Poe the man, linking him to the unhealthy nature of his poems.

"THE POETICAL *Works of Edgar Allan Poe, with a Notice of His Life and Genius*. By James Hannay, Esq. With Twenty Illustrations."—Some of these
twenty illustrations are gracefully fantastic. The biographical notice is per-
versely sentimental. The story of Poe's life was told by himself so largely
and loudly to the public by the daily papers of America, that to attempt
to colour over its shames with sympathy and apology is idle.—The poems, with their strange, unwholesome, unequal vigour (night-mare verses,
if such things can be) speak for themselves. Their writer, apart from his
works, had best be forgotten.

Anonymous, *Athenaeum*, 25 December 1852: 1425.

"Authors and Books. Edgar Poe." (1854)

"Apollodorus" [George Gilfillan]

George Gilfillan, writing here under the pseudonym Apollodorus, was a prominent Scottish literary critic during the 1850s, who published accounts of many writers of his, and other, days. Given Gilfillan's strong—if narrow, uninformed, and rigid—moral outlook, there is no wonder in his composing a devastating sketch of Poe, which was widely read and influential in keeping the conception of an almost monstrous figure before the reading public, as was typical of much else published about Poe during this era. Gilfillan's comparison of Poe with Richard Savage, who died in squalid poverty, and Thomas Dermody (1775–1802), an Irish poet, whose demise occurred in kindred circumstances, seems calculated to blast Poe's reputation. Gilfillan's allusion to the *Edinburgh Review* refers to Francis Jeffrey's slashing commentary in that magazine [8 (April 1806): 159–167] on James Grant Raymond's biography of Dermody. Gilfillan's sketch was reprinted in *Littell's Living Age*, in an abridged form in the *Southern Literary Messenger*, and in Gilfillan's third *Gallery of Portraits* (1855). Since Dermody and Savage may be unfamiliar figures today, the best recent information about their alcoholism and deaths appears respectively in Reiman, v, ix; and Tracy, 146–152.

WE HAVE SOMETIMES amused ourselves by conjecturing, had the history of human genius run differently—had all men of that class been as wise and prudent and good as too many of them have been improvident, foolish, and depraved—had we had a virtuous Burns, a pure Byron, a Goldsmith with common-sense, a Coleridge with self-control, and a Poe with sobriety—what a different world it had been; what each of these surpassing spirits might have done to advance, refine, and purify society; what a host of "minor prophets" had been found among the array of the poets of our own country! For more than the influence of kings, or rulers, or statesmen, or clergymen—though it were multiplied tenfold—is that of the "Makers" whose winged words pass through all lands, tingle in all ears, touch all hearts, and in all circumstances are remembered and come humming around us—in the hours of labour, in the intervals of business, in trouble, and sorrow, and sickness, and on the bed of death itself; who enjoy, in fact, a kind of omnipresence—whose thoughts have over us the threefold grasp of beauty, language, and music—and to whom at all times "all power is given" in the "dreadful trance" of their genius, to move our beings to their foundations, and to make us better or worse, lower or higher men, according to their pleasure. Yet true it is, and pitiful as true, that these "makers"—themselves made of the finest clay—have often been "marred," and that the history of poets is one of the saddest and most humbling in the records of the world—sad and humbling especially because the poet is ever seen side-by-side with his own ideal, that graven image of himself he has set up with his own hands, and his failure or fall are judged accordingly. There is considerable truth in the remark made by poor Cowper. He says in his correspondence: "I have lately finished eight volumes of Johnson's *Lives of the Poets*; in all that number I observe but one man whose mind seems to have had the slightest tincture of religion, and he was hardly in his senses. His name was Collins. But from the lives of all the rest there is but one inference to be drawn: that poets are a very worthless, wicked set of people." This is certainly too harsh, since these lives include the names of Addison, Watts, Young, and Milton; but it contains a portion of truth. Poets, as a tribe, have been rather a worthless, wicked set of people; and certainly Edgar Poe, instead of being an exception, was probably *the* most wicked of all his fraternity.

And yet we must say, in justice, that the very greatest poets have been good as well as great. Shakspere—judging him by his class and age—was undoubtedly, to say the least, a respectable member of society, as well as a warm-hearted and generous man. Dante and Milton we need only name. And these are "the first three" in the poetic army. Wordsworth, Young, Cowper, Southey, Bowles, Crabbe, Pollock, are inferior but still great names, and they were all, in different measures, good men. And of late years, indeed, the instances of depraved genius have become rarer and rarer: so much so that we are disposed to trace a portion of Poe's renown to the fact that he stood forth an exception so gross, glaring, and defiant, to what was fast becoming a general rule.

In character he was certainly one of the strangest anomalies in the history of mankind. Many men as dissipated as he have had warm hearts, honourable feelings, and have been loved and pitied by all. Many, in every other respect worthless, have had some one or two redeeming points; and the combination of "one virtue and a thousand crimes" has not been uncommon. Others have the excuse of partial derangement for errors otherwise monstrous and unpardonable. But none of these pleas can be made for Poe. He was no more a gentleman than he was a saint. His heart was as rotten as his conduct was infamous. He knew not what the terms honour and honourable meant. He had absolutely no virtue or good quality, unless you call remorse a virtue and despair a grace. Some have called him mad; but we confess we see no evidence of this in his history. He showed himself, in many instances, a cool, calculating, deliberate blackguard. He was never mad, except when in delirium tremens. His intellect at all other times was of the clearest, sharpest, and most decisive kind. A large heart has often beat in the bosom of a debauchee; but Poe had not one spark of genuine tenderness, unless it were for his wife, whose heart, nevertheless, and constitution, he broke—hurrying her to a premature grave, that he might write *Annabel Lee* and *The Raven*! His conduct to his patron, and to the lady mentioned in his memoirs, whom he threatened to cover with infamy if she did not lend him money, was purely diabolical. He was, in short, a combination, in almost equal proportions, of the fiend, the brute, and the genius. One might call him one of the Gadarene swine, filled with the devil, and hurrying down a steep place to perish in the waves; but none could deny that—to use an expression applied first to a celebrated female author of the day—he was a "swine of genius."

He has been compared to Swift, to Burns, to Sheridan, to De Quincey, and to Hazlitt; but in none of these cases does the comparison fully hold. Swift had probably as black crimes on his conscience as Poe; but Swift could feel and could create in others the emotion of warmest friendship, and his outward conduct was irreproachable—it was otherwise with the Yankee Yahoo. Burns had many errors, poor fellow! but they were "all of the flesh, none of the spirit:" he was originally one of the noblest of natures; and during all his career nothing mean or dishonourable or black-hearted was ever charged against him; he was an erring man—but still a *man*. Sheridan was a sad scamp, but he had a kind of *bonhommie* about him which carried off in part your feeling of disgust; and although false to his party, he was in general true to his friends. De Quincey is of an order so entirely different from Poe that we must apologize for introducing their names into the same sentence—the one being a very amiable, and the other having been the most hardened and heartless of men; the only point of comparison in fact between them being their poverty. Hazlitt's faults were deep and dark; but he was what Poe was not—an intensely honest and upright man; and he paid the penalty thereof in unheard-of abuse and proscription. In order to parallel Poe we must go back to Savage, and Dermody. If our readers will turn to the first or second volumes of the *Edinburgh Review*, they will find an account of the last-mentioned, which will remind them very much of Poe's dark and discreditable history. Dermody, like Poe, was an habitual drunkard, licentious, false, treacherous, and capable of everything that was mean, base, and malignant; but unlike Poe, his genius was not far above mediocrity. Hartley Coleridge, too, may recur to some as a case in point; but, although he was often, according to a statement we heard once from Christopher North, "dead drunk at ten o'clock in the morning," he was, both out of and in his cups, a harmless being, and a thorough gentleman— amiable, and, as the phrase goes, "no body's enemy but his own."

How are we to account for this sad and miserable story? That Poe's circumstances were precarious from the first—that he was left an orphan— that without his natural protector he became early exposed to temptation—that his life was wandering and unsettled;—all this does not explain the utter and reckless abandonment of his conduct, far less his systematic want of truth, and the dark sinistrous malice which rankled in his bosom. Habitual drunkenness does indeed tend to harden the heart; but if Poe had possessed any heart originally, it might, as well as in the case of other dissipated men of genius, have resisted, and only in part yielded to the induration; and why *did* he permit himself to become the abject slave of the vice? The poet very properly puts "lust hard by hate" (and hence, perhaps, the proverbial fierceness of the bull), and Poe was as licentious as he was intemperate; but the question recurs, why? We are driven to one of two suppositions: either that his moral nature was more than usually depraved *ab origine*—that, as some have maintained, "conscience was omitted" in his constitution; or that, by the unrestrained indulgence of his passions, he, as John Bunyan has it, "tempted the devil," and became the bound victim of infernal influence. In this age of scepticism such a theory is sure to be laughed at, but is not the less likely to be true. If ever man in modern times resembled at least a demoniac, "exceeding fierce, and dwelling among tombs"—possessed now by a spirit of fury, and now by a spirit of falsehood, and now by an "unclean spirit"—it was Poe, as he rushed with

[177]

his eyes open into every excess of riot; or entered the house of his intended bride on the night before the anticipated marriage, and committed such outrages as to necessitate a summons of the police to remove the drunk and raving demon; or ran howling through the midnight like an evil spirit on his way to the Red Sea, battered by the rains, beaten by the winds, waving aloft his arms in frenzy, cursing loud and deep Man—Himself—God—and proclaiming that he was already damned, and damned for ever. In demoniac possession too, of a different kind, it was that he fancied the entire secret of the making of the universe to be revealed to him, and went about everywhere shouting "Eureka"—a title, too, which he gave to the strange and splendid lecture in which he recorded the memorable illusion. And when the spirit of talk came at times mightily upon him—when the "witch element" seemed to surround him—when his brow flushed like an evening cloud—when his eyes glared wild lightning—when his hair stood up like the locks of a Bacchante—when his chest heaved, and his voice rolled and swelled like subterranean thunder—men, admiring, fearing, and wondering, said, "He hath a demon, yea, seven devils are entered into him." His tongue was then "set on fire," but set on fire of hell; and its terrific inspiration rayed out of every gesture and look, and spake in every tone.

"Madness!" it will be cried again; but that word does not fully express the nature of Poe's excitement in these fearful hours. There was no incoherence either in his matter or in his words. There was, amid all the eloquence and poetry of his talk, a vein of piercing, searching, logical, but sinister thought. All his faculties were shown in the same lurid light, and touched by the same torch of the furies. All blazed emulous of each other's fire. The awful soul which had entered his soul formed an exact counterpart to it, and the haggard "dream was one." One is reminded of the words of Aird, in his immortal poem *The Demoniac*:—

> Perhaps by hopeless passions bound
> And render'd weak, the mastery a demon o'er him found:
> Reason and duty all, all life, his being all became
> Subservient to the wild, strange law that overbears his frame;
> And in the dead hours of the night, when happier children lie
> In slumbers seal'd, he journeys far the flowing waters by.
> And oft he haunts the sepulchres, where the thin shoals of ghosts
> Flit shiv'ring from death's chilling dews; to their unbodied hosts

[178]

That charm through night their feeble plaint, he yells; at the red morn
Meets the great armies of the winds, high o'er the mountains borne,
Leaping against the viewless rage, *tossing his arms on high*,
And hanging balanced o'er sheer steeps against the morning sky.

We are tempted to add the following lines; partly for their Dantesque power, and partly because they describe still more energetically than the last quotation such a tremendous possession as was Herman's in fiction and Poe's in reality:—

He rose; a smother'd gleam
Was on his brow; with fierce motes roll'd his eye's distempered beam;
He smiled, 'twas as the lightning of a hope about to die
For ever from the furrow'd brows of Hell's eternity;
Like sun-warmed snakes, *rose on his head a storm of golden hair*,
Tangled; and thus on Miriam fell hot breathings of despair:
"Perish the breasts that gave me milk! yea, in thy mould'ring heart,
Good thrifty roots I'll plant, to stay next time my hunger's smart.
Red vein'd derived apples I shall eat with savage haste,
And see thy life-blood blushing through, and glory in the taste."

Herman, in the poem, has a demon sent into his heart, in divine sovereignty, and that he may be cured by the power of Christ. But Poe had Satan substituted for soul, apparently to torment him before the time; and we do not see him ere the end, sitting, "clothed, and in his right mind, at the feet of Jesus." He died, as he had lived, a raving, cursing, self-condemned, conscious cross between the fiend and the genius, believing nothing, hoping nothing, loving nothing, fearing nothing—himself his own God and his own devil—a solitary wretch, who had cut off every bridge that connected him with the earth around and the heavens above. This, however, let us say in his favour—he has died "alone in his iniquity;" he has never, save by his example (so far as we know his works), sought to shake faith, or sap morality. His writings may be morbid, but they are pure; and, if his life was bad, has he not left it as a legacy to moral anatomists, who have met and wondered over it, although they have given up all attempt at dissection or diagnosis, shaking the head, and leaving it alone in its shroud, with the solemn whispered warning to the world, and especially to its stronger and brighter spirits, "Beware."

A case so strange as Poe's compels us into new and more searching forms of critical, as well as of moral analysis. Genius has very generally been ascribed to him; but some will resist and deny the ascription—proceeding partly upon peculiar notions of what genius is, and partly from a very natural reluctance to concede to a wretch so vile a gift so noble, and in a degree, too, so unusually large. Genius has often been defined as something inseparably connected with the *genial* nature. If this definition be correct, Poe was not a genius any more than Swift, for geniality neither he nor his writings possessed. But if genius mean a compound of imagination and inventiveness, original thought, heated by passion, and accompanied by power of fancy, Poe was a man of great genius. In wanting geniality, however, he wanted all that makes genius lovely and beloved, at once beautiful and dear. A man of genius, without geniality, is a mountain, clad in snow, companioned by tempests, and visited only by hardy explorers who love sublime nakedness, and to snatch a fearful joy from gazing down black precipices; a man whose genius is steeped in the genial nature of an Autumn landscape, suggesting not only images of beauty, and giving thrills of delight, but yielding peaceful and plenteous fruits, and in which the heart finds a rest and a home. From the one the timid, the weak, and the gentle retire in a terror which overpowers their admiration; but in the other the lowliest and feeblest find shelter and repose. Even Dante and Milton, owing to the excess of their intellectual and imaginative powers over their genial feelings, are less loved than admired, while the vast supremacy of Shakspere is due not merely to his universal genius, but to the predominance of geniality and heart in all his writings. You can envy and even hate Dante and Milton— and had Shakspere only written his loftier tragedies, you might have hated and envied him too; but who can entertain any such feelings for the author of the *Comedy of Errors* and *Twelfth Night*, the creator of Falstaff, Dogberry and Verres? If Genius be the sun, geniality is the atmosphere through which alone his beams can penetrate with power or be seen with pleasure.

Poe is distinguished by many styles and many manners. He is the author of fictions, as matter-of-fact in their construction and language as the stories of Defoe, and of tales as weird and wonderful as those of Hoffman—of amatory strains trembling, if not with the heart, with passion, and suffused with the purple glow of love—and of poems, dirges either in form or in spirit, into which the genius of desolation has shed its dreariest essence— of verses, gay with apparent, but shallow joy, and of others dark with a misery which reminds us of the helpless, hopeless, infinite misery which sometimes visits the soul in dreams. But, amid all this diversity of tone and of subject, the leading qualities of his mind are obvious. These consist of strong imagination—an imagination, however, more fertile in incidents, forms, and characters, than in images; keen power of analysis, rather than synthetic genius; immense inventiveness; hot passions, cooled down by the presence of art, till they resemble sculptured flame, or "lightning in the hand of a painted Jupiter;" knowledge rather *récherché* and varied than strict, accurate, or profound; and an unlimited command of words, phrases, musical combinations of sound, and all other materials of an intellectual workman. The direction of these powers was controlled principally by his habits and circumstances. These made him morbid; and his writings have all a certain morbidity about them. You say at once, cool and clear as most of them are, these are not the productions of a healthy or happy man. But surely never was there such a calm despair—such a fiery torment so cased in ice! When you compare the writings with the known facts of the author's history, they appear to be so like, and so unlike, his character. You seem looking at an inverted image. You have the features, but they are discovered at an unexpected angle. You see traces of the misery of a confirmed debauchee, but none of his disconnected ravings, or of the partial imbecility which often falls upon his powers. There is a strict, almost logical, method in his wildest productions. He tells us himself that he wrote *The Raven* as coolly as if he had been working out a mathematical problem. His frenzy is a conscious one—he feels his own pulse when it is at its wildest, and looks at his foaming lips in the looking-glass. You are reminded of the figure of Mephistopheles in Retzsch's illustrations of Faust, sitting on the infernal steed, which is moving at the pace of the whirlwind, with the calm of perfect indifference.

Poe was led by a singular attraction to all dark, dreadful, and disgusting objects and thoughts—mahlstroms [*sic*], mysteries, murders, mummies, premature burials, excursions to the moon, solitary mansions, surrounded by mist and weighed down by mysterious dooms, lonely tarns, trembling to the winds of autumn and begirt by the shivering ghosts of woods. These are the materials which his wild imagination loves to work with, and out of them to weave the most fantastic and dismal of worlds. Yet there's "magic in the web." You often revolt at his subjects; but no sooner does he enter on them, than your attention is riveted, you lend him your ears—nay, that is a feeble word, you surrender your whole being to him for a season, although it be as you succumb, body and soul, to the dominion of a nightmare. What greatly increases the effect, as in *Gulliver's Travels*, is the circumstantiality with which he recounts the most amazing and incredible things. His tales, too, are generally cast into the autobiographical form, which adds much to their living vraisemblance and vivid power. It is Coleridge's "Old Mariner" over again. Strange, wild, terrible, is the tale he has to tell; haggard, woe-begone, unearthly, is the appearance of the narrator. Every one at first, like the wedding guest, is disposed to shrink and beat his breast; but he holds you with his glittering eye, he forces you to follow him into his own en-chanted region,—and once there, you forget everything, your home, your friends, your creed, your very personal identity, and become swallowed up like a straw in the mahlstrom of his story, and forget to breathe till it is ended, and the mysterious tale-teller is gone. And during all the wild and whirling narrative, the same chilly glitter has continued to shine in his eye, his blood has never warmed, and he has never exalted his voice above a thrilling whisper.

Poe's power may perhaps be said to be divisible into two parts—first, that of adding an air of circumstantial verity to incredibilities; and sec-ondly, that of throwing a weird lustre upon commonplace events. He tells fiction so minutely and with such apparent simplicity and sincerity, that you almost believe it true; and he so combines and so recounts such inci-dents as you meet with every day in the newspapers that you feel truth to be far stranger than fiction. Look, as a specimen of the first, to his Descent into the Mahlstrom, and to his Hans Pfaal's Journey to the Moon. Both are impossible; the former as much so as the latter; but he tells them with such Dante-like directness, and such Defoe-like minuteness, holding his watch and marking, as it were, every second in the progress of each stupendous lie—that you rub your eyes at the close, and ask the question, Might not all this actually have occurred? And then turn to the Murders in the Rue St. Morgue [*sic*], or to the Mystery of Marie Roget, and see how, by the disposition of the drapery he throws over little or ordinary incidents, con-nected indeed with an extraordinary catastrophe, he lends

The light which never was on sea or shore

to streets of revelry and vulgar sin, and to streams whose sluggish waters are never disturbed save by the plash of murdered victims, or by the plunge

[182]

of suicides desperately hurling their bodies to the fishes, and their souls to the flames of Hell.

In one point, Poe bears a striking resemblance to his own illustrious countryman, Brockden Brown—neither resort to agency absolutely supernatural, in order to produce their terrific effects. They despise to start a ghost from the grave—they look upon this as a cheap and *fade* expedient—they appeal to the "mightier might" of the human passions, or to those strange unresolved phenomena in the human mind, which the terms mesmerism and somnambulism serve rather to disguise than to discover, and sweat out from their native soil superstitions far more powerful than those of the past. Once only does Poe approach the brink of the purely preternatural—it is in that dreary tale, the "Fall of the House of Usher;" and yet nothing so discovers the mastery of the writer as the manner in which he avoids, while nearing the gulf. There is really nothing after all in the strange incidents of that story, but what natural principles can explain. But Poe so arranges and adjusts the singular circumstances to each other, and weaves around them such an artful mist, that they produce a most unearthly effect. He separates the feeling of supernatural fear from the consciousness of supernatural agency, and gives you it entire, "lifting the skin from the scalp to the ancles." Perhaps some may think that he has fairly crossed the line in that dialogue between Charmian and Iras, describing the conflagration of the world. But, even there, how admirably does he produce a certain feeling of probability by the management of the natural causes which he brings in to produce the catastrophe. He burns his old witch-mother the earth, scientifically! We must add that the above is the only respect in which Poe resembles Brown. Brown was a virtuous and amiable man, and his works, although darkened by unsettled religious views, breathe a fine spirit of humanity. Poe wonders at, and hates man—Brown wonders at, but at the same time pities, loves, and hopes in him. Brown mingled among men like a bewildered angel—Poe like a prying fiend.

We have already alluded to the singular power of analysis possessed by this strange being. This is chiefly conspicuous in those tales of his which turn upon circumstantial evidence. No lawyer or judge has ever equalled Poe in the power he manifests of sifting evidence—of balancing probabilities—of finding the *multum* of a large legal case in the *parvum* of some minute and well-nigh invisible point—and in constructing the real story out of a hundred dubious and conflicting incidents. What scales he carries with him! how fine and tremulous with essential justice! And with what a microscopic eye he watches every foot-print! Letters thrown loose on the mantel-piece, bell-ropes, branches of trees, handkerchiefs, &c. become to him instinct with meaning, and point with silent finger to crime and to punishment. And to think of this subtle algebraic power, combined with such a strong ideality, and with such an utterly corrupted moral nature! It is as though Chatterton had become a Bow-street officer. Surely none of the hybrids which geology has dug out of the graves of Chaos, and exhibited to our shuddering view, is half so strange a compound as was Edgar Poe. We have hitherto scarcely glanced at his poetry. It, although lying in a very short compass, is of various merit: it is an abridgement of the man in his strength and weakness. Its chief distinction, as a whole, from his prose, is its peculiar music. *That*, like all his powers, is fitful, changeful, varying; but not more so than to show the ever-varying moods of his mind, acting on a peculiar and indefinite theory of sound. The alpha and omega of that theory may be condensed in the word "reiteration." He knows the effect which can be produced by ringing changes on particular words. The strength of all his strains consequently lies in their chorus, or "oure turn," as we call it in Scotland. We do not think that he could have succeeded in sustaining the harmonies or keeping up the interest of a large poem. But his short flights are exceedingly beautiful, and some of his poems are miracles of melody. All our readers are familiar with the *Raven*; it is a dark world in itself; it rises in your sky suddenly as a cloud, like a man's hand in the heaven of Palestine, and covers all the horizon with the blackness of darkness. As usual in his writings, it is but a common event idealised; there is nothing supernatural or even extraordinary in the incident recounted; but the reiteration of the one dreary word "nevermore;" the effect produced by seating the solemn bird of yore upon the bust of Pallas; the manner in which the fowl with its fiery eyes becomes the evil conscience or memory of the lonely widower; and the management of the time, the season, and the circumstances—all unite in making the Raven in its flesh and blood a far more terrific apparition than ever from the shades made night hideous, while "revisiting the glimpses of the moon." The poem belongs to a singular class of poetic uniques, each of which is itself enough to make a reputation, such as Coleridge's *Rime of the Anciente Marinere* [*sic*] or *Christabel*, and Aird's *Devil's Dream upon Mount Acksbeck*—poems in which some one new and generally dark idea is wrought out into a whole so strikingly complete and self-contained as to resemble creation, and in which thought, imagery, language, and music combine to produce a similar effect, and are made to chime together like bells. What entirety of effect, for instance, is produced in the *Devil's Dream* by the unearthly theme, the strange title, the austere and terrible figures, the large rugged volume of verse, and the knotty and contorted language; and in the *Rime of the Anciente Marinere* by the ghastly form of the narrator—the wild rhythm, the new mythology, and the exotic diction of the tale he tells! So Poe's *Raven* has the unity of a tree blasted, trunk, and twigs, and root, by a flash of lightning. Never did melancholy more thoroughly "mark for its own" any poem than this. All is in intense keeping. Short as the poem is, it has a beginning, middle, and end. Its commencement how abrupt and striking—the time a December midnight—the poet a solitary man, sitting "weak and weary," poring in helpless fixity, but with no profit or pleasure, over a black-letter volume; the fire half expired; and the dying embers haunted by their own ghosts, and shivering upon the hearth! The middle is attained when the raven mounts the bust of Pallas, and is fascinating the solitary wretch by his black glittering plumage, and his measured, melancholy croak. And the end closes as with the wings of night over the sorrow of the unfortunate, and these dark words conclude the tale:—

> And my soul from out that shadow that lies floating on the floor,
> Shall be lifted Nevermore.

You feel as if the poem might have been penned by the finger of one of the damned. Its author has fallen below the suicide point; death opens up no hope for him; the quarrel is not with *life* on earth—it is with *being* anywhere.

The same shadow of unutterable woe rests upon several of his smaller poems, and the effect is greatly enhanced by their gay and song-like rhythm. That madness or misery which *sings* out its terror or grief, is always the most desperate. It is like a burden of hell set to an air of heaven. "Ulalume" might have been written by Coleridge during the sad middle portion of his life. There is a sense of dreariness and desolation as of the last of earth's Autumns, which we find no where else in such perfection. What a picture these words convey to the imagination:—

> The skies they were ashen and sober;
> The leaves they were crisped and sere—

The leaves they were withering and sere,
It was night in the lonesome October
Of my most immemorial year.
It was hard by the dim lake of Auber,
In the misty mid-region of Weir—
It was down by the dank tarn of Auber
In the ghoul-haunted woodland of Weir.

These to many will appear only words; but what wondrous words. What a spell they wield,—what a withered unity there is in them! Like a wasted haggard face, they have no bloom or beauty; but what a tale they tell! Weir—Auber—where are they? They exist not, except in the writer's imagination, and in yours; for the instant they are uttered a misty picture, with a tarn, dark as a murderer's eye, below, and the thin, yellow leaves of October fluttering above,—exponents both of a misery which scorns the name of sorrow, and knows neither limit nor termination—is hung up in the chamber of your soul for ever. What power, too, there is in the "Haunted Palace," particularly in the last words, "*They laugh, but smile no more!*" Dante has nothing superior in all those chilly yet fervent words of his, where "The ground burns frore, and cold performs the effect of fire."

We must now close our sketch of Poe; and we do so with feelings of wonder, pity, and awful sorrow, tempted to look up to heaven, and to cry, "Lord, why didst thou make this man in vain?" Yet perhaps there was even in him some latent spark of goodness, which may even now be developing itself under a kindlier sky. If man, even at his *best* estate, be altogether vanity, at his *worst* he cannot be much more. He has gone far away from the misty mid-region of Weir; his dreams of cosmogonies, &c. have been tested by the searching light of Eternity's truth; his errors have received the reward that was meet; and we cannot but say, ere we close, peace even to the well-nigh putrid dust of Edgar Poe.

APOLLODORUS

Apollodorus [George Gilfillan], "Authors and Books. Edgar Poe," *Critic* (*London Literary Journal*), 1 March 1854: 119–121.

"Preface" to *Works of the Late Edgar A. Poe* (1856)

RUFUS WILMOT GRISWOLD

> This item is consequential because it acknowledges Poe's own high estima-
> tion of his comic writings and acknowledges *Pym* and "Maelzel's Chess-
> Player" as being among Poe's "remarkable productions"—and is all the more
> significant because of Griswold's antipathies toward Poe. Commenting on
> *The Narrative of Arthur Gordon Pym*, Griswold ignores Poe's other attempt at
> sustained narrative, "The Journal of Julius Rodman," perhaps because once
> it was serialized it never appeared in hardcover volume form. Not all of Gris-
> wold's comments about Poe were hostile or belittling, as is attested in what
> follows. Moreover, this opinion concerns the importance of Poe's ventures
> into humorous writing, and so it indicates that one on the contemporaneous
> scene could readily recognize Poe's humor, a feature in his fiction that con-
> tinues to occasion disputes that touch on the writings and on biographical
> issues.

THE PRESENT VOLUME contains some of Mr. Poe's most remarkable productions. The nautical story of "Arthur Gordon Pym" was written at an early
period of his literary life, is the longest of his fictions, and the only exhibition we have of his abilities in a protracted and sustained narrative. The
humorous tales which follow, were, in the author's own opinion, among the
most perfect and successful of his performances; and all readers will agree
that the discussion respecting the Automaton Chess Player of Maelzel is
characteristically ingenious and conclusive.

The publisher has now finished the complete collection of the Works of
Edgar A. Poe, originally contemplated. The series of volumes, of which
this is the fourth, embrace, it is believed, everything written by him which
he himself would have wished thus to preserve.

New York, Feb. 13, 1856

Rufus Wilmot Griswold, "Preface" to Volume Four of *The Works of the Late Edgar A. Poe*, [v].

"Edgar Allan Poe: A Letter to the Editor of *The Train*" (1857)

WILLIAM MOY THOMAS

William Moy Thomas, a British journalist who frequently contributed critiques of writers and literary topics, sounds a note of skepticism concerning Griswold's portrayal of Poe, and, as such, his opinion is significant as a calling into question of Griswold and followers' hostility, and as a faceoff to Gilfillan's recent and influential negative commentary on Poe.

THE POEMS AND tales of Edgar Allan Poe are now so well known to English readers; the story of his life and character has been so often told, in magazine articles and prefaces to reprints of his works, that I purpose here to do nothing more than say a few words upon what has already been said upon this subject. I have, indeed, no new story to tell, or fact to add, to what is written in memoirs long extant and accessible to all; nor am I ashamed to confess that I have little acquaintance with American literature, and that I do not go so far in my admiration of Poe, as the most ardent of his friends. But, from the first day that I heard a rumour of this Transatlantic genius, and of his reputed wild and dissolute life, I have felt some curiosity concerning him; for I fancied that he must, at least, fill a gap in American literary history—a gap, which but for him might perhaps never have been filled. The lettered scamp of the first order (have we not heard it a hundred times?) will leave few bones or imprints of himself in this latest formation of the literary world. He was going out, when the maxims of Poor Richard first came to us as a token of the future respectability of the literature of His Majesty King George's Plantations in America. I am not aware that any American city has, or ever had, a Grub Street. Of the Otways and Savages, the Gildons, the Chattertons, the Smarts and Dermodys, America had, I presume, no knowledge, save what we sent her, until at length this native name arose, outdarkening all that had been yet recorded. Presuming this to be so, I had, as I have said, some curiosity to know more about this strange anachronism in literary history. Knowing as I did, how tenderly modern biography deals with the departed, I was curious, I say, to learn what honest tongue had dared to tell these unpalatable truths. It would not be difficult for me to put in a foot-note to this sentence some names of men of genius, who even of these better days, even of this last stratum of literary life, owe something of their respectable fame to the indulgent pen of the biographer, the critic, or the literary executor. You know, Sir, that, when little Button the Antiquarian, or poor Tom Grub the Poet is taken from us, it is not the fashion to be hard upon him. We drag no frailties from their dread abode. The reader of the present day, not initiated into that esoteric doctrine which sometimes reveals itself among ourselves by nods, or shrugs, or compassionate ejaculations, must, I fancy, miss the wicked men, as the little child missed them in the churchyard. Perhaps some critic, whose great-grandmother is yet in swaddling clothes, may one day rake and pry, as we now rake and pry into the lives of Pope and Swift, and Steele and Young, and Mallet and Boswell, and may glean some few things that we have missed or have not cared to tell. For who among us likes to be called a flunkey, a valet-soul, a miserable puppy, who takes a wanton delight in defiling the illustrious dead? It would be a pitiful, a foolish, and an unprofitable ambition. In fact, our sins lie not on that side. I would rather say, that we are a trifle too large-hearted—have a trifle too much love in public towards our kind. Let me mention the case of Ringlett, that well-known epic poet. It is no secret to me or you that he ran away from Mrs. Ringlett, for Potosi, a year or two ago—that he still lives there, a prosperous gentleman, and that he has never yet dreamed of sending poor Mrs. R. anything, save three small portraits of his own inspired countenance, in lieu of board and clothes, and lodging. Well, if Ringlett were to die to-morrow, should we be found wanting in Christian charity? I should say not. There was, I know, the other day, when the diary of a dead poet was published, a little squabble between editor and critic, in which some things were blurted out before their time; but the indiscreet critic was an old man, and a Tory of another age.

Now, knowing all these things, and many more of the kind, and having upon me, I suppose, the habit and prejudice of these times, it did, I say, fill me with wonderment and curiosity, when I heard what was said of this American Poet. Granting all to be true,—what man, within a few months after his decease, had been brave enough to paint the author of the "Raven" as a liar, a cheat, a libertine, a drunkard, a slanderer, and a coward? He presented himself to my mind, I confess, as a problem no less wonderful than Poe himself. Greater still was my surprise, when I learned that he was the literary executor of the deceased poet, selected by the latter himself, to give the public an account of his warfare upon earth. Surely this was a case of stern devotedness to truth, which could find few parallels in the world's history. Here is a Christian Clergyman—a Reverend Rufus Griswold—announcing himself as a personal friend of the deceased, intrusted with the task of editing his works, who does his duty with such bitter honesty, as puts the whole race of mealy-mouthed and pliant critics and biographers to shame. For I took it for granted that there was no known enmity between Poe and Griswold—I took it for granted that the biographer's motives were unquestionable—the facts of his melancholy story too recent and too notorious, to be made the subject of "historic doubts." Had not Poe himself chosen this man? Were not the poet's most ecstatic friends all silent? Did not memoir after memoir reproduce, without one doubtful line or softened feature, the original portrait of the Reverend Editor and Executor, till all the world has seen and knows it at first sight? Such indeed were my impressions when I first became interested in the subject. Yet, knowing that Poe's miserable story rested wholly upon Griswold's Memoir—that all since him have followed Griswold with the exactness of a Hebrew copyist, trembling at the prophet's curse upon all who should add to or take away one tittle of the text—it did appear to me to be an important and an interesting point, to learn what explanation, if any, Griswold himself had given of the reasons which had determined him to fulfil his painful task. How had he conquered that unwillingness, which the sternest moralist among us might have felt in such a case?—how had he escaped that tender casuistry that might have haunted the best and wisest, to turn them from their purpose? You and I, Sir, have far too much honesty—far too great a reverence for the truth, to flatter the living or the dead; but let us imagine ourselves in Griswold's place, and let us try to conceive what temptations might have beset us to gloss or to suppress. We might have thought of some persons living, who still perhaps remembered him with sorrow, or with an unreasoning affection—some who, knowing him better, or being more closely allied to him than we were, could think of his failings with more compassion than the world could feel—some, perhaps, to whom the truest story we could tell, would for his sake even cause more pain than all the wrongs he had done them. We might, with a diffidence at other times foreign to our nature, have mistrusted our own judgment, or suspected ourselves of some secret bias—or have nourished an illogical and superstitious notion that it is possible to do a wrong towards the dead, who cannot answer from their graves. We might have fancied that some stranger was better qualified for this task than we, who had so lately heard his voice or held his hand in ours. We might have thought that time would bring a better judgment, and weakly taken the middle course of silence.

God forbid that I should be in haste to say that Mr. Griswold has done wilful injustice to the memory of Poe; but this matter is too important to humanity to be settled without question. That a man may "love beauty only," and become a glorious devil, large in heart and brain; that he may attain the highest culture, yet be in daily life the vilest—is a fact of which, if true, few men, I hope, would desire to multiply the proofs. Now it is right that English readers should know, what even American readers appear to have forgotten, that when Mr. Griswold's Memoir was first published, its assertions were denied by many who had known Poe—that no person corroborated the worst parts of his story—that some went so far as to impugn his motives; and that others, who had known, and had closer relations with the poet, gave accounts differing materially from Griswold's.

Mr. George R. Graham, in what the Reverend Biographer calls "a sophomorical and trashy, but widely circulated letter," denounced the Memoir as "the fancy sketch of a jaundiced vision," and "an immortal infamy;" and Mr. John Neal, a literary name well known on both sides of the Atlantic, asserted that there was a long, intense, and implacable enmity between Poe and Griswold, which disqualified him for the office of his biographer.

The particulars of that controversy will be found in the third volume of the collected edition of Poe's works, published in New York in 1850. They are inserted by Mr. Griswold himself, in his own justification, and I can therefore be guilty of no injustice in quoting and commenting upon them. Mr. Griswold admits that when the news of Poe's death first reached him, he announced the fact in the *Tribune* Newspaper in the following terms:— "Edgar Allan Poe is dead. This announcement will startle many, *but few will be grieved by it.*"

And again: "Passion in him comprehended many of the worst emotions that militate against human happiness. You could not contradict him but you raised quick choler; you could not speak of wealth, but his cheek paled with gnawing envy. [. . .] Irascible, envious, bad enough, but not the worst, for these salient angles were varnished over with a cold repellent cynicism. His passions vented themselves in sneers," &c.

He had not then been informed of his appointment to the duty of liter-ary executor; but, "I did not," he says, "suppose I was debarred from *the expression of any feelings or opinions* in the case, by the acceptance of this office."

I think it must be evident to you and all other unbiassed persons, that the tone of these extracts did not indicate any intention to conceal or palliate the errors of the deceased. We trace here no unwillingness to enter on his task of accuser—no regret that the stern duty should have fallen to him. Mr. Griswold admits that he had been long at enmity with Poe; but he shows that a reconciliation had taken place, and points triumphantly to the poet's wish that he should edit his Remains. But was every spark of that enmity extinguished? Had the biographer examined his own heart, or ever doubted of himself? That there was a time during their quarrel when Poe would have been unwilling to hand himself over to the critical mercies of his future editor, is shewn by the published Letters. The enemies of Poe, unhappily, appear to have been not few. Any one who will turn to his ad-mirable criticism upon Mr. Dickens's "Barnaby Rudge,"—a paper which drew from Mr. Dickens himself a letter of acknowledgment to the writer—will see that Poe was no common critic. But he had not always such a theme as Barnaby Rudge, and he had little tenderness for the sins of authorship. The more refined productions of his genius were sometimes overwhelmed for awhile, by the deluge of American bookmaking, and he had a natural impatience of literary quackery. He attacked it openly, and with a savage pleasure which made him many foes. Now, the Reverend Rufus Griswold—not without a reverend counterpart on this side of the Atlantic—appears to be an active manufacturer of editions of the poets, and such books, whose style of comment on the poets may be judged from the fine sentences above quoted. I can imagine Poe reading this posthumous sketch of himself from the pen of his Literary Executor:—

"He walked the streets in madness or melancholy, with lips moving in indistinct curses, or with eyes upturned in passionate prayer—never for himself, for he felt, or professed to feel, that he was already damned; but for their happiness, who at the moment were the objects of his idolatry—or with his glances introverted to a heart gnawed with anguish, and with a face shrouded in gloom he would brave the wildest storms, and all night, with drenched garments, and arms beating the winds and rains, would speak as 'if to spirits,' " &c.

I can, I say, imagine Poe reading this, and being stirred with other feelings than those of anger. Mr. Griswold is, I presume, a prosperous man. He tells us that he undertook the task of editing Poe with reluctance, being then engaged in a work, in which "many thousand dollars were invested." It is possible that Poe, in a bitter mood, may have looked upon his gains with "a cheek paled with gnawing envy." It is possible that, wounded, as he said, by a report that Griswold had attacked him, he may have said some disagreeable things of the tawdry sentences of his reverend friend. We know only that he commented upon some work of Mr. Griswold in a public lecture, and that the result was open enmity between them. Shortly afterwards, a work of Mr. Griswold's called the "Prose Writers of America" being in the press, Poe wrote to him, saying: "With your present feelings you can hardly do me justice in any criticism, and I shall be glad if you will simply say after my name, 'Born 1811; published Tales of the Grotesque and Arabesque in 1839; has resided latterly in New York.'" A reconciliation ensued, and Poe asked forgiveness for some absurd jokes at his expense in the Lecture: they were based, he said, upon the malignant slander of a mischief-maker by profession—upon a false imputation of a "beastly article." So the quarrel was patched up; but his reverend friend would not allow him any judgment as a critic. Two years after the reconciliation, he declares that Poe's "chief skill lies in the dissection of sentences." Four years after their reconciliation, it is evident that he was in the habit of still harping privately upon the "Lecture." "They lied," says Poe, in a letter to him, "(*if you told ——— what he says you told him*) upon the subject of my *forgotten lecture*." Now I think there was in all this sufficient to give a man who has ever reflected upon the subtlety of human motives, some misgivings as to his qualification for the task which Mr. Griswold did not hesitate to accept. You and I, whose calling has no particular sanctity about it, might have asked ourselves what the world would say, when they found that we had no good thing to tell about our hero. We should not, perhaps, have liked to have begun our task with an anecdote of his childhood, to "explain that morbid self-esteem which characterized the author in after-life." When we told of his gambling and intemperance at the university, we might not have liked to round off our sentence with an allusion to "other vices," which we omitted to name. We might have been unwilling to quote an anonymous and exaggerated paragraph accusing him of "a sin that wanted name or precedent," and of which there should not "remain any register but that of Hell." When Poe won the prize for an essay, we might have felt that it might be considered ungenerous to ascribe the fact to his penmanship rather than literary skill; or, in quoting a letter from the poet telling of his own illness, and the illness of his wife—of which, it appears, that she died a few weeks afterwards—we might have shrunk from saying, that "this was written for effect."

I have little more to say upon this subject. My purpose was merely to call attention to what any one may read for himself, and form his own judgment upon. I felt it just and right to remind English readers, that there are portraits of Poe less repulsive than that one which is best known. That Poe's errors were many cannot be doubted; they find some excuse in the story of his early training. That in his poverty and vagabondage, in early life, he contracted a fatal habit of intemperance, is admitted by all; but there are traces even in the Memoir of his literary executor of many a struggle to subdue temptation, of long periods when he did his duty bravely; glimpses of him in an orderly and happy home—or watching tenderly and long by the side of a sick wife. His fine culture and acquirements are in themselves the best evidences of many days well spent. There were surely some who saw him to the last with other eyes. The story of the untiring devotedness of her who knew him best—the mother of his wife—is touchingly related by Mr. N. P. Willis in his notice of Poe's death, which should always be printed with Mr. Griswold's Memoir. "I have this morning," she wrote, "heard of the death of my darling Eddie. [. . .] Ask Mr. —— to come, as I must deliver to him a message from my poor Eddie. I need not ask you to notice his death, and to speak well of him—I know you will; but say what an affectionate son he was to me, his poor desolate mother."

I cannot think of the history of this unhappy lady, without remembering how many such have been, who, by testimony like this, have, in truth, borne witness to little, save their own patient long suffering and inexhaustible forgiveness. Yet, let us not say that this is all; but rather think that, in their deeper sympathy and closer knowledge, some things are visible to them, which are not the less there, because many see them not.

William Moy Thomas, "Edgar Allan Poe: A Letter to the Editor of *The Train*," *Train: A First-Class Magazine*, April 1857: 193–198.

From "Edgar Allan Poe"
in *Edinburgh Review* (1858)

BRYAN W. PROCTOR

> This article, from Bryan W. Proctor, another influential British writer and
> critic, might have come from Griswold's pen, given its emphatic vilification of
> Poe. Generally hostile, it links him to William Godwin and Charles Brockden
> Brown. Its appearance in an influential British periodical no doubt helped to
> maintain a negative image of Poe among British readers, although somewhat
> later defenders such as John Henry Ingram, Poe's first English biographer,
> sprang up and were found sensible by many.

EDGAR ALLAN POE was incontestably one of the most worthless persons of
whom we have any record in the world of letters. Many authors have been
as idle; many as improvident; some as drunken and dissipated; and a few,
perhaps, as treacherous and ungrateful; but *he* seems to have succeeded in
attracting and combining, in his own person, all the floating vices which
genius had hitherto shown itself capable of grasping in its widest and most
eccentric orbit. As the faults of this writer present themselves more upon
a level with the ordinary gaze than the loftier qualities which his friends
ascribe to him, we shall venture to introduce him to the reader, in the first
instance, by his humbler every day actions; satisfied that it is not of much
moment how a picture has been commenced, if the proportions prove correct at last. Fuseli, as we know, preferred beginning his sketch of the human figure at the lowest point, and worked from the foot upwards. In like
manner, we shall begin with the defects,—or, to give them their true title,
with the substantial vices of Edgar Poe,—proposing to ourselves to ascend
ultimately to his virtues, should we discover any; at all events, to those rare
qualities and endowments, the demonstration of which has entitled him to
no mean place on the rolls of the Temple of Fame.

He was, as we have said, a blackguard of undeniable mark. Yet his
chances of success at the outset of life were great and manifold. Nature was

bountiful to him; bestowing upon him a pleasing person and excellent talents. Fortune favoured him; education and society expanded and polished his intellect, and improved his manner into an insinuating and almost irresistible address. Upon these foundations he took his stand; became early very popular amongst his associates; and might have erected a laudable reputation, had he possessed ordinary prudence. But he defied his good Genius. There was a perpetual strife between him and virtue, in which virtue was very triumphant. His moral stamen was weak, and demanded resolute treatment; but instead of seeking a bracing and healthy atmosphere, he preferred the impurer airs, and gave way readily to those low and vulgar appetites, which infallibly relax and press down the victim to the lowest state of social abasement.

He arrived at the end of his descent, after many alarms, many warnings, that might have deterred him, and induced him to try another course. For the most instructive teaching of Edgar Poe was in the roughest school of life. He had, indeed, for a brief period the advantage of some grave counsel at Charlottesville. But he left that place early, when his intellect was merely in its adolescent state. It was in his subsequent transit through poverty and degradation, when he had to battle not only with the world, but also with those compunctious visitors that force their way into the most obstinate bosom, that he received his most valuable lessons. The natural soil, however, was barred of good. The seed was sown upon a rock; or, if the reader prefer it, upon one of those shifting unprofitable sands which no culture will bring into fertility.

It seems impossible to have kept him upright. His tendency was decidedly downwards. He was, time after time, cautioned, forgiven, punished. All tender expostulation, all severe measures, were alike unavailable. The usual prizes of life,—reputation, competency, friendship, love,—presented themselves in turn; but they were all in turn neglected or forfeited,— repeatedly, in fact, abandoned, under the detestable passion for drink. He outraged his benefactor, he deceived his friends, he sacrificed his love,—he became a beggar,—a vagabond,—the slanderer of a woman,—the delirious drunken pauper of a common hospital,—hated by some—despised by others—and avoided by all respectable men. The weakness of human natures has, we imagine, its limit; but the biography of Poe has satisfied us that the lowest abyss of moral imbecility and disrepute was never attained until he came, and stood forth a warning to the times to come.

We say all this very unwillingly; for we admire sincerely many things that Mr. Poe has produced. We are willing to believe that there may have been, as Mrs. Osgood has stated, an amiable side to his character, and that his mother-in-law had cause to lament his loss. We learn, moreover, from Mr. Willis, that at one time, in the latter portion of his life, "he was invariably punctual and industrious." The testimony of that gentleman and Mr. Lowell (both men of eminence in literature) tempted us at first to suspend our opinion of the author; but the weight of evidence on the darker side proved overwhelming, and left us no choice but to admit the fact upon record, and to stigmatise with our most decided reprobation those misdeeds that seem to have constituted almost the only history of his short career.

And, here, let it not be surmised that Poe was an "enemy only to himself." His was, as Mr. Griswold states, a "shrewd and naturally unamiable character." We refuse our assent to the argument of one of his advocates, that "his whole nature was reversed by a single glass of wine;" and that "his insulting arrogance and bad heartedness" had no deeper origin than a modicum of that agreeable liquid. We lean rather to the ancient proverb, which asserts that Truth is made manifest upon convivial occasions. Moreover, his ingratitude and insults towards Mr. Allan, Mr. White, Mr. Burton, and his affianced wife,—his harsh and dishonest criticisms upon Mr. Osborn and Mr. Jones (each, in fact, contradicted by himself) and others, were not momentary flashes of ill humour; while his long and elaborate deprecation of Mr. Longfellow (one part of it meriting particular condemnation), and finally his deliberate threats of publicly slandering a lady merely because she claimed the return of a loan of money, cannot by possibility be referred to so feeble and temporary an impetus as "a single glass of wine." They sprang undoubtedly from what Mr. Griswold calls "his naturally unamiable character."

To this and to his moral weakness must be ascribed the melancholy and poverty which we are told overshadowed his life. That he was very often unhappy we have no doubt; but that condition of mind was obviously referable to his excesses. It was the collapse after the high-strained revel. That he was frequently poor enough is also very probable; and yet, what is that but saying that he shared the ordinary fortunes of authors, many of whom too readily barter for the pleasures of writing and popularity, or the remote chances of future fame, those material comforts which are found to spring generally from regular mechanical industry, or other unexciting employments of common life. Some of these men, however, endure poverty very bravely; some with little help and no sympathy; some for years,—some for all their humble and laborious days. They begin life with bright hopes and resolute hearts. They see above them Parnassus or Helicon, quite accessible. There is El Dorado also, in the misty distance. Yet they work on, from hour to hour, from week to week, without much repining. And, at the end of many years, perhaps, they discover that their only reward has been in the shape of a vulgar payment,—a loaf of bread, a pot of beer, and an empty garret. Finally, they die without an historian to chronicle their labours, or even to notice their having once existed. Their very comrades content themselves with looking out for better fare to-morrow, and will pass on to another friend.

We turn now, without more ado, to the biography and Works before us. In the front of the first volume is the portrait of the author. It deserves note. His friends speak of his pale and beautiful face. Upon ourselves the impression made is very different. It seems rather to confirm the opinion derived from his history and writings. It seems to us pinched, painful, jealous, irritable, and weak; and is altogether wanting in that frank, manly, generous character which takes the fancy of the beholder at the first glance.

Edgar Allan Poe, we are told, was the son of an American father and an English mother. On the death of his respectable parents, which event occurred when he was about six years of age, he was thrown penniless upon the world. Providence decreed that he should be adopted by a rich and benevolent merchant, Mr. John Allan. This gentleman took him to England; placed him at a school there for four or five years; and, on his return to the United States, entered him at the University of Charlottesville. Here the youth broke loose from the trammels of authority, and distinguished himself not only by his talents, but by the wildest excesses. It is argued, in his excuse, that the manners of the University at this time were extremely dissolute. Poe, however, young as he was, exceeded all his fellows. Not only, it is said, was he "the wildest and most reckless student of his class;" but he mastered the most difficult problems with ease, and kept "all the while in the first rank for scholarship." He would, in fact, have "graduated in the highest honours, had not his gambling, intemperance, and other vices induced his expulsion from the University." Thus early did the demon disclose itself which was to have such an overwhelming influence on his future life.

His allowance of money at Charlottesville had been liberal; yet he quitted that place very much in debt, and when Mr. Allan refused to pay some of his losses at gaming, he wrote him an abusive letter and left his house.

For about a year he seems to have wandered through Europe; but at the end of that time he contrives to reach St. Petersburgh, where the American minister (Mr. Middleton) is summoned one day to save him from the penalties of a drunken debauch. Through this gentleman's kindness Poe is enabled to return to America. Mr. Allan (although he is now not so cordial as formerly) declares himself still willing to serve the culprit, and, at his request, exerts his interest and obtains a scholarship in the military academy. Here Poe works assiduously for some months, but his habits of dissipation are renewed, and in "ten months from his matriculation he is cashiered."

Upon this second expulsion he goes once more to the house of Mr. Allan, at Richmond, who is even then disposed to treat him as a son, but Poe, by some very offensive act, forces his old patron to close his doors against him. At this time it appears that Mr. Allan had married, for his second wife, a Miss Paterson, who was considerably younger than himself. Poe's own account of this offence is that *he only ridiculed this marriage of his benefactor*, and had a quarrel with his wife. But a much darker story is told on the other side, and one that is said to be damnatory to Poe's character. That the offence was very grave is undoubted, inasmuch as Mr. Allan, hitherto so repeatedly forgiving, thought it necessary to banish the "adopted son" from his house, and refused to see him again. On the gentleman's death in 1834, it was found that of his large property, "not a mill" was bequeathed to Poe.

Our future author now endeavours to earn his bread by printing a volume of poems, and by contributing to the journals. The result is a failure; and his next step is to enlist as a private soldier, and then—to desert. His friends surmise that he probably did not like the "monotony of a soldier's life." It does not appear that he encountered the punishment which he deserved for his breach of military discipline; but that he had to fare hardly is clearly the case. For he subsequently contests for, and (almost as a matter of course) obtains, a certain prize offered by the proprietor of "The Baltimore Saturday Visitor;" and upon the occasion comes forward in a state of the most squalid poverty. His destitute condition, indeed, operates so effectually on some compassionate people, especially on a Mr. Kennedy, that he is sent to a clothing store, and afterwards to a bath, in order to enable him to recover, outwardly at least, the appearance of a gentleman.

By the help of his new friends he obtains the editorship of a "Richmond Magazine," but after a short time is found "in a condition of brutish drunkenness," which "results in his dismissal." His employer at this time was a Mr. White, a gentleman evidently kind and long-enduring, but who at the same time speaks very plainly to "Edgar;" consenting to take him back as an assistant, only on condition that he will "promise to separate from the bottle." This promise is of course speedily made,—and as speedily broken.

We are not able to ascertain the precise date at which he borrowed a poem from Professor Longfellow, imitated it, and afterwards *denounced the author as a plagiarist from himself, the Simulator.* The mimic poem is called "The Haunted House," and is one of Poe's best pieces of verse. The original is "The Beleaguered City," of Mr. Longfellow. There are, necessarily, statement and counterstatement in this case; but while we have the most entire reliance on Mr. Longfellow's word, we confess that we place none whatever on the assertion of Edgar Poe.

Poe's next appearance is as a writer in a magazine established by Mr. Burton, in Philadelphia. He remains with this gentleman till June 1840, more than a year. This long lapse into sobriety is followed by the usual fit of intemperance. "On one occasion returning after the regular day of publication, he [Mr. Burton] found the number unfinished, and Poe incapable of duty." Notwithstanding this the wretched culprit is forgiven, and accepted again as a coadjutor in the magazine, his employer however addressing to him some words of counsel, from which may be discerned a fresh and not very favourable feature in Poe's character.

"You must get rid," Mr. Burton advises, "of *your avowed ill-feelings toward your brother authors.* You say the people love havoc. I think they love justice. I think you yourself would not have written the article on Dawes, in a more healthy state of mind. I am not trammelled by any vulgar consideration of expediency. I would rather lose money than by such undue severity wound the feelings of a kind-hearted and honourable man. I regret your word-catching spirit."

This letter, at once so sensible and so honourable to its writer, was productive of no good result. It would seem rather to have generated, or to speak more correctly, to have encouraged the growth of some of those seeds of malignity and ingratitude which had been slumbering in the breast of his correspondent; for,

In two or three months afterwards Burton went out of town to fulfil a professional engagement, leaving material and directions for completing the next number of the magazine in four days. He was absent nearly a fortnight, and on his return he found that his printer in the meanwhile had not received a line of copy; but that Poe had prepared the prospectus of *a new monthly, and obtained transcripts of his subscription and account books, to be used in a scheme for supplanting him!*

From the house of Mr. Burton our author migrates to that of Mr. Graham, where he is installed as editor of "Graham's Magazine." He works there for a short time, and is again dismissed. He then tries to establish a journal of his own, called "The Stylus," but fails, and eventually, in 1844, removes to New York. Here he distinguishes himself by borrowing fifty dollars from a "celebrated literary lady." On failing to repay them on the day promised, and being asked for an acknowledgment of the debt, to be shown to the lady's husband, he at once denies all knowledge of the transaction, and threatens to exhibit, *to* the husband, a correspondence which, as he states, "*would make the woman infamous if she said any more on the subject.*" Such correspondence had never existed!

After being made acquainted with this act, which could only have emanated from a creature in the very lowest condition of depravity, the reader will naturally dismiss from his breast all sympathy with the good or bad fortune of Mr. Edgar Poe.

The few remaining incidents of his life afford little or no variety or relief from the foregoing history. They are all tinged by the same gloom. His wife, whom he had married when residing at Richmond, dies. During her last illness, her mother is met going about from place to place, in the bitter weather, half-starved and thinly clad, with a poem or some other literary article, which she was striving to sell; or otherwise she was begging for him and his poor partner, both being in want of the commonest necessaries of life.

Nevertheless, even after this prostration, Poe seems to have arisen for a short period, and to have signalized himself by some more literary activity. He wrote an essay, entitled "Eureka," delivered lectures, and—his wife being then dead—engaged himself to marry "one of the most brilliant women of New England." This engagement, however, is one that he means to break. "Mark me," he says, "I shall not marry her." In furtherance of this gentlemanlike decision, he deliberately gets drunk, and on the evening before the appointed bridal is found "reeling through the streets, and in his drunkenness commits, at her house, such outrages, as render it necessary to summon the police." He went from New York with a *"determination thus to induce the ending of the engagement," and—succeeded.*

His last journey is now to be taken. He travels as far as Baltimore, but never returns. He is seen a short time afterwards in that city, in such a state as induced by long-continued intoxication, and after "a night of insanity and exposure," he is carried to a hospital, and there, on the evening of Sunday, the 7th day of October, 1849, he dies, at the age of thirty-eight years!

One of his biographers concludes with the words, "It is a melancholy history." We trust that it will prove a profitable one; for unless we are mistaken, it involves a moral that may be studied with advantage by future authors.

We have now to offer an opinion on the peculiar features and literary value of Poe's productions in prose and verse. In reference to the former, we are disposed to think that we can trace his inspiration in a great measure to the writings of Godwin and Charles Brockden Browne. There is in each the same love of the morbid and improbable; the same frequent straining of the interest; the same tracing, step by step, logically as it were and elaborately, through all its complicated relations, a terrible mystery to its source. These authors pursue events through all their possible involutions, but seldom deal with character. There is indeed a singular want of the dramatic faculty in all these eminent persons. Godwin, it is true, in his "Fleetwood" and "Mandeville," and Browne in "Ormond," and "Arthur Mervyn," made an effort to draw forth some human peculiarities; but their personages are a little more, after all, than stately abstractions of impersonations of certain moods or guesses of their own minds, the results of solitary thinking. Whatever latent qualities they possess, each of their figures reminds one somewhat of the cocoon,—a thing drawn from the entrails of its parent, with no apparent vitality about it.

Notwithstanding the appearance of originality, due perhaps more to the eccentricity of his life and the deformity of his moral character than to the vigour or freshness of his intellect, it is easy to trace throughout Edgar Poe's writings impressions derived from authors he had chanced to read or contrivances which had dwelt in his memory. So little indeed can he be considered a truly original writer, that he perpetually reminds us of something we have read before. Sometimes he imitates the matter-of-fact precision that gives such reality to the fiction of Defoe; sometimes he pursues the fantastical or horrible night mares of Hoffmann; sometimes a thought visits him from the highly wrought philosophy of Novalis, or the huge and irregular genius of Jean Paul; sometimes he loses himself, like the Louis Lambert of Balzac, in the labyrinth of transcendental speculation. But though he resembles these writers in his love of the marvelous, and in his ingenious treatment of it, he is inferior to the least of them in depth. His reading was doubtless curious rather than accurate, desultory rather than wide; and his genius grew rank in a half-cultivated soil.[1]

Considered apart from his poetry, Poe's fictions seem to resolve themselves for the most part into two classes:—one like those to which we have already adverted, where a series of facts woven mysteriously out of some unknown premises are brought apparently to a logical result; the other, where the author deals strictly with a single event; where there is little or no preliminary matter, but the reader is at once hurried into a species of catastrophe, or conclusion of the most exciting character. These last-mentioned fictions are necessarily short, because the sympathy of the reader could not possibly remain at the high point of tension to which he is raised by the torture of the scene. In a few instances we encounter merely a gloomy scene, (sometimes very highly wrought and picturesque,) or a human being fashioned out of the most ghastly materials,—a tale, in short, without any result, properly speaking. We look in at the death-bed of a man; we see him writhe—utter a few words referable to some imperfectly disclosed event; or he professes to expound, under mesmeric influence, while he is dying, or *when he is dead*, certain things which the human mind in its wakeful healthy state is quite incapable of comprehending.

It should not be forgotten that in some of these sketches, which are the most mysterious in their treatment, the author has contrived to absolve himself from the necessity of verifying, in his usual manner, the rationale of his design. He ascends into the cloudiest regions of metaphysics, of speculation,—of conjecture,—of dreams! God, as we learn, amongst other things, from "Mesmeric revelation," is "unparticled matter." From M. Valdemar we collect that a man, thrown into a mesmeric state just before death, will not only speak after death, but will remain unaltered for some months afterwards, and only betray the frail and crumbling evidence of his mortality, when a few "mesmeric passes" have succeeded in restoring him to his real decayed condition. He then falls to pieces and dissolves, "a mass of loathsome putrescence."—That such sketches were considered by the author as unimportant, and not as a grand or final effort to ensure himself a name in the literature of his country, we can really believe. Nevertheless there is something very morbid in all these fancies and prolusions of the intellect.

There can be no question but that Edgar Poe possessed much subtlety of thought; an acute reasoning faculty; imagination of a gloomy character, and a remarkable power of analysis. This last quality, which from its frequent use almost verges upon disease, pervaded nearly all his stories, and is in effect his main characteristic. Other persons have drawn as unreservedly from the depths of horror. But few others, with the exception of Browne and Godwin, have devoted themselves to that curious persevering analysis of worldly mysteries by which Poe has earned so large a portion of his reputation. The impression made upon the mind of the reader by the apparently wonderful solutions of the most difficult problems will not easily be forgotten. Yet, on examining the marvel more attentively, he will divest himself of a good deal of his admiration, by reflecting (as Dr. Griswold justly observes) that the ingenuity is displayed "in unraveling a web which has been woven for the express purpose of unravelling." Every man, in fact, is able readily to explain the riddle which he himself has fabricated, however laborious the process of manufacturing it may have been.

How far the thrilling interest which Poe infused into his stories may be traced to the acute sensations which he himself endured in a state of excitement or despondency, we have no means of knowing. But we think that no writer would have resorted so incessantly to the violent measures and extreme distresses which constitute the subject of his narratives, in a good sound condition of health. His imagination appears to have been absolutely embarrassed by a profusion of visionary alarms and horrors. We rise up from his pages as from the spectacle of some frightful disaster,—relieved because the worst is over, happy that we are left at last to partake of less stirring pleasures, and to return to the calmer sensations of ordinary life.

Edgar Poe had no humour, properly so called. His laugh was feeble, or it was a laugh of ill-temper, exhibiting little beyond the turbulences of his own mind. He was carping and sarcastic, and threw out occasionally a shower of sharp words upon the demerits of his contemporaries; but of that genial humour which shines through a character, fixes it in a class, and shows by what natural gradations it moves, and by what aspects and impulses it claims to resemble the large brotherhood of man, he possessed nothing.

The ordinary incidents of life—the domestic affections, the passions, the intermixture of good and evil, of strength and weakness, in the great human family who pass by our doors every day, and who sit beside us, love us, serve us, maltreat us (as the varying mood prompts), were unknown to him, or disregarded. Yet these things constitute the staple—the best and most essential parts of the modern novel. They intrude themselves, in fact, into our acquaintance, so frequently, so intimately, that we cannot ignore their existence. In the present case, we are at a loss to understand how a person so acute as our author could have neglected to place upon record what must have so incessantly forced itself upon his observation; nay, what must have met and jostled him so frequently in his rough journey through life.

Of the tales in which the analytical power of the author is more obviously exerted, the least unpleasant are "The Purloined Letter," and "The Golden Bug." "The Murders in the Rue Morgue," and "The Mystery of Marie Roget," are, like too many of his other fictions, saturated with blood. In order that the reader may satisfy his curiosity as to the construction of these plots, the stories themselves must be read. It is quite impossible, in the space at present at our command, to transcribe either of these stories, and without such complete transcription the mysterious minute details, in which and in the tracing and solution of which the merit resides, cannot be explained. . . .

The poetical works of the author need not detain us long. With one remarkable exception, his verses do not differ materially from others of the same time. They are neither very good nor very bad. They do not exhibit much depth or graphic power, and but little tenderness—nor do they, in fact, possess any of those distinguishing qualities which lift a man up beyond his contemporaries. The blank verse is not good; but some of the smaller pieces have a smoothness and liquid flow that are pleasant enough. One short poem, said to have been written at the age of fourteen, and addressed "To Helen," is full of promise.

Of all Mr. Poe's poems, however, "The Raven" is by far the first. It is, like the larger part of the author's writings, of a gloomy cast; but its merit is great; and it ranks in that rare and remarkable class of productions which suffice *singly* to make a reputation. Whether or not it was manufactured in the deliberate way stated by the writer in his article on "The Philosophy of Composition," we do not know; but the passage in which he dissects with anatomical precision what might otherwise pass for the offspring of impulse and of genius, is curiously characteristic of his analytical disposition. The poem itself, however, deserves to be remembered by all lovers of verse. In the United States its popularity is universal, but we believe it still to be far less known in this country than it ought to be. . . .

We do not propose to enter into the accuracy of the numerous investigations which Mr. Poe appears to have instituted into the publications of his brother and sister authors. To say the truth, we do not estimate his powers as a critic very highly. His essays on Criticism were, we imagine, written on the spur of the moment, without much consideration, and were more than sufficiently imbued with those prejudices with which he was so apt, we are told, to view the works of contemporary writers. Some of his essays are very slight and brief; some flippant; some distinguishable for that remarkable power of analysis which he carried into all his productions. His review of "Barnaby Rudge," in the third volume of this collection, is an extraordinary instance of his subtle and discriminating research into the very elements of fiction. It is impossible to trace out with greater nicety the very germ of a plot, and the finest artifices of invention. But here the interest of Edgar Poe's criticisms stops: few of them enter into the question of the peculiar genius of the author reviewed, of the class to which he belongs, of the way in which education and events have moulded him, of his habits of every day life, or of those impulses or physical circumstances which have impelled his intellect to assume that particular shape in which it presents itself before the world. . . .

Without entering into some such considerations, the critic can scarcely place his author fairly on his pedestal. We feel, even in the case of Mr. Poe, that it would have been more desirable if a fuller biography had accompanied his works. Honest and able, as far as it goes, and glancing upon the more prominent events of his life, it leaves us without information on many matters from which much might have been gathered to form an accurate judgment. Perhaps we are, after all, copying the deformities only of the man, at a time when we are anxious to submit all that was good as well as bad to the reader's judgment. The roughnesses that were so conspicuous on the surface of Poe's character would naturally attract the notice of his biographers in the first instance. But, underneath, was there nothing to tell of?—no cheeriness in the boy—no casual acts of kindness—no adhesion to old friendships—no sympathy with the poor or the unhappy, that might have been brought forward as indicative of his better nature? Even he himself has done nothing to help us. His sketches and stories are singularly deficient in all reference to his own private life. It is strange that a man who did and suffered so much should have left nothing for the historian's hands! The petty acts are indeed before us, but perhaps "the greatest is behind." For no man is thoroughly evil. There must be slumbering virtues—good intentions undeveloped,—even good actions, claiming to have a place on the record. Generosity, sympathy, charity have often their abodes in lowly and unexpected places—in poor, thoughtless, humble bosoms—in the hearts of those who have deeply sinned.

The influence of his faults was limited and the penalty (such as it was) he only had to bear. But the pleasure arising from his writings has been shared by many thousand people. In speaking of himself personally, we have felt bound to express our opinions without any subterfuge. But we are not insensible that, whilst he grasped and pressed hardly on some individuals with one hand, with the other he scattered his gifts in abundance on the public. These gifts are by no means of a common order, and on balancing the account of the author with posterity, he ought to have credit for their full value.

Fortunately for Edgar Poe, his personal history will be less read, and will be more short-lived than his fictions, which will probably pass into many hands, unaccompanied by the narrative of his personal exploits. For one reader who carefully weighs the actions of an author's life, there are a hundred who plunge into the midst of his works without any previous injury. The sempstress revelling in "The Mysteries of Udolpho" neither knows nor cares anything about the comfortable, domestic Mrs. Radcliffe. And the young man, intent on cheering his leisure hour with the adventures of Mrs. Amelia Booth, or Mr. Abraham Adams, has never heard perhaps that Henry Fielding (the noblest member of the house of Denbigh) was as often reduced to shifts as one of his own heroes, and that he died poor, and in a foreign land.

Note

1. It is a curious example of his superficial acquaintance with the literature of other lands, that in recapitulating the titles of a mysterious library of books in the "House of Usher," he quotes among a list of cabalistic volumes Gresset's "Vertvert," evidently in complete ignorance of what he is talking about. Gresset's "Vertvert" is the antipodes of Poe's "Raven"; but the comic interest of the former poem, and the tragic interest of the latter, turns alike on the reiteration of bird-language: and it is not impossible that Poe may have had in his mind some vague impression or recollection of Gresset's celebrated parrot.

From Bryan W. Proctor, "Edgar Allan Poe," *Edinburgh Review*, April 1858: 419–442.

"Editorial Etchings" (1858)

[ANONYMOUS]

> Following are anecdotes about Poe's everyday life, recorded in a once popu-
> lar art publication several years after his death. As was customary in Poe's
> day, a direct connection between his life and writings is presumed.

A FRIEND TOLD US, the other day, of one of Edgar A. Poe's sarcasms, which is
worth repeating. Poe had been told that certain ladies in the literary world
had resolved to *expose* him, for some of his misdemeanors. He answered:
"they are very good at *exposures*!" Those who have frequented some literary soirees, will especially appreciate the significance of the sarcasm.

Poe was once dunned savagely for a grocer's bill long overdue. He immediately sat down, penned one of his most savage onslaughts upon one
of "the literati," and upon the *strength* of it borrowed the amount needed
to free him from the grocer. "There, sir!" said he, "grow, sir, you grocer
puppy, into a dog, sir, and may you then be dogged, sir, as you have dogged
Poe, sir. Now, go sir, and be —— to you." This, properly expressed,
would look very like a Poe-stanza. It goes to show that some of his conceptions may have originated in moments of high-feeling, instead of having all
been coolly "coined," with great labor, as he intimates they were.

"Editorial Etchings." *Cosmopolitan Art Journal* [New York City], December 1858: 51.

From "Nathaniel Hawthorne" (1860)

[Anonymous]

> During the nineteenth century Poe and Hawthorne were repeatedly com-
> pared as fiction writers. My brief comment here provides information about
> Poe's supposed literary principles, which in turn reflect on his philosophical
> outlook. (I quote only a short passage from the lengthy original.)

THE REVIEWER CATEGORIZES Hawthorne's fiction variously, commenting
that the "Imaginative and Fantastic" sketches bear "the greatest resemblance to Poe, because it is in these that he is least moral, though always
more so than that singular writer."

Quoted material from "Nathaniel Hawthorne," *Universal Review* June 1860: 747 (entire
article 742–771).

"Reminiscences of Edgar Poe" (1863)

MARY GOVE NICHOLS

> Mary Gove Nichols's reminiscences of a visit to Poe and his family at their home in then rural Fordham is revealing portraiture of Poe's domestic life. The effects of Virginia's and Poe's deaths on Mrs. Clemm provide other interesting biographical details. Since many other recollections of Poe center on his activities and ideas of an entirely literary type, Nichols's sensible memories should not be ignored.

SOME SIXTEEN YEARS AGO, I went on a little excursion with two others—one a reviewer, since dead, and the other a person who wrote laudatory notices of books, and borrowed money or favours from their flattered authors afterwards. He was called unscrupulous by some, but he probably considered his method a delicate way of conferring a favour upon an author or of doing him justice without the disagreeable conditions of bargain and sale. It is certain that he lived better and held his head higher than many who did more and better work. The reviewer petted him, relied upon him, and gave him money when he failed to get it elsewhere.

We made one excursion to Fordham to see Poe. We found him, and his wife, and his wife's mother—who was his aunt—living in a little cottage at the top of a hill. There was an acre or two of greensward, fenced in about the house, as smooth as velvet and as clean as the best kept carpet. There were some grand old cherry-trees in the yard, that threw a massive shade around them. The house had three rooms—a kitchen, a sitting-room, and a bed-chamber over the sitting-room. There was a piazza in front of the house that was a lovely place to sit in in summer, with the shade of cherry-trees before it. There was no cultivation, no flowers—nothing but the smooth greensward and the majestic trees. On the occasion of this my first visit to the poet, I was a good deal plagued—Poe had somehow caught a full-grown bob-o'-link. He had put him in a cage, which he had hung on a nail driven into the trunk of a cherry-tree. The poor bird was as unfit to live in a cage as his captor was to live in the world. He was as restless as his jailer, and sprang continually in a fierce, frightened way, from one side of the cage to the other. I pitied him, but Poe was bent on training him. There he stood, with his arms crossed before the tormented bird, his sublime trust in attaining the impossible apparent in his whole self. So handsome, so impassive in his wonderful, intellectual beauty, so proud and reserved, and yet so confidentially communicative, so entirely a gentleman on all occasions that I ever saw him—so tasteful, so good a talker was Poe, that he impressed himself and his wishes, even without words, upon those with whom he spoke. However, I remonstrated against the imprisonment of "Robert of the Lincoln Green."

"You are wrong," said he, quietly, "in wishing me to free the bird. He is a splendid songster, and as soon as he is tamed he will delight our home with his musical gifts. You should hear him ring out like a chime of joy bells his wonderful song."

Poe's voice was melody itself. He always spoke low, even in a violent discussion, compelling his hearers to listen if they would know his opinion, his facts, fancies, or philosophy, or his weird imaginings. These last usually flowed from his pen, seldom from his tongue.

On this occasion I was introduced to the young wife of the poet, and to the mother, then more than sixty years of age. She was a tall, dignified old lady, with a most ladylike manner, and her black dress, though old and much worn, looked really elegant on her. She wore a widow's cap of the genuine pattern, and it suited exquisitely with her snow-white hair. Her features were large, and corresponded with her stature, and it seemed strange how such a stalwart and queenly woman could be the mother of her almost petite daughter. Mrs. Poe looked very young; she had large black eyes, and a pearly whiteness of complexion, which was a perfect pallor. Her pale face, her brilliant eyes, and her raven hair gave her an unearthly look. One felt that she was almost a disrobed spirit, and when she coughed it was made certain that she was rapidly passing away.

The mother seemed hale and strong, and appeared to be a sort of universal Providence for her strange children.

The cottage had an air of taste and gentility that must have been lent to it by the presence of its inmates. So neat, so poor, so unfurnished, and yet so charming a dwelling I never saw. The floor of the kitchen was white as wheaten flour. A table, a chair, and a little stove that it contained, seemed to furnish it perfectly. The sitting-room floor was laid with check matting;

four chairs, a light stand, and a hanging bookshelf completed its furniture. There were pretty presentation copies of books on the little shelves, and the Brownings had posts of honour on the stand. With quiet exultation Poe drew from his side pocket a letter that he had recently received from Elizabeth Barrett Browning. He read it to us. It was very flattering. She told Poe that his "poem of the Raven had awakened a fit of horror in England." This was what he loved to do. To make the flesh creep, to make one shudder and freeze with horror, was more to his relish (I cannot say more to his mind or heart) than to touch the tenderest chords of sympathy or sadness.

On the book-shelf there lay a volume of Poe's poems. He took it down, wrote my name in it, and gave it to me. I think he did this from a feeling of sympathy, for I could not be of advantage to him, as my two companions could. I had sent him an article when he edited the Broadway Journal, which had pleased him. It was a sort of wonder article, and he published it without knowing its authorship, and he was pleased to find his anonymous contributor in me. He was at this time greatly depressed. Their extreme poverty, the sickness of his wife, and his own inability to write, sufficiently accounted for this. We spent half an hour in the house, when some more company came, which included ladies, and then we all went to walk.

We strolled away into the woods, and had a very cheerful time, till some one proposed a game at leaping. It must have been Poe, as he was expert in the exercise. Two or three gentlemen agreed to leap with him, and though one of them was tall, and had been a hunter in times past, Poe still distanced them all. But alas! his gaiters, long worn and carefully kept, were both burst in the grand leap that made him victor. I had pitied the poor bob-o'-link in his hard and hopeless imprisonment, but I pitied Poe more now. I was certain he had no other shoes, boots, or gaiters. Who amongst us could offer him money to buy a new pair? Surely not the writer of this, for the few shillings that I paid to go to Fordham must be economized somewhere and somehow, amongst my indispensable disbursements. I should have to wear fewer clean shirts, or eat a less number of oyster stews. In those days I never aspired to a broil. It is well that habit is a grand ameliorator, and that we come to like what we are obliged to get accustomed to. But if any one had money, who had the effrontery to offer it to the poet? When we reached the cottage, I think all felt that we must not go in, to see the shoeless unfortunate sitting or standing in our midst. I had an errand, however—I had left the volume of Poe's poems—and I entered the house to get it. The poor old mother looked at his feet, with a dismay that I shall never forget.

"Oh, Eddie!" said she, "how did you burst your gaiters?"

Poe seemed to have come into a semitorpid state as soon as he saw his mother.

"Do answer Muddie, now," said she, coaxingly.

"Muddie" was her pet name with her children.

I related the cause of the mishap, and she drew me into the kitchen.

"Will you speak to Mr.——," said she, "about Eddie's last poem?"

Mr.—— was the reviewer.

"If he will only take the poem, Eddie can have a pair of shoes. He has it—I carried it last week, and Eddie says it is his best. You will speak to him about it, won't you?"

We had already read the poem in conclave, and Heaven forgive us, we could not make head or tail to it. It might well have been in any of the lost languages, for any meaning we could extract from its melodious numbers. I remember saying that I believed it was only a hoax that Poe was passing off for poetry, to see how far his name would go in imposing upon people. But here was a situation. The reviewer had been actively instrumental in the demolition of the gaiters.

"Of course they will publish the poem," said I, "and I will ask C—— to be quick about it."

The poem was paid for at once, and published soon after. I presume it is regarded as genuine poetry in the collected poems of its author, but then it bought the poet a pair of gaiters, and twelve shillings over.

At my next visit, Poe grew very confidential with me.

"I write," said he, "from a mental necessity—to satisfy my taste and my love of art. Fame forms no motive power with me. What can I care for the judgment of a multitude, every individual of which I despise?"

"But, Mr. Poe," said I, "there are individuals whose judgment you respect."

"Certainly, and I would choose to have their esteem unmixed with the mean adulation of the mob."

"But the multitude may be honestly and legitimately pleased," said I.

"That may be possible," said Poe, musingly, "because they may have an honest and legitimate leader, and not a poor man who has been paid a hundred dollars to manufacture opinions for them and fame for an author."

"Do reviewers sell their literary conscience thus unconscionably?" said I.

"A literary critic must be loath to violate his taste, his sense of the fit and the beautiful. To sin against these, and praise an unworthy author, is to him an unpardonable sin. But if he were placed on the rack, or if one he loved better than his own life were writhing there, I can conceive of his forging a note against the Bank of Fame, in favour of some would-be poetess, who is able and willing to buy his poems and opinions."

He turned almost fiercely upon me, his fine eyes piercing me, "Would you blame a man for not allowing his sick wife to starve?" said he.

I changed the subject and he became quiet, and we walked along, noting the beauties of flowers and foliage, of hill and dale, till we reached the cottage.

At my next visit Poe said, as we walked along the brow of the hill, "I can't look out on this loveliness till I have made a confession to you. I said to you when you were last here, that I despised fame."

"I remember," said I.

"It is false," said he. "I love fame—I dote on it—I idolize it—I would drink to the very dregs the glorious intoxication. I would have incense ascend in my honour from every hill and hamlet, from every town and city on this earth. Fame! glory!—they are life-giving breath, and living blood. No man lives, unless he is famous! How bitterly I belied my nature, and my aspirations, when I said I did not desire fame, and that I despised it."

Suggestive that the utterance on both occasions might be true to the mood that suggested them. But he declared that there was no truth in his first assertion. I was not as severe with him as he was with himself.

The autumn came, and Mrs. Poe sank rapidly in consumption, and I saw her in her bed chamber. Everything here was so neat, so purely clean, so scant and poverty-stricken, that I saw the sufferer with such a heartache as the poor feel for the poor. There was no clothing on the bed, which was only straw, but a snow white spread and sheets. The weather was cold, and the sick lady had the dreadful chills that accompany the hectic fever of consumption. She lay on the straw bed, wrapped in her husband's great-coat, with a large tortoise-shell cat on her bosom. The wonderful cat seemed conscious of her great usefulness. The coat and the cat were the sufferer's only means of warmth, except as her husband held her hands, and her mother her feet.

Mrs. Clemm was passionately fond of her daughter, and her distress on account of her illness and poverty and misery, was dreadful to see.

As soon as I was made aware of these painful facts, I came to New York, and enlisted the sympathies and services of a lady, whose heart and hand were ever open to the poor and miserable. A featherbed and abundance of bed-clothing and other comforts were the first fruits of my labour of love. The lady headed a subscription, and carried them sixty dollars the next week. From the day this kind lady saw the suffering family of the poet, she watched over them as a mother watches over her babe. She saw them often and ministered to the comfort of the dying and the living.

"My poor child," said Mrs. Clemm, "my blessed and beloved, who has gone before me. Mrs. ——— was so good to her. She tendered her while she lived, as if she had been her dear sister, and when she was dead she dressed her for the grave in beautiful linen. If it had not been for her, my darling Virginia would have laid in her grave in cotton. I can never tell my gratitude that my darling was entombed in lovely linen."

It seemed to soothe the mother's sorrow in a wonderful way, that her daughter had been buried in fine linen. How this delicate raiment could add so much to her happiness, I was not able to see, but so it was.

The same generous lady gave the bereaved mother a home for some time after the death of the poet. I think she only left her house to go to her friends in the South.

Soon after Poe's death, I met the aged mother on Broadway. She seized me by both hands, regardless of the passers by.

"My Eddie is dead," she sobbed, hardly able to speak. "He is gone—gone, and left his poor Muddie all alone."

And then she thought of his fame, and she clung to me, speaking with pathetic and prayerful earnestness. "You will take care of his fame," said she; "you will not let them lie about him. Tell the truth of my Eddie. Oh, tell the truth—tell the world how great and good he was. They will defame him—I know they will. They are wicked and envious; but you will do my poor, dear Eddie justice." She pressed my hands convulsively. "Say that you will take my Eddie's part," said she, almost wildly.

"I can never do him injustice," said I; "I assure you I never will."

"I knew you never would," said she, seeming greatly comforted.

I have said nothing of Poe's genius. His works are before the world. Those who are able to judge of them will do so. There is no need to manufacture fame for the poet now. He cannot be pleased or benefited by it.

Poe has been called a bad man. He was his own enemy, it is true; but he was a gentleman and a scholar. His clear and vivid perception of the beautiful constituted his conscience, and unless bereft of his sense by some poison, it was hard to make him offend his taste.

People may be starved, so that they will eat coarse, disgusting, and unhealthy viands, and a poet has human liabilities. We may be sure if Poe sold his poems, to be printed as the productions of another, or if he eulogized what he despised, that the offence brought with it sufficient punishment. Poor Poe! If the scribblers who have snapped like curs at his remains, had seen him as his friends saw him, in his dire necessity and his great temptation, they would have been worse than they deem him to have written as they have concerning a man of whom they really knew next to nothing.

Requiescat in pace!

Mary Gove Nichols, "Reminiscences of Edgar Poe," *Sixpenny Magazine*, February 1863: 471–474.

From *American Art* (1864)

JOHN FRANKENSTEIN

> This bit of verse follows the viewpoint that Poe's morality and personality in-
> spired his writings, and that both were lurid. Since the author was not impar-
> tial, his attitude toward Poe is one more in a long line of hostile portrayals.

Come! Be by searching truth's tribunal tried!
Come forth! If you've got sober since you died,
You, drunken mad-dog **Edgar Allan Poe**—
Is it my fault that I must call you so?
Your works, like you, are borne of alcohol;
Horrid monstrosities, distortions all;
It needs no doctor's gallipot or jar,
Filled with that stuff, to keep them as they are;
Soaked with its strange and strong, insidious power,
Your tales the many eagerly devour;
The Barnum of the Western Museum, Franks,
Here, for apt illustration shall have thanks;
He fitted up a noted murderer's room,
Of victims, too, which they sent to the tomb,
Wax figures with authentic, gaping gashes,
The weapons that made all these hideous slashes;
An hundred dollars covered the expense—
Three thousand dollars was his recompense!
You, *Poe*, through all your nature most debased,
You pandered to this craving tiger-taste;
King Alcohol through you once ruled our realm
Of literature, you staggered at its helm;
By English critics, too, were recognized,
A fact which was by us most highly prized.
You, with an impudence sublimely brazen,

In Art your frantic fumes must largely blazon;
Here I've a crow to pick with you, my friend—
Your poor, poor raven that rhymes without an end?
No, mad dog, no! but do you recollect
How at my pictures once you picked and pecked?
They were done soberly, with anxious care,
No time, no labor on them did I spare,
All *that* nigh any fool could have seen there,
Nor was the labor lost, they were well painted;
Then *you*, with every fiber liquor-tainted—
You, **YOU**, who all your life could not walk straight,
With swaggering ignorance my work berate?
When in the gutter the last time you lay,
When death disgusted, almost turned away,
When you with rot-gut whisky stunk,
And thus into God's presence reeled, **Dead-Drunk**—
I tell you, mad dog, when I heard all this,
I helped outraged humanity, to hiss!
You need not say now nothing should be said,
That I am living and that you are dead—
You drank yourself to death; must I forego,
Be balked of justice and revenge? Not so;
In prose to prick me you chose your own time,
And I choose mine to pay you back in rhyme;
Avaunt! And *nevermore* to me come nigh—
I do believe you stink of whisky yet—good bye!

From John Frankenstein, *American Art: Its Awful Attitude. A Satire*. Cincinnati, 1864: 84–86.

"Autobiographic Notes. Edgar Allan Poe." (1867)

Elizabeth Oakes Smith

Elizabeth Oakes Smith, wife of the humorist Seba Smith, was well informed about the literary scene in her day. Her portraiture of Poe, championing him as someone much misunderstood, differs in many respects from those that try to make him a raving lunatic, a wholly immoral person, or some other creature beyond the pale of usual humanity, whose personal emotions and activities infiltrated his writings. Portraying him as more "spectral" than human, Smith's notes contain several inaccuracies but are provocative. For an account of Mrs. Smith's viewpoints on Poe, see Ljungquist and Nickels.

I GIVE THE Allan in this name because it is generally so written; but I think the middle one should be at once and forever dropped; since it is that of a man who had befriended the poet—protected and educated him, but who finally abandoned him to his fate, leaving him to battle with the world as best he could, he, totally unable to compete with the world, with no understandable weapons for the contest, born with vast, gloomy premonitions, shadowy intimations of grandeur, stupendous day-dreams, which had no visible relation to what was passing around him—weird, unearthly visions which shut out the real—gorgeous idealisms overmastering the actual; a *demonized* man, in the fullest sense; and when his guardian—this wealthy, conventional, every-day man—assumed the responsibility of taking such a boy in charge, he had no right to abandon him.

It may be said that the errors of Poe drove his friends from him, compelled them to abandon him; this is no excuse at all to a TRUE man. *The greater his faults the more need of the friend.* I do not believe one tithe of what is said about the moral obliquities of Edgar Poe; and, even were he as guilty as his worst traducers represent him, there was that pale, sorrowful face of his always pleading for palliation, always seeming to say, "I do not comprehend it all; I am beyond, above, or below it! I am *not of it!*"

More than all this, the very appearance of the man gave the lie to these slanders. He was, to the last degree, refined in look and manner. I knew him for years—met him at my own house and in society, and never once saw any of those reprehensible aspects of character which have been imputed to him. I never once saw him when he had even looked upon the wine-cup. With his delicate organization, I am sure that a very small quantity would affect him; but I am convinced he was not habitually *addicted* to any kind of intoxicating drink, and am well persuaded that a very little might excite nearly to madness a brain of such volume and delicacy of fiber.

Others have given currency to wild tales of orgies, in which they must have also partaken, or at least encouraged. I remember to have heard a Philadelphian poet, the author of Endymion, describe a scene of the kind. To him it was amusing—to me most painful. He remarked that, "the real contempt which Poe felt for his contemporaries came out at once under the influence of the wine-cup, and he ridiculed, satirized, imitated and abused them right and left without mercy." I did not think the presence of such a stimulant at all necessary for such a development; for the bearing of the man at all times, the curl of his lip, the cold sarcasm, the covert smile, each and all told of a man who measured himself with his fellows, only to feel his own superiority. And why should he not?

Yes, I repeat, why should he not? I must and will speak of this man, not as he manifested himself to the world, but by the measure of his intimations, by his own estimate of himself, which is a truer mode of judgment than the world knows. Yes, this man knew what was in himself, and this it was that sustained him through all the perplexities and disheartenments of poverty, and all the abuse heaped upon him by the cruelty and malice of his enemies; and it is this faith in himself which enabled him to command the respect even of those critical in judgment and austere in practice, and which sustained him to the last, and is now fast redeeming his memory.

Edgar Poe found persons of noble penetration, who could worthily estimate him. I find among my letters the following, from Sarah Helena Whitman, of Providence, R. I. I had written a critique upon Mr. Poe, published in the *United States Magazine*, to which she refers:

"It is said that all men have two natures—a higher and a lower—a divine and a demoniac sphere of life. It has been so painful for me to contemplate the lower sphere of *his* life, that I have habitually turned away from it to look at the other nobler or more interior nature. In this I believe, and would fain ignore the rest. . . . From any other point of view, I see that your estimate is a most kind and tolerant one. I like, especially, the passage commencing,

'We listen as to a dirge, but it is not of mortal sounding,' and that in which you speak of his manner toward women. I do not think with you, that his manner gave the impression of habitual insincerity. On the contrary, he seemed to me—in his private character—simple, direct and genuine, beyond all other persons that I have known. . . . I believe, too, that in the artistic utterance of poetic emotion he was profoundly, passionately genuine; genuine in the expression of his utter desolation of soul—his tender, remorseful regret for the departed; his love, his hate, his pride, his perversity, and his despair. He was, it is true, vindictive, revengeful, unscrupulous in the use of expedients to attain his ends; but never false and fair-seeming from an inherent perfidy and hollowness of heart. . . . I feel sure that your notice will be read with interest, and will help to remove from his memory some undeserved imputations."

It is now seventeen years since Edgar Poe laid aside the earthly garment, and entered within the veil, yet, so far from sinking to oblivion, we find that every year awakens a new interest in his genius. Left without a stone to mark his place of burial, his own mind has created an imperishable monument.

He was born in the city of Baltimore, in January, 1811, and died in the same place, October 7th, 1849.

His father was studying law in Baltimore, when he became fascinated with an English actress named Elizabeth Arnold, with whom he eloped, and afterward married. It has been asserted that this girl was the daughter of the traitor Arnold—I do not know upon what authority. She seems to have been pretty and vivacious, but nothing more. The husband abandoned the law for the stage, and the two played together perhaps a half-dozen years, without acquiring either fame or money, and then died, leaving three children, two of whom fell into total eclipse, for we hear only of Edgar, the second boy.

When death entered the little dim, dingy green-room of the theater, and dropped the tinsel curtain forever between this world and the young, reckless pair, who left three helpless, uncared-for little ones to the tender mercies of men, which are often only cruelty, a merchant of Richmond, Virginia, by the name of Allan, adopted little Edgar as his own child. He was a spirited, handsome boy, precocious in intellect, and of arrogant, self-willed temper. Here was, certainly, fine material upon which to work—the germs of the scholar or the hero. But nature is stronger than education. I do not believe the blood of father or mother were of the best quality to produce the most reliable results. The excitements and exhaustions of the profession are not favorable to the best maternity—the tawdry accessories of the stage are not the most desirable associations for the growing mind and heart of a young child, who has everything to learn.

Mr. Allan was childless and wealthy, and, it would seem, injudiciously indulgent to the boy, yielding quite too much to his arrogance, and far too lenient to his outbreaks of temper. But it must be borne in mind that the young Edgar was living in a society in which spirit was ranked as the test of manliness, where coercion was reserved, like the whip, for the slave only, and where the assertion that "he who ruleth himself is greater than he who taketh a city," is a musty, old-fogy view, unbecoming a gentleman.

At length Mr. Allan, tired of the caprices and outrages of the boy-genius, and having married a second time, and now become a father, turns him out of doors, without a cent in the world; and so this child of genius, reared in luxury, after having been born in the hot-bed of excitement, with his keen, precocious intellect and sensitive nerves, is a houseless beggar.

Mr. Allan died, as rich men can, peacefully in his bed; and men praise him as the "patron" of Edgar Poe. To my eyes he committed a grievous wrong. When he had once assumed the responsibility of this boy, it was his duty to carry it through, and to see how the world went with him. After he had denuded him by his indulgence, it was the height of cruelty for him to cast him, defenseless as he was, upon the hard bosses of the world.

It must be borne in mind that he was but a boy of sixteen, and if this youth had become such a monster, he had been ripened under the very eye of his guardian. Where was the fault?

At the time when he was associated in Richmond with the excellent and simple-hearted Dr. White, as editor of the *Southern Literary Messenger*, he was but nineteen. Thus, three years after having been turned adrift in the world by his guardian, he is of sound mind enough and respectable enough in appearance to be taken into the family of Mr. White as assistant editor.

Even then he had written much, not only in prose but verse also—had written great quantities of the latter before his guardian abandoned him.

One little gem of his was addressed, at this time, to Lizzie White, the daughter of his host—a fair-haired, blue-eyed girl, with a cast of mind not unlike that of Poe in some of its aspects—singularly quick, subtle, and impassioned.

This poem, by the way, was afterward presented to Fannie Osgood, and appears as a tribute to that lovely woman. Let not that surprise the reader, for I have known poets to compel their verses to do duty to scores of fine women!

This is the poem in question, as I saw it in the delicate chirography of Edgar Poe, with date, etc., in the hands of Lizzie White:

"To E. W.

> "Thou wouldst be loved? then let thy heart
>> From its present pathway part not!
> Being every thing which now thou art,
>> Be nothing which thou art not.
>
> "So with the world thy gentle ways,
>> Thy grace, thy more than beauty
> Shall be an endless theme of praise,
>> And love—a simple duty."

This does not sound like a young profligate of nineteen—a Catullus, a Moore, enrapturing the senses, nor an Iago, unimpassioned but malignant; on the contrary, it is as ideal in its purity as Byron's

> "She walks in beauty like the night
>> Of cloudless climes and starry skies,
> And all that's best of good and bright
>> Meets in her aspect and her eyes," etc.

Or Shelley's

> "The desire of the moth for the star,
>> Of the night for the morrow,
> The devotion to something afar
>> From the sphere of our sorrow."

It is easy to see lines of genius akin to the gloomy discontent of Byron, the unearthly melody of Shelley, and the gorgeous echoes from the Halls of Eblis in [Beckford], permeating the warp and woof of the mind of Edgar Poe.

Before Mr. Poe came to New York, he traveled much, both at home and abroad; he had been partially educated at West Point, but his mind was neither mathematical, military, nor subordinate to soldierly discipline, as might have been conceived, and for this cause his relation therewith was dissolved, though he always retained the air inseparable from military training. It was said he made his way to Russia, and got into some difficulty there; be that as it may, he could not have sunk himself very low, for his looks and manner bore not the shadow of a trace of any irregularity.

If he did make the mistakes imputed to him, I can only say that Edgar Poe was right royally organized, when he could rise so above every vestige of disorder, as the lion shakes the dew from his mane.

While in Richmond he married his own cousin, and she a child of fourteen. Here was another error. But let us draw the veil over it, for it produced for him in the person of his aunt, and now mother-in-law, Mrs. Clemm, one devoted, untiring, long-suffering friend, without whom his career would have been even sadder than it was.

It must have been in 1842 that Poe first came to reside permanently in New York. He was at once admitted into its literary circles, where his superior address and remarkable conversational powers at once attracted attention. Then there was more prestige attached to literature than at present exists. The field is now so over-filled, and the persons of marked genius so comparatively few, that the desire for companionship with literary persons is much less.

At that time, at the houses of Rev. Dr. Dewey, Miss Anna C. Lynch, Mr. James Lawson, and others of scarcely less celebrity, might be found some of the finest spirits of any age, whose brilliancy entitled them to all the homage they received. It was in these circles that I first met Edgar Poe. He had criticised myself and some others, who could well survive it, very severely, but not entirely ungenerously, and I harbored no malice against him. His wife was at this time much an invalid, and rarely went out, but he was fond of naming her, and dwelling upon her loveliness of character. His manners at these reunions were refined and pleasing, and his scope of conversation that of the gentleman and the scholar. Whatever may have been his previous career, there was nothing in his look or manner to indicate the debauchee.

The first time I spoke with him, I had been talking with Catherine Sedgwick, author of several works of much merit, and now arrived at that happy age when vanity or adulation are out of the question. I was not prepared to be pleased with Mr. Poe. That he had not very much praised *me* in his critique I did not much care; but I felt that he had done my husband injustice—he had neither appreciated his genius nor his character—and this had prejudiced me against him.

Gradually the conversation became animated, and Mr. Poe entered into it warmly; then I saw that a mind like his would not by any method of thought either understand or appreciate a mind that would produce the Major Downing letters. I saw that the "Raven" was really Mr. Poe—that he did not go out of one state of mind to conceive another in which he placed his "Lenore," "Raven," or other poems—but that he was *what he wrote*, his own idiosyncrasy, "that and nothing more." Then I laid aside my personal pique and accepted the poet.

"I am afraid my critique on your poems did not please you," he said, with his great eyes fixed upon mine, with a childlike anxiety in them.

I was half inclined to tell him the real truth, and now I wish I had done so, but, at the time, I thought to myself, "it is useless, he would not understand it," and so I answered:

"I have no right to complain; you doubtless wrote as you thought."

"I wrote honestly, and meaning great praise," he answered.

After his death, a small volume of his annotations, was sent me by Dr. Griswold, which were more flattering than his public notice.

Poe was an enigma to himself no less than to others, and was only happy in the few hours snatched from the actual, and irradiated by the ideal. He used to take his paper on which to write, and cut it into strips; these he would glue together as he wrote, and convert them into rolls, often measuring many yards in length. His penmanship was fine, even to the utmost elegance—clear and distinct, as if from the hand of a graver. He was not an idle man. He studied much, and his contributions to the literary world comprised several volumes. They always were original and startling. His somber pictures and intricate machinery have a peculiar fascination which few can resist, while a weird, unearthly light, half angel, half devil, like his own poor self, wrought a wizard spell upon the mind. He obtained several prizes for these, and his articles generally were in demand. Indeed, we all recollect the interest felt in every thing emanating from his pen—the relief it was from dullness of ordinary writers—the certainty of something fresh and suggestive.

His critiques were read with avidity, not that he convinced the judgment, but because people felt their ability and their courage; he took the public idols so by the beard and knocked them right and left, till people saw they were no gods at all but miserable shams. Sometimes he found the genuine, and attempted the same process with a cool hardihood; but he is a pigmy in giant's armor who does not come out magnified by the blows of an assailant. These critiques of Edgar Poe were live productions; he did not play with his pen, but wielded it. Right or wrong, all was real at the time. He was terribly in earnest. He was carried away as by an avalanche of words and emotions. Men and women with their books under their arms marched in grand procession before him, and he discovered the rich goods of one, the thefts of another, the divine art, the heavenly beauty, the profound meanings of some, while others were totally enigmatical and unrevealed to him.

He was himself in the highest degree original and unique, hence he could not abide either twaddle or plagiarism. Some of his strictures upon these grounds will long be remembered; and by-and-by, when the accounts of certain authors are made up, it will be seen that he was more than three-quarters right. We need now, in this day of mawkish adulation, a critic with a trenchant pen like that of Edgar Poe's. We need an eagle to swoop down upon the noisy brood of geese and crows and jackdaws, to set their feathers fluttering. It was a sad day that took Edgar Poe out of the world of letters, just at the time when his powers were ripening, his judgment maturing, and I believe, his deeper and better intimations assuming shape and urgency. Though late, that part of his character was rapidly developing.

As a prose writer, his stories are finished in the highest artistic manner; they are so carefully and artistically completed, that they cease to be fictions, and not being facts, they assume the aspect of a lie. Indeed, Poe believed his own fictions for the time being, or he would have you think so; he became a part of them; he filled up incident, and iterated congruities like a man who is savagely intent upon making you believe him, while underneath he carries a Mephistophelean smile that can not be hidden. We have no sympathy with his characters or their surroundings, but he holds us, nevertheless, as the Ancient Mariner held his victim; we read on with a ghastly interest, we hurry on to the close, we can not escape him; we are not pleased but fascinated, and that is his power, a sort of serpent-holding which we can not resist. He was truly a demonized man—a man possessed: in other words, a man of genius. He will be remembered when better writers, healthier, and more beneficent, are forgotten, for though sometimes incoherent, always morbid, and reckless of results, he touched a vein to which all will more or less respond.

As a poet, he may not be placed in the higher ranks, although his wondrous command of a weird, startling vocabulary, always will raise his readers to the high, cold realms of the imaginative, where we yield instinctively as to a wizard spell. The dainty ring of his chimes, the exquisite sweetness and iterating flow of his numbers, can rarely if ever be equaled. When we have said this much, we have said all, for he awakens no hopefulness in the heart, no noble aspirations, only a lone, melancholy reminiscence, more painful than beautiful, more sorrowful than dear. We listen to a dirge, but it is not of mortal sounding; it is as if a lost spirit stood beside some awe-engirdled lake, where funeral manes walk to and fro slowly, and the silence is unbroken even by the waters that kiss the gray pebbles, and there we hear the chant of a deep-toned requiem. Witness the following from a poem entitled a "Dream with a Dream" [text of this poem follows].

Here is nothing forced or unnatural; on the contrary, the words are simple and few, yet it makes the heart ache.

He was haunted by the dim region of sleep and the mystery of dreams; we find it in his poetry; it hung about his eyes, and imparted a something like mystery to his appearance. He made you think of one weighed by the awe of his own being—like a child who was floated into an unknown realm, and who can not well open his eyes to read and understand what is before him; he has vague, incomprehensible visions of love; undefined yearnings, as the poet must have of love, only love, and he falls back haunted by phantoms. His loves are all ideal—there is no flesh-and-blood tenderness about them, but a dreamy phantasmagoria of gleaming eyes and angel wings. He says:

> "For the moon never beams without bringing me dreams
>   Of the beautiful Annabel Lee;
> And the stars never rise, but I feel the bright eyes
>   Of the beautiful Annabel Lee."

This is as cold and ideal as the lines of Byron, quoted above,

> "She walks in beauty, like the night," etc.

The "Raven" is a poem so unique that we accept it unquestioning. We do not ask whether it will abide the hard nib of the critic, but impressed, we know not, care not why—we move onward to its stately march, and repeat its melancholy refrain, with a sympathy, challenged we hardly know how. In spite of the foolish manner in which Poe pretends it was written, all for effect, it is probably the most entirely spontaneous production he ever wrote. It is the very expression of this dirge-like quality of his muse. It is greater than he knew. It expresses more than he meant. We know he loved to repeat it to himself and to hear it spoken of. It was the one poem of which he was himself *fond*.

He was pleased to see that I had an admiration for it; and one morning, when my canary alighted upon the head of an Apollo in my room, I pointed out, and said,

"See, Mr. Poe, I do not keep a raven, but there is song to song: why did you not place an owl upon the head of Pallas?"

He smiled faintly—I never saw him laugh—and replied,

"There is a mystery about the Raven," and then his eyes took the introverted, abstract look so common to them, as if he were pursuing an idea that eluded his grasp. Then he roused himself and said,

"You and Helena Whitman ought to live together—and you ought to be installed as queens and poets; all artists should be privileged to pay court to you. They would grow wise and holy in such companionship."

"Will not women be thus installed as teachers—ay, even as protectors, in the true, ideal development of society?"

"We shall see it only as Hamlet saw it, in the mind's eye."

I have said I never heard him laugh: I never saw him eat; indeed, he never made one think of any mortal necessity.

And now I must touch upon a subject delicate in itself, upon which I should choose to be silent did I not believe that great injustice has been done Edgar Poe in this relation.

He was, it is said, treacherous to women, while at the same time they felt his irresistible fascinations. It is time this miserable cant were ended. Women of elevation and nobleness are not apt to compromise themselves. It is said letters written anonymously by their authors were found with the real name indorsed in the handwriting of Edgar Poe. If this be true, it is a burning shame to manhood.

It should be remembered that a man who would indorse the name of a woman upon a communication which she had seen fit to render anonymous, would be just as likely to indorse a false as a true name. He is not to be trusted in any respect.

[228]

And here I wish to say that the inordinate desire evinced by biographers to drag the relations of the sexes from the obscurity in which they have modestly chosen to enshroud them, and spread abroad names and persons, sacred to God and love, is a gross and reprehensible act. Lewes, in his recent life of Goethé, while he palliates the vices and strives to cover the moral obliquities of the great man, is wholly unscrupulous in the use he makes of the names and of the reputations of the women who became in any way associated with his career. In this respect he has exhibited not only a lack of delicacy, but of justice also. Women must correct this phase of literature, they must teach authors to ignore the relations of the sexes in their biographies, or to remember that, abstractly, moral delinquencies are no more venal in the one sex than the other.

I do not believe that Poe ever was the all-subduing man to the sex which the vanity of some and the falsehood of others have sought to represent him as being. It should be borne in mind that always there is something arbitrary in these things—the great laws of God are always stronger in all persons, than any mere act of volition. A man may be as desirous to please, and as unprincipled in his action as it is possible to conceive; he may regard every woman as only so much human aliment to his vanity or his voluptuousness, and yet over and above all this recklessness on his part he must have certain genuine qualities which inspire confidence and engage the affections no less than those which excite the fancy.

Now it is well known that Edgar Poe was an adroit and elegant flatterer. His language was refined, and abounded in the finer shades of poetry and those touches of romance so captivating to the womanly character. He was always deferential—he paid a compliment to the understanding of a woman no less than to her personal charms. He had an exquisite perception of all the graces of manner and the shades of expression. He was an admiring listener—an unobtrusive observer, and delighted in the society of the superior of the sex. If there ever were exceptions to this—if ever Poe presented oblations upon an inferior shrine, it must be imputed to his poverty for the time being, which left him no choice; for, instinctively, he sought only the loveliest and best.

In saying this I do not mean to assert more than this was due to him; but now to the point of distinction. Women, however their vanity may be flattered by the attention of a poet, and however much their admiration of such may win a certain superficial response, are never deeply affected except by that which is wholly and entirely genuine. The true heart responds only to the true. Of the myriad of little loves which have made up the experience of the world, not one in a million is of magnitude sufficient to be in any way noteworthy. Made up of the irregular demonstrations of the mind as they are, by vanity, selfishness and spleen, to trumpet them before the world, to talk of them, revive names and characters doomed to perpetual obscurity, is a piece of foolish malice, or unjustifiable scandal, as weak as it is petty and wicked.

Now, Edgar Poe had one radical defect of character, which large-minded and large-hearted persons will at once comprehend. He never inspired confidence. That was something, which lawyers call *malice prepense*, not to be mistaken in him. He always seemed to have a design—*to be acting a part*. This, a woman of penetration never forgives. It is an insult to her womanhood which she resents for herself as well as her sex. No woman with a particle of self-respect encounters this in a man without an invincible repugnance, and therefore I assert that Poe might be a bad man to frivolous or intriguing women, but dangerous to no others; and, unfortunately, society affords but too many facilities for the practice of intrigue and deception.

In person, Poe was of medium hight, slender and refined in organization. Nature designed this man little lower than an angel, for his exquisite machinery rebelled at any and every violation of the laws of his creation. He should have respected these laws. Delicate, almost, as fine as a woman, he had no aptitude for the life of the debauchee, and those who willfully and recklessly led this man into the habits of dissipation, knowing his infirmity, were guilty of a crime. It is not enough to say that people must take care of themselves; there are myriads of persons incapable of this, and therefore it is the duty of the strong to help the weak. I have been told that it was an amusement in some quarters for persons to present Poe with wine for no purpose but to watch its effect upon his sensitive nerves. This was nothing less than devilish, for it took little to move him from his proprieties.

The Raven of Mr. Poe evidently was written in one of those weird states of mind which were normal to him. I do not believe he had any fixed plan of construction. It created a deep sensation, not only among the literati, but among ordinary readers. Mr. Hoffman read it to me with much feeling, immediately it appeared.

"It is greater than Poe realizes," he remarked, as he folded the magazine.

"I feel there is a shadowy significance in the poetry, but it is not clear as yet."

"*It is despair brooding over wisdom*; the bust of Pallas becomes the perch of the Raven."

I have heard no one else read it this way, and it was startlingly just, I think. I do not conceive that Poe understood his own oracle.

Mr. Poe was pleased with the impression produced; he was sensitive to blame or praise, at all times, and at this time had many causes for uneasiness.

He was present at the theater, he told me, when the principal actor, I forget who, interpolated the words "*never more*." A thrill seemed to pass through the whole audience, and the sensation, together with its cause, were not to be mistaken.

How still, and with what an unearthly look of pleasure, Poe told me this. His large, open eyes fixed upon vacancy, and his clear intellectual face radiant. He then saw supernal lights, and heard supernal voices.

"You have read the Raven?" Ralph Waldo Emerson asked me.

"Yes, everybody reads it."

"What do you think of it? *I* can see nothing in it."

"To me it is wonderful. I do not care to fully interpret it; its merits are not to be estimated by the ordinary rules of poetry, but by the impression it produces upon the individual reader."

Mr. Emerson did not pursue the subject; *he* is *not* imaginative; his poems belong more to the realm of fancy gathering facts than to the ideal which so eminently distinguishes that of Mr. Poe.

I never read the Raven, or recall it to my memory as a fact in literature, without a sense of solemnity strangely mingled with dread; the word even creates a vision as of a vast, silent solemn cathedral; I walk its aisles alone, when forth from the dim, shadowy, spectral silence issues the "never more" from an unearthly visitant.

To me Poe was more spectral than human, and I used often to feel a deep sadness when I heard persons of ordinary perceptions and little idealism speak of him with severity. In this country there is no niche for the men of genius; everybody writes verses, but we have few *poets*, and very few with singleness of purpose to admire the patient toil of the student in the realms of Art. In Europe it is otherwise; there the severe rules of common life are not applied to the child of genius. He is recognized as exceptional, and fostered with genial care. The hardening process necessary to adapt our poets to the requirements of the Republic, is most likely to destroy the finer threads of his being, and by becoming "practical" he ceases to be ideal. Some few giants in literature are able to combine the actual and the ideal; but there exists a large class who are not strong, but are most lovely—stars of the lesser magnitude, which it is sorrowful to contemplate as fading stars, beautiful Alcyones, obliterated from the glittering galaxies of Art.

There were many rumors as to the parentage of Poe, which it is of little consequence to consider, for the fact must remain, that father and mother, one or both, must have possessed organizations exquisitely fine and intellectual. Their child was a poet in every sense; certainly he was not like any other person we ever met; he was entirely original, if the worse for it, and without any adaptability to the circumstances around him. I do not know how it would have fared with him had he not found one true, patient, devoted friend in the person of his wife's mother, Mrs. Clemm. She never wearied in her love and thoughtfulness for him.

"But madam," somebody says, "you do not consider that Poe was a man, and ought himself to have been the protector."

I know that is the traditional and conventional opinion of the masculine sex, which I, from my stand-point of observation, do not think is at all carried out in the experience of life. I am not telling of *manly* men, able to brunt the fight, but of a class by no means adapted to its rough encounters, although every one of these men, ay, and these women too, have an ideal of themselves, justified, too, by some internal consciousness, by which they could meet the utmost that may befall humanity without a groan; and I think they would have done so. It was the dull canker of everyday life which fretted and corroded them.

Mr. Hoffman used to say,

"I could easily die for a cause, when I could not live for it."

"You think, then, that heroism is an impulse—a momentary madness?" I said.

"By no means; the last act may be sudden, but it must proceed from a heroic make, just as cowardice may exist in the man undetected, till the emergency betrays it. Our acts are prompted by what lies deeper than ordinary observation."

Mr. Poe was spiritual, abstract, intellectual; he had a manly sense of independence, which rendered *patronage* of any kind repugnant to him. I do not think he ever found any appropriate sphere in this life; genial moments, green oases in the dreary waste he certainly found, for he, in one phase of character, had an almost childish desire for companionship. I have often thought how happily such a man as Poe, and some others, might have been, placed in an atmosphere of taste and appreciation, in some little court—like that of Bavaria for instance, which so fostered the genius of Goethé and Schiller; but in our country the life of genius is a perpetual struggle.

His marriage had been, as I have said, premature, to his cousin, a sweet, stag-eyed girl, who devoted herself to him in the way that she would have devoted herself to a greyhound or any other handsome pet, but who could add little to his mental or moral growth. I have always regarded this marriage as an unfortunate one for the poet, who needs a more profound sympathy always, if he would sound the depths of his own genius. That he loved her tenderly none will deny, and some of his sweetest lyrics owed their inspiration to her delicious eyes and girlish affection. She was his playmate, his pretty child-wife, for she was but fourteen at the time of her marriage.

Later in life, after the death of this child-wife, Mr. Poe became greatly attached to a lady of rare genius and deep spiritualism. The engagement was broken off, perhaps wisely on the part of the lady. A story is in circulation to the purport that Poe, repenting of the engagement, visited the lady in a state of intoxication, in the hope her disgust would release him. I do not place any reliance whatever upon the motive of this visit. That he might have visited her in this unfortunate state is more than possible, and that such might have been the consequence also; but that it was from no such design upon the part of the unfortunate poet I am equally confident.

He may have talked wildly and in unmanly wise, after such result, but it was nothing more than the reckless language of a child who has marred some precious work. He found then, as always, persons ready to listen to the wild, mortified language of genius, and to go away and report it; but the *better* soul of Poe disclaimed it altogether.

One of his most touching and significant poems was addressed to this lady, and I am happy to say she, who was so well able to read and understand the true soul of a poet, despite of all that may mar the harmony of its demonstrations, has not failed to cherish tenderly his memory. She is worthy of the "Lines to Helen."

I once heard him say,

"Had I known Helena sooner, I should have been very different from what I have been. I am fond of the society of women—poets always are; and I have found enough to play into my foibles and palliate my defects; but a true woman, with superior intellect and deep spiritualism, would have transformed my whole life into something better."

The remark has force in more ways than one. It indicates the sincerity of regret which the man must have felt in view of the past, and is also a fine tribute to the angel-mission of woman. This was uttered but a few weeks before his death, when his last work, *Eureka*, upon which he had expended much time and thought, was beginning to attract some attention. He had expected more. He had thought this deep utterance of a poetic soul would be hailed as a revelation, and his chagrin was not to be concealed. He was ill at ease at this time. He felt his best life had not been realized. He was always grave, now he was melancholy. Circumstances painful and mortifying had transpired, and he reviewed them with grief.

He called upon me one morning and found me preparing to start for Philadelphia, where I was engaged for a course of lectures, and our interview was necessarily short. He seemed disappointed—grieved.

"I have so much—so much I wished to say."

I recall his look of pain, his unearthly eyes, his emaciated form, his weird look of desolation with a pang, even now. Little did either suppose the grave was so soon to hide all that was mortal in him from human sight. Peace to his ashes!

It is asserted in the American Cyclopedia, that Edgar Poe died in consequence of a drunken debauch in his native city. This is not true.

At the instigation of a woman, who considered herself injured by him, he was cruelly beaten, blow upon blow, by a ruffian who knew no better mode of avenging supposed injuries. It is well known that a brain fever followed; his friends hurried him away, and he reached his native city only to breathe his last.

Mr. Poe, near the close of his life, lived in a little band-box of a house at Fordham, and there his wife died. The Brothers of the Jesuits' College, in that place, contrary to their wont, gave him free access to their groves and gardens, and there he unquestionably passed the happiest years of his life. His simplicity of manners and studious habits endeared him to the good Brothers, who often saw him at midnight as they passed to their vigils, moving silently under the lofty trees, too absorbed in meditation to notice their presence.

I have more than once sat spell-bound under the Shakesperean illusion of Edwin Booth as *Hamlet*, and always in the grove scene I thought of Poe. The same deep thoughtfulness—the profound expression of sadness—the weird silence and gloom which harmonize so wonderfully with the character of the shadowy Dane, served to reproduce the image of Edgar Poe.

Mrs. E. O. Smith

Elizabeth Oakes Smith, "Autobiographic Notes. Edgar Allan Poe," *Beadle's Monthly*, February 1867: 147–156.

"The Facts of Poe's Death and Burial" (1867)

Joseph E. Snodgrass

Joseph E. Snodgrass, a physician who preferred literary to medical pursuits, initiated the *American Museum*, a Baltimore publication (1838–1839), where Poe's "Ligeia" and "The Signora Psyche Zenobia" and its pendant, "The Scythe of Time" (republished, revised, respectively as "How to Write a Blackwood Article" and "A Predicament"), first appeared. Later Snodgrass edited the *Saturday Visiter*, another Baltimore periodical, in which Poe's "MS. Found in a Bottle" and "The Coliseum" had appeared, in October 1833. The two men remained on friendly terms for many years. What follows, an expansion of an earlier commentary by Snodgrass on Poe's death, challenges some aspects of Elizabeth Oakes Smith's writings on Poe. Snodgrass gives an incorrect date for the notification that Poe needed help. The correct date is Wednesday, 3 October 1849.

Clarification concerning the (often inaccurately presented) circumstances of Poe's funeral and burial appears in Christopher Scharpf. "Where Lies a Noble Spirit?—An Investigation into the Curious Mystery of Edgar Allan Poe's Grave in Baltimore," in *Masques, Mysteries, and Mastodons: A Poe Miscellany*, ed. Benjamin F. Fisher. Baltimore: Edgar Allan Poe Society, 2006: 194–222.

The first paragraph in the following article is the original editor's note.

THE FOLLOWING COMMUNICATION from a gentleman fully cognizant of what he writes, we give, not only because of its intrinsic though most painful interest, but for the further reason that it seems to us necessary in order for ever to settle the controversy in regard to the manner of the poet's death, and the circumstances attending his burial. The article in our magazine, to which it refers, was from the pen of Mrs. E. Oakes Smith, whose memories of Poe were those of a friend, and who wrote of him as one who revered his genius; yet we are sure, knowing her desire to be correct in statements of fact, the lady wrote what were not only her own impressions regarding his death, but also expressed the impressions and feelings of many friends of

Poe, who question the truth of Dr. Griswold's "Memoir," in many of its essential features.

In *Beadle's Monthly*, for February, I find some statements respecting the cause and manner of the death of Edgar Allan Poe, and, as a possessor of the facts of the case, I feel it to be due to the truth of history that I should narrate them.

The first statement to which I refer is in these words:

"It is asserted in the *American Cyclopedia* that Edgar Poe died in consequence of a drunken debauch. This is not true."

I regret to say, with due respect to the author of this assertion, and at the same time to the memory of one who was my personal friend, that it is, alas! too true. The facts of the case are simply these: On Tuesday, November 1, 1849, a wet and chilly day, I received a note bearing a signature which I recognized as that of a printer, named Walker, who had set type for the *Baltimore Saturday Visiter* while I was editing it, and thus became aware of my deep interest in Mr. Poe. It stated that a man claiming Poe's name, and to be acquainted with me, was at Cooth & Sergeant's tavern in Lombard street, near High street, (Baltimore), in a state of beastly intoxication and evident destitution, and that he had been heard to utter my name as that of an acquaintance.

I immediately repaired to the drinking-saloon—for such it was, although dignified by the designation of tavern—and, sure enough, there was Edgar Allan Poe, in a condition which had been but too faithfully described by Mr. Walker. He was in the bar-room, sitting in an arm-chair, with his head dropped forward, so stupefied by liquor and so altered from the neatly-dressed and vivacious gentleman which he was when I last had the pleasure of a call from him, that, unaided, I should not have distinguished him from the crowd of less-intoxicated men, whom the occasion of an election had called together at the tavern, as the voting-place of the ward in which it was located.

Knowing from observation on a former occasion, when he presented himself at my editorial rooms while intoxicated, that the strain of his conversation would be neither agreeable to me nor creditable to my unfortunate friend, if able to converse at all, and considering the company of unsympathetic tipplers who stared at me as I entered their Bacchanalian haunt, I thought it best not to attempt to arouse him from his stupidity. Instead of so doing, I at once ordered a room for him. I had already accompanied a waiter up-stairs, with a view to selecting a sufficiently retired apartment, and had done so, and was returning to the bar-room for the purpose of having the evidently undesired guest conveyed to his allotted chamber, when I was met, at the head of the stairway, by Mr. H——, a relative of Mr. Poe's by marriage. He suggested a hospital as a better place for him than the tavern.

I admitted the correctness of this suggestion. But, some remark of mine having caused his relative to explain why he had not suggested a still better place—his own dwelling—he stated the reason to be, that Mr. Poe had "so frequently abused his hospitality by the rudeness as well as vulgarity of his bearing while drunk, toward the ladies of his household," that he "couldn't think, for a moment, of taking him to his house in his present besotted condition."

For a moment, I confess, I felt resentful toward his friend; but I subsequently became satisfied that he was justified in the course he pursued. The Washington College Hospital having been fixed upon, a messenger was dispatched to procure a carriage. While awaiting its arrival, I had an opportunity to observe, more closely than I had taken time to do previously, the condition and apparel of the strangely metamorphosed being in the bar-room, who wore a name which was a synonym for genius—the first glance at whose *tout ensemble* was well calculated to recall Poe's own so-frequently hinted doctrine of the *metempsychosis*. His face was haggard, not to say bloated, and unwashed, his hair unkempt, and his whole physique repulsive. His expansive forehead, with its wonderful breadth between the points where the phrenologists locate the organ of ideality—the widest I ever measured—and that full-orbed and mellow, yet soulful eye, for which he was so noticeable when himself, now lusterless and vacant, as shortly I could see, were shaded from view by a rusty, almost brimless, tattered and ribbonless palmleaf hat. His clothing consisted of a sack-coat of thin and sleazy black alpaca, ripped more or less at several of its seams, and faded and soiled, and pants of a steel-mixed pattern of cassinette, half-worn and badly-fitting, if they could be said to fit at all. He wore neither vest nor neck-cloth, while the bosom of his shirt was both crumpled and badly soiled. On his feet were boots of coarse material, and giving no sign of having been blacked for a long time, if at all.

The carriage having arrived, we tried to get the object of our care upon his feet, so that he might the more easily be taken to it. But he was past locomotion. We therefore carried him to the coach as if he were a corpse, and lifted him into it in the same manner. While we were doing this, what was left of one of the most remarkable embodiments of genius the world has produced in all the centuries of its history—the author of a single poem, which alone has been adjudged by more than one critic as entitling its producer to a lasting and enviable fame—was so utterly voiceless as to be capable of only muttering some scarcely-intelligible oaths, and other forms of imprecation, upon those who were trying to rescue him from destitution and disgrace.

The carriage was driven directly to the hospital, where its unconscious occupant was assigned to the care of its intelligent and kindly resident physician. Of the numerous and strangely contradictory memoirs of Mr. Poe that I have preserved, there lies one before me, which states that "insanity ensued, and that *next morning* he died, a miserable, raving maniac." As to *time*, this is not true. He lived nearly a week, instead of dying "next day" as one account has it, or "in a few hours" as another records it, dying on the 7th of the same month—Monday. Besides it might convey the idea that he had no lucid moments. But he had, and in one of these an incident transpired which, while its mention may serve to extend the already long as well as interesting record of the last words of noted men, it will be recognized as any thing but characteristic of Mr. Poe, who was always haunted by a terrible though vague apprehension of death and the grave. When the hospital physician became satisfied that the author of "William Wilson"—a favorite tale of Mr. Poe—and of "The Raven" had written his last story and his last poem, he addressed him, concernedly and kindly, saying:

"Mr. Poe, it is my painful duty to inform you that you have, in my judgment, only a short time to live. If you have any friends whom you would like to see, name them, and your wish shall be gratified; I will summon them."

"Friends!" exclaimed the dying son of genius—"Friends!"—repeating the word for a moment, as if it had no longer a definite meaning; "*my* best friend would be he who would take a pistol and blow out these d——d wretched brains!" pressing his hand to his forehead as he uttered the awful imprecation.

During the six days of Mr. Poe's survival after he was placed in the hospital, he had only a few intervals of rationality, one of which was availed of as just described. That his disease was *mania a potu*, I have never for a moment doubted. Being this, and following as it so soon did upon his "drunken debauch," it struck me with amazement, when I came to the above-quoted statement in the usually reliable *Beadle's Magazine*, to observe that it was put forth so unqualifiedly and so flatly in contradiction of a work so justly accepted as high authority as the *New American Cyclopedia*.

Glad should I be, as a sincere friend as well as an enthusiastic admirer of the writings of Edgar Allan Poe, could the assignment of such an agency as the actual cause of his death be made with truthfulness. Unreliable as I had personal reason to know Rufus W. Griswold to be where there was half as much temptation as arose from his well-known jealousy of Poe, to tell a lie instead of the truth, I am bound to say that he failed to exaggerate, in his biography of him, as to this point. Nor can I see what is to be gained by these frequent attempts to gloss over the facts of biographical history, while I can see very clearly where a great deal is to be lost. May I not go further, and say that, not only is there the negative result of a loss, but a positive damage to the cause of truth and social progress? The most enthusiastic of all the admirers and defenders of Mr. Poe, who knew him more intimately than the writer whose doubtless unintentional misstatement it is the purpose of this article to correct, herself saw that her eloquent plea might be considered to have made the path he trod less abhorrent to others. Hence the words of assurance, in her "Edgar Allan Poe and his Critics," that, had she believed it would certainly have this effect, she "never would have proffered" that plea at all.

I can understand, and to some extent appreciate, the force of the Pagan maxim, "*De mortuis nil nisi bonum.*" But, when Christians follow its inculcations, I do not expect them to go *beyond* them, and not only omit to say any thing evil of the dead, but to make truth-straining attempts to say good things of them, to the misleading [of] the public mind and doing positive injury to the cause of good morals.

I come, now, directly to the inference drawn by the writer already referred to, that Poe's death was caused by "brain fever," as the result of a "beating." I am positive that there was no evidence whatever of any such violence having been used upon his person, when I went to his rescue at the tavern. Nor was there any given at the hospital, where its detection would have been certain, if external violence had really been the cause of his insanity, for there would have been some physical traces of it on the patient's person.

In this view of the question, I respectfully submit that it is high time that the hypothesis of a beating were dropped. As an isolated fact, the probabilities do not sustain it, to say nothing of its alleged fatal results.

I now proceed to give the true version of the place and manner of Mr. Poe's burial. Among the false statements I have met with was one to the effect that he had been "buried in the Potter's Field of his native city." As one of only three, or perhaps four, persons—not counting the undertaker and the drivers of the hearse and a single carriage, which made up the entire funeral train of the author of "The Raven"—who followed the body to the grave, I am happy to be able to testify that the truth, bad enough as it is, does not sustain this story. The burying-place of Poe was an old one belonging to the "Westminster Presbyterian Church," which had ceased to be used much, in 1849, because of its location in a populous portion of Baltimore—in Green street. There were many old vaults in it; and, when our little cortege reached it, I naturally consoled myself with the thought that his relatives—two of whom were present, and one of these the officiating clergyman—had secured him at least a temporary resting-place in one of those family tombs. But it proved to be otherwise. A grave had been dug among the crumbling mementos of mortality. Into this the plainly-coffined body was speedily lowered, and then the earth was shoveled directly upon the coffin-lid. This was so unusual even in the burials of the poor, that I could not help noticing the absence of not only the customary box, but even of the commonest boards to prevent the direct contact of the decomposing wet earth with it. I shall never forget the emotion of disappointment, mingled with disgust and something akin to resentment, that thrilled through my whole being as I heard the clods and stones resound from the coffin-lid and break the more than ordinarily solemn stillness of the scene, as it impressed me. It seemed as if Heartlessness, too often found directing the funeral rites of the poor and forsaken ones of earth, had suddenly become personified into a malign goddess, and that she had ordered those awfully discordant sounds as best befitting her own unearthly mood.

At the head and foot of the grave a place of common undressed pine board, as unlettered as unsuited, was placed—

"Only this and nothing more!"

Nor has any more befitting head or footpiece ever been substituted for the ones I have described, although there has been much *talk* about "rescuing the remains of the author of 'The Raven' from their obscurity, and building a monument worthy of his genius," etc. Recently a "Poe Monument Association" has been started in Baltimore, and some well-intended but rather spasmodic efforts have been made, through lectures or concerts, to raise the funds necessary to build the proposed memento, but I believe with very inconsiderable results. But it is hoped that *Beadle's Monthly* will prove to have furnished a channel of influence upon the public mind, not only in the most concerned city of Baltimore—the birth-place as well as the death and burial-place of Poe—through which a fresh stimulus shall be applied more widely and successfully than heretofore, resulting in the erection of the proposed monument at no very distant day.

This is the second time, since the death of Poe, that the writer of this has called attention to the condition of his remains in the hope of doing something toward the "consummation so devoutly to be wished." And I beg leave to remind such as may be inclined to assist in such an undertaking that the necessary ground was long since proffered by the "Baltimore Cemetery," on the condition that a creditable monument were erected over the grave. This was, then, a new cemetery, and it could afford to be generous. I doubt not its directors would be found ready to fulfill their promise, even at this late day. With the improvements made in this city of the dead since then, and in consideration of its accessibility as well as its attractiveness, it strikes me that no more appropriate place of final repose could be selected. The fact of its bearing the name of the city itself, where was born the deceased son of genius, whose memory its earlier directors stood ready to honor—and, may I not say, to be honored at the same time?—would seem to add to rather than detract from its appropriateness for the purpose in view.

In saying this, I do not wish to be understood as doubting the judgment or taste of those of my former fellow-citizens who are so creditably exerting themselves to secure the desired removal and more creditable disposition of Poe's remains. My only motive is a desire to forward their well-conceived and no doubt faithfully prosecuted enterprise, by arousing a renewed interest in it—for I feel, with them, that it is a melancholy shame that the bones of such a transcendently gifted writer as Edgar Allan Poe should have so long been permitted to molder in an unmarked grave in an abandoned graveyard, and that in the city of his birth and of the earliest triumphs of his matchless pen!

It was not my purpose, in this paper, to write a word about the living career of my deceased friend, beyond what has necessarily been already said in connection with its lamentably unfortunate close. But the mention of the earlier triumphs of his pen in his native city, just made, has reminded me of an incident which has been overlooked, seemingly, by most of his biographers, and yet one peculiarly illustrative of not only the fact that he was gifted, by nature, with rare capacity as a writer in the field of the ideal, but—what is nearly as equally important, in most cases, to early success— he was *conscious* of this himself; and hence dared to do what few youthful aspirants would have dreamed of accomplishing. The fact to which I here refer, I will now give as a conclusion to this article.

The *Baltimore Visiter* had offered money-prizes for a first and a second best tale. At that early day, especially in provincial places, such as Balti- more was then, fiction-writers seldom ventured to publish their articles over their real names. Young Poe had not dared to depart from the prevail- ing custom. Hence he was known, in a literary capacity, only to a small circle of friends. Imagine the surprise, then, with which the reading public was startled, when the prizes aforesaid were awarded, by the announce- ment that a single pen had won them both, and that it had been wielded by a mere youth, named Poe!

One of these prize-winning tales was "The Gold Bug." The title of the other I do not now recall. Although always regarded and referred to with evident satisfaction by himself, "The Gold Bug" was not its author's favor- ite in after life, but "William Wilson," as he gave others of his friends be- sides myself to understand—the reason being that the latter was what the former was not, viz., a reflex of his so greatly altered selfship, considered in relation to his intellectual and physical state at the time it was penned. For, whatever may have been the original tendency of Edgar Allan Poe's mind, no one who ever had opportunities to receive light from himself on the sub- ject, could doubt that his views of man, in his relations to the universe, had undergone a great change after the commencement of his literary career, so that readers who might look for his later weird and unearthly erections in "The Gold Bug," or others of his earlier productions, would seek them there in vain. He himself was so fully conscious of this change in the tone as well as the philosophy of his productions, that, in collecting his volume, entitled "Tales of the Grotesque and Arabesque," he left out more than one story which had proved most effectual in the line of the descriptive and the sensational, because of its lacking the peculiar characteristics of the latter-day creations of his singularly enchanting pen.

J. E. Snodgrass, M.D.

Joseph E. Snodgrass, "The Facts of Poe's Death and Burial," *Beadle's Monthly*, March 1867: 283–287.

"Another View of Edgar A. Poe" (1867)

Margaret E. Wilmer

> This estimate of Poe is interesting because it alludes to several previous items, challenging the portraiture offered by Dr. Joseph E. Snodgrass. Wilmer is (correctly) unsympathetic toward the hostile portraiture of George Gilfillan. Moreover, Margaret Wilmer, daughter of one of Poe's early associates who remained a steadfast friend, had access to information about Poe, from a direct source, who would have comprehended both Poe the man and Poe the writer.

WE HAVE READ with much interest an article upon Poe, the poet, by Mrs. E. Oakes Smith, recently published in *Beadle's Monthly*; and also another communication, upon the same subject, by Dr. Snodgrass. Of these, we will only remark that Mrs. Smith's article, even if mistaken in some of its representations, evidently was inspired by a generous feeling toward a dead man, whose memory has been very hardly dealt with; and that the statement of Dr. Snodgrass, though doubtless a correct one, evinced in its details a greater regard for historical accuracy than tenderness for the frailties of an unfortunate friend. We have, also, an essay on Poe, in a book by George Gilfillan, entitled "A Third Gallery of Portraits," and in this there may be said to have been summed up all that has ever been said against one of the "best abused" of men. According to Gilfillan, "Poe was no more a gentleman than he was a saint. His heart was as rotten as his conduct was infamous. He knew not what the terms 'honor' and 'honorable' meant. He had absolutely no virtue or good quality, unless you call remorse a virtue and despair a grace." [. . .] "He was, in short, a combination, in almost equal proportions, of the fiend, the brute, and the genius. One might call him one of the Gadarene swine, filled with a devil, and hurrying down a steep place to perish in the wave." [. . .] "Poe had Satan substituted for soul."

On reading whole pages of raving abuse like this, we stand amazed to think that a man who plainly claims to be a Christian, and expects to be judged by divine justice, even as he judges his fellow-man, should use such language about a person of whose real history he actually knew next to nothing. But we are able to speak understandingly on the subject.

The writer's father, Lambert A. Wilmer, was a man who made the study of human nature his constant pursuit, and he was one of the last persons to be imposed upon by any false appearances. At the same time, he was distinguished by a strictness of morals that, to some, appeared like austerity. We make these remarks by way of introduction to the statement that for more than twelve years, Mr. Wilmer was the most intimate friend and valued associate of Edgar A. Poe. Both belonged to the literary profession, and there was but a slight difference in their ages. Their friendship commenced at the period when Mr. Poe had just made his regular entrance upon the profession of authorship. Mr. Wilmer has often and solemnly averred, and has left a written statement to the effect that, during this period of twelve years, he never knew Poe to be intoxicated, or to be guilty of any immorality of conduct. In fact, his behavior was remarkably precise, and his conversation singularly pure and correct in its nature. It is certain that, whatever Mr. Poe may have become in his last years, his natural character, and that which he manifested during the longest portion of his life, had in it nothing beastly or degraded.

We have seen and heard it asserted that Mr. Poe "broke his wife's heart," and, in this statement, there is not a shadow of truth. Virginia Poe was of a very delicate constitution, and once, while singing to entertain some visitors, she ruptured a blood-vessel. This did not immediately prove fatal, but her health declined thenceforth, until at length, she died of consumption. Her husband watched over her with devoted solicitude, and neglected no means which affection could suggest, to restore her health or to promote her comfort. All of Mr. Poe's biographers agree that his mother-in-law, Mrs. Clemm, never ceased to regard him with affection; but would this excellent woman have been thus devoted to a man who had broken the heart of her only and idolized daughter?

It seems to be considered as a trifling merit that there is no taint of immorality in any of the writings of Edgar A. Poe, but we can not so regard it. The private character, even of a literary man, must, of course, be of the most importance to his own prosperity and his soul's salvation; but it is with his *writings* that the world has to do, and, according to the nature of what he has written, shall his influence upon posterity be good or evil.

What appears most singular to us is, that people should consider the character and fate of Poe as being so *extraordinary*. Others, as well as Gilfillan, can make of him nothing but a "moral monster"—"a demoniac 'exceeding fierce, and dwelling among the tombs' "—"an awful soul, touched by the torch of the Furies," and so on. He is described as a sort of terrific, supernatural being, striding over the earth, and casting "the blackness of his own vast shadow" upon its trembling and bewildered inhabitants. What does all this mean? Deprived of his idolized wife, finding his gifts of mind all unappreciated by his contemporaries, bound down to poverty and toil, uncheered and unsupported by a practical religion, is it so strange that thus, a weak-hearted man of genius should sink into dissipation, that we must call upon the heavens to be astonished and the earth to quake at it?

Most people, on reading the wild, awe-inspiring, gloom-diffusing productions of Poe, seem to think that the man must be just like his writings, though every one who has read the lives of authors ought to know that this is very far from being the rule. Instead of writing "in a frenzy," Mr. Poe "built up" (as he himself said) his composition in a remarkably deliberate and methodical manner. But, if there are people who can not understand how a poet may write in a wildly imaginative vein, and yet not be a lunatic or a demoniac, we do not undertake to make the matter clear to their comprehension. Those who talk or write of what they do not understand, often work their bewildered imaginations up to such a pitch that "vaulting ambition overleaps itself" and the subject, too. Thus, many writers upon Shakespearean character have put into the minds of Hamlet and Macbeth a host of reflections, and purposes, and secrets, that the illustrious bard himself never thought of; and as critics may be said to have created a new Shakespeare, so biographers have truly made up a new Edgar Allan Poe.

And now, as we have seen that Poe's early career has been so grossly misrepresented, is it not a thousand to one that there is great exaggeration in most accounts of those faults and follies which marked his later years? Clearly, he was one whose fate it was,

> "In life and death, to be the mark where wrong
> Aimed with her poisoned arrows;"

And every honorable soul will shrink from a complicity in the hideous baseness of slandering the helpless dead, or heaping wanton indignity upon the already too much "injured shade" of Edgar Allan Poe.

Margaret E. Wilmer, "Another View of Edgar A. Poe," *Beadle's Monthly*, April 1867: 385-386.

From *Edgar Allan Poe* (1891)

WILLIAM GOWANS

> This posthumous account, by William Gowans, a bookseller who saw much
> of Poe during the writer's time in New York City, throws glimpses onto Poe's
> domestic life that counter many less sympathetic accounts, thus furnishing a
> corrective to much that was slanderous. Gowans's championing of Poe would
> have been dear to the heart of John Henry Ingram, Poe's English biographer,
> who was firm in his perception that Poe was a much maligned man.

THE CHARACTERS DRAWN of Poe by his various biographers and critics may
with safety be pronounced an excess of exaggeration; but this is not to be
much wondered at, when it is taken into consideration that these men were
rivals either as poets or prose writers, and it is well known that such are
generally as jealous of each other as are the ladies who are handsome, or
those who desire to be considered to be possessed of the coveted quality. It
is an old truism and as true as it is old, "that in the midst of counsel there
is safety."

I, therefore, will also show you my opinion of this gifted but unfortunate
genius. It may be estimated as worth little, but it has this merit—it comes
from an eye and ear witness; and this, it must be remembered, is the very
highest of legal evidence. For eight months or more, "one house contained
us, us one table fed!" During that time I saw much of him, and had an opportunity of conversing with him often; and I must say, that I never saw him
the least affected with liquor, nor ever descend to any known vice, while he
was one of the most courteous, gentlemanly, and intelligent companions I
have met with during my journeyings and haltings through diverse divi-
sions of the globe; besides, he had an extra inducement to be a good man
as well as a good husband, for he had a wife of matchless beauty and liveli-
ness; her eyes could match that of any houri, and her face defy the genius of
a Canova to imitate; a temper and disposition of surpassing sweetness; besides, she seemed as much devoted to him and his every interest as a young

mother is to her first born. . . . Poe had a remarkably pleasing and prepossessing countenance, what the ladies would call decidedly handsome.

From John Henry Ingram, *Edgar Allan Poe: His Life, Letters, and Opinions* (1891): 116–117, quoting William Gowans (in the *New York Evening Mail*, 10 December 1870).

"Edgar Poe" in *Temple Bar* (1874)

John Henry Ingram

> Another piece by Ingram served (perhaps intentionally) to prepare the way
> for his book-length biography, published in 1880. Like many of Ingram's writ-
> ings about Poe, this article champions Poe the man and the writer against
> Griswold's slanders. At this time Ingram had obviously not ascertained all
> the facts about Poe—for example, his birth date, his return from England to
> Richmond (was 1820, not 1822), his foreign travels, when the first Mrs. Allan
> died, the correct age of John Allan's second wife—though he subsequently
> marshalled important factual information for his edition of Poe writings and
> for his biography.

UNTIL THE PRESENT MOMENT Dr. Griswold's "Memoir" of Edgar Poe has
been accepted, almost unquestioned, in Europe: in America its correctness
has been frequently and authoritatively impugned. Baudelaire in France,
and Mr. Moy Thomas in England,[1] it is true, have ventured to question the
truth of the reverend gentleman's account of Poe's life, but, twenty-four
years after the poet's decease, we still find ourselves the first in this country
to appear before the public with any proofs of the thorough untrustworthi-
ness of the said "Memoir." The present is not an occasion for a full and
critical examination of the biography by Dr. Griswold, but we confidently
believe that enough evidence can be adduced here to prove that when
Mr. Graham styled it "the fancy sketch of a jaundiced vision," he was but
giving utterance to the truth. Writers in search of a sensational subject are
prone to resort to Poe's life for a point to their moral; but we must content
ourselves with the barest and most unsophisticated narration of his career,
as gathered from fresh evidence, merely pointing out on our course his biographer's more palpable deviations from the fact.

Edgar Poe could boast of gentle lineage; a fact, probably, of little value,
save that it explains to some extent the delicacy of his feelings and fancies.
Descended from the old Norman family of the Le Poers, the race would
appear to have retained its position in society until our hero's father for-

sook jurisprudence to elope with an actress. After having "donned the sock" himself for a few years, David Poe died, and within a few weeks of his youthful bride, leaving three children, Henry, Edgar, and Rosalie, utterly destitute. Mr. John Allan, a wealthy merchant, and a friend of the family, having no children of his own, following a common American custom, adopted the boy Edgar and his sister Rosalie. Of this girl we learn no more, save that she is still alive and in a state of utter destitution.[2]

Edgar Poe was born in Baltimore, but when is still doubtful. Griswold, and other biographers copying him, say in January, 1811, and this date is alleged to have been taken from a letter of the poet's, but those who have investigated the "Memoir" will probably be inclined to question its correctness. Poe, in his wonderful story of "William Wilson," speaks of passing the third lustrum of his life at Dr. Bransby's, and if that might be accepted as a fact it would, by antedating his birth some few years, get rid of several singular anomalies in his biography. Griswold frequently overlooks the necessity of being accurate in his dates. On the very first page of his "Memoir," in order to avail himself of a ridiculous anecdote communicated to him by "an eminent and estimable gentleman," of Poe's conduct at a school in Richmond, Virginia, when he "was only six or seven years of age," he disregards the fact that, according to his own account, his hero was then and had been for two years past in England.

Accepting the date recorded by all his biographers, his adopted parents brought Poe to England in 1816, and placed him at the Manor House School, Church Street, Stoke Newington. The school was then kept by the Rev. Dr. Bransby, and would appear to have been situated in grounds of considerable extent, although now sadly shorn of their proportions. The poet's description of the place must be taken *cum grano salis*, and the oft quoted recollections of "William Wilson" may well be referred to the usually exaggerated dimensions of childhood's reminiscences. In 1822, after a residence of five years in England, he returned to the United States, and, says Griswold, "after passing a few months at an academy in Richmond, entered the University at Charlottesville, Virginia, where he led a very dissipated life. The manners which then prevailed there were extremely dissolute, and he was known as the wildest and most reckless student of his class; but his unusual opportunities, and the remarkable ease with which he mastered the most difficult studies, kept him all the while in the first rank for scholarship." The "gambling, intemperance, and other vices," which "induced," says this biographer, "his expulsion from the university," must have been the result of extraordinary precocity, because, if this authority is reliable in his dates, Poe was now in the eleventh or twelfth year of his age!

If the "William Wilson" theory may be accepted, and the statement of Mr. Powell, in his sketches of "The Authors of America," that Poe went to "various academies" previous to entering the Charlottesville University, be borne in mind, the poet's age would be from fifteen to twenty during his collegiate career. Notwithstanding his alleged dissoluteness, this precocious boy, according to his more reliable biographers, actually found means to obtain the first honours of his college, and at the conclusion of his university career, instead of being expelled, as Griswold asserts, left *alma mater* with the intention of aiding the Greeks in their struggles for independence. A mere boy, Poe would appear to have joined in the various pastimes of his fellow students, but that he made himself notorious by "his gambling, intemperance, and *other* vices," would appear to be in direct contradiction to all unprejudiced evidence now obtainable. Griswold admits that at this period Poe was noted for feats of hardihood, strength and activity, and that "on one occasion, in a hot day of June, he swam from Richmond to Warwick, seven miles and a half, against a tide running probably from two to three miles an hour." Certainly a wonderful performance for a dissolute youth, and one that if not vouched for on good authority, might well have been relegated to the depths of the Doctor's imagination. Apart from his athletic feats, Poe's great abilities enabled him to maintain a respectable position in the eyes of the professors. "His time," remarks Powell, "was divided between lectures, debating societies, rambles in the Blue Ridge mountains, and in making caricatures of his tutors and the heads of the colleges." He was a clever draughtsman, and is stated to have had the habit of covering the walls of his dormitory with rough charcoal sketches. "Rousing himself," adds Powell, "from this desultory course of life, he took the first honours of the college, and returned home."

Poe left the Charlottesville University with the intention of emulating Byron in his efforts on behalf of the Greeks. In conjunction with an acquaintance, Ebenezer Burling, the future poet purposed proceeding to Greece to take part in the struggle against the Turks, but his companion's heart failing him, Poe had to undertake the perilous journey alone. This act of chivalry on the part of the youthful adventurer was undertaken in 1827, when, according to his biographers, he had attained the prematurely mature age of sixteen! The would-be warrior got no further than St. Petersburg, where he was arrested in consequence of an irregularity in his passport, and was only saved from further difficulty through the exertions of the American consul, by whose friendly assistance he was, moreover, enabled to return to his native land, the recognition of Greece by the allied powers rendering *his* aid no longer necessary. It should be noted that Griswold states his young countryman's troubles in St. Petersburg arose "from penalties incurred in a drunken debauch;" but this allegation was denied directly it appeared in print; its author never attempted to support it by evidence of any description, and every other native biographer gives the story as we have told it.

On his return home poor Poe found a sad change. Mrs. Allan, who seems to have acted a mother's part to him, and whom he would appear to have regarded with a deep affection, was dead. He was too late even to take a last farewell of his only friend, her funeral having taken place the day before he reached Richmond. Mrs. Allan died on the 27th of February, 1829, and from that day his biographers very justly date all his misfortunes. Mr. Allan, who does not appear to have manifested much pleasure at his adopted son's return, when Poe declared his resolution of devoting himself to a military life seems to have assisted him in obtaining an appointment in West Point Military Academy. "Here he entered upon his new studies and duties," remarks Powell, "with characteristic energy, and an honourable career was opened to him; but the fates willed it that Mr. Allan should marry a girl young enough to be her husband's granddaughter;" and this event Poe was soon made to feel as a deathblow to his hopes of succeeding to his adopted father's property, in accordance with that person's oft-expressed intention. Here again it is necessary to revert to Mr. Griswold's "Memoir" to contradict his emphatic statement that Mr. Allan, on his second marriage, so far from being sixty-five years of age, as "stated by all Poe's biographers . . . was in his forty-eighth year." He seems to have re-married in a twelvemonth after his first wife's death, and yet the careless recorder of the event, forgetting on the very next page his declaration of the "forty-eighth year," allows him to die in the spring of 1834, or barely four years later, at fifty-four instead of fifty-two years of age.[3] The point is hardly worth quibbling over save that it is another specimen of Griswold's want of accuracy. Common sense would show that a man who had been so long married and so hopeless of offspring as to have adopted two non-related children in 1814–15 was more likely to be nearer sixty-five than forty-eight in 1830.

[254]

Whether the truth lies with all the other biographers or with the Doctor, as regards this circumstance, matters little; it suffices to say that Poe but too speedily discovered, after Mr. Allan's second marriage, that affairs had altered to his detriment at home. The birth of a son to his adopted father was made the means of completely alienating that man from his hitherto reputed heir, and poor Edgar found all his pecuniary prospects suddenly blighted. The unfortunate cadet's allowance being entirely withdrawn he was compelled to leave West Point, and resolved to proceed to Poland, to aid the patriots of that nation in their struggle to shake off the Russian yoke. Here again it is requisite to refer to a statement of Griswold's, to the effect that Poe parted in anger from Mr. Allan, who refused in any way to assist him further, because, "according to Poe's own statement, he ridiculed the marriage of his '*patron*' [4] with Miss Patterson and had a quarrel with her; but a different story, scarcely suitable for repetition here, was told by the friends of the other party." The different story is then referred to in a note as hinted at by the writer of an "Eulogium" upon the life and genius of Mr. Poe, in the "Southern Literary Messenger," for March, 1850. To this "Eulogium" and its author, we shall again refer, merely contenting ourselves now with stating that this tale can only be spoken of as unsupported by a tittle of evidence.

On the 6th of September, 1831, the unequal conflict in Poland was ended by the fall of Warsaw. The news reached the chivalric poet in time to prevent his departure, but left him once more aimless, and almost resourceless. In 1827, in happier times, Poe had published a small volume of poems, which ran through three editions—a fact Dr. Griswold forgets to mention—and which appears to have received the warm commendations of local critics. Griswold asserts that it included "Al Aaraaf" and "Tamerlane," pieces since republished in the collected edition; but this would not appear to have been the case; and the poet's own reference to those poems being "reprinted *verbatim* from the original edition"—as if to refute his biographer's suggestion that they had been constantly revised—applies to the volume of 1830–31. Of the former work the only poem preserved would appear to be the sweet little lyric "To Helen," embalmed by Lowell in his sympathetic sketch of its author. Encouraged by this illusory success, Poe started for Baltimore, where he turned to literature as a means of subsistence. He quickly found that the waters of Helicon were anything but Pætolian; and although some of his finest stories were written at this time, and accepted

[255]

by the magazines, they were scarcely ever paid for, and at last the unfortunate man was absolutely and literally *starving*.

At this period of the terrible tale, as frightful as the most dramatic of his own stories, Poe, according to Griswold, enlisted as a private soldier, was recognised by some officers who had known him at West Point, and who made efforts, with prospects of success, to obtain a commission for him, when it was discovered by his friends that he had deserted. About the whole of this story there is that air of improbability which the reverend doctor is so fond of. Of the many lives of the poet, by friends and foes, published in America, Griswold alone mentions the circumstance, and as his "Memoir" has been authoritatively stigmatised by Mrs. Sarah Whitman, and others, for containing anecdotes which "are utterly fabulous," it must be regarded with grave suspicion. There is one fact which renders it very improbable: Poe went to Baltimore in 1830, and was in that city in 1833. Griswold places the affair between those dates, stating, "how long he remained in the service I have not been able to ascertain." Is it likely that a man so well known as Poe would have enlisted, deserted, and yet have remained in a place where he was so generally known? or that his friends would not have encouraged him to remain in the army to wait the result of their exertions?

In 1833, the proprietor of the "Baltimore Saturday Visitor" offered premiums for the best prose story and the best poem, and to adjudicate upon the mass of papers sent in three well known men were obtained. The committee included the Honourable John P. Kennedy, author of the well known fiction, "Horse-Shoe Robinson." "The umpires," remarks Powell, "were men of taste and ability, and after a *careful consideration* of the productions, they decided that Poe was undoubtedly entitled to both prizes. As Poe was entirely unknown to them, this was a genuine tribute to his superior merit." The poem sent was "The Coliseum," and it was accompanied by six stories for selection; "not content with awarding the premium, they (i.e. the committee) declared that the worst of the six tales referred to was better than the best of the other competitors." Griswold, enlarging upon the "Eulogium" already referred to, tells the story of the award in the following manner. We leave our reader to judge the value of Dr. Griswold's "Memoir" by this fact alone, if he will compare the extract we now give with the official report given below:

"Such matters are usually disposed of in a very off-hand way. Committees to award literary prizes drink to the payer's health in good wines, over unexamined MSS., which they submit to the discretion of publishers, with permission to use their names in such a way as to promote the publisher's advantage. So, perhaps, it would have been in this case, but that one of the committee, taking up a little book remarkably beautiful and distinct in caligraphy, was tempted to read several pages; and becoming interested, he summoned the attention of the company to the half-dozen compositions it contained. It was unanimously decided that the prizes should be paid to 'the first of geniuses who had written legibly.' Not another MS. was unfolded. Immediately the 'confidential envelope' was opened, and the successful competitor was found to bear the scarcely known name of Poe."

Thus runs the printed report of the committee, published with the award on the 12th of October, 1833, and republished in the "Southern Literary Messenger," previous to Poe's assuming the editorial management of that magazine:

"Amongst the prose articles were many of various and distinguished merit, but the singular force and beauty of those sent by the author of 'The Tales of the Folio Club,' leave us no room for hesitation in that department. We have accordingly awarded the premium to a tale entitled the 'MS. found in a Bottle.' It would hardly be doing justice to the writer of this collection to say that the tale we have chosen is the best of the six offered by him. We cannot refrain from saying that the author owes it to his own reputation as well as to the gratification of the community, to publish the entire volume ('Tales of the Folio Club'). These tales are eminently distinguished by a wild, vigorous, and poetical imagination, a rich style, a fertile invention, and varied and curious learning.

(Signed)
"JOHN P. KENNEDY,
"J. H. B. LATROBE, and
"JAMES H. MILLER."

Comment on this is needless.

From this time Poe's affairs mended, and his writings were not only sought after but paid for by the publishers. In the spring of the year following (1834) Mr. Allan died, and of his property, to quote the elegant words of Griswold, "not a mill was bequeathed to Poe," and, it is alleged, the widow of his adopted father "even refused him his own books." Early in 1835, the poet began to contribute poems, tales and reviews to the "Southern Literary Messenger," a newly-established monthly magazine. Mr. Kennedy, after a year and a half's friendship with Poe, had advised him to forward a paper to Mr. White, the proprietor of the above publication. He did so; became a regular contributor, and in May, 1835, he was made editor, at a salary of five hundred dollars per annum. The accession of the new editor worked wonders in the "Southern Literary Messenger," in a short time raising its circulation from four hundred to three thousand. Its success was partially due to the originality and fascination of Poe's stories, and partially owing to the fearlessness of his trenchant critiques. He was no respecter of persons, and already began to rouse the small fry of bookmakers by his crucial dissection of their mediocrities. "He had a scorn," says Powell, "of the respectable level trash which has too long brooded over American literature. Poe did not like tamely to submit to the dethronement of genius. . . . What gods and men abhor, according to Horace, a certain class of critics and readers in America adore." Amongst the best of his productions at this period was the "Adventure of Hans Pfaal," which appeared in the "Literary Messenger" three weeks previous to the appearance of Mr. Richard Lock's "Moon Story," which indeed it probably suggested, although, from the way in which Griswold alludes to "Hans Pfaal" being "in some respects very similar to Mr. Lock's" story, one is led to believe our poet the copier instead of the copied.

In September, 1835, Poe, who had hitherto performed his editorial duties at a distance, found it necessary to leave Baltimore for Richmond, where the "Messenger" was published. Again amongst his kindred, he met his cousin Virginia Clemm, a girl in years, and already manifesting signs of consumption; but undeterred by this or by their poverty, the poor poet was wedded to his kinswoman. He continued the direction of the "Messenger" until January, 1837, when he left it for the more lucrative employment of assisting Professors Anthon, Hawkes, and Henry, in the management of the "New York Quarterly Review." Griswold, it is true, states that he was dismissed from the "Messenger" on account of his irregularities, and he quotes a goody letter from its *deceased* proprietor, upbraiding him for getting drunk, but promising to allow him to "again become an assistant in my office" on condition that he forswore the bottle. Unsupported by other evidence, we should doubt the truth of this extract. Undated, addressed to a gentleman who has raised his publication to a profitable and famous circulation, and who would appear at the time to have been married, is it probable that Poe would have been termed "an assistant in my office," and offered "quarters in my house," by Mr. White, who, like all the authorities referred to by this biographer in corroboration of his allegations, save the writer of the aforementioned "Eulogium," unfortunately dies before the charge is brought?

In 1837 Poe wrote some of his slashing critiques for the "New York Review," and by them, says Powell, "made many enemies." In July of the same year, he also completed and published his wonderful narrative of "Arthur Gordon Pym." Griswold displays his usual animus by stating that "it received little attention," and that in England, "being mistaken at first for a narrative of real experiences, it was advertised to be reprinted, but a discovery of its character, I believe, prevented such a result." In truth, it was in a short interval twice reprinted in England, and did obtain considerable notice, "the air of truth" which, it is suggested, was only in the attempt, having excited much interest in the book.

The heavy "Review" work was not in Poe's line, and at the end of a year he left New York for Philadelphia, where he was engaged on the "Gentleman's Magazine," since merged into "Graham's." In May 1839 he was appointed editor of this publication, and, as usual, "came down pretty freely with his critical axe." At the same time he contributed tales and papers to various other magazines, so that, although obliged to labour severely, he began to get a fair livelihood. In the autumn of this year he published a collection of his best stories, in two volumes, under the title of "Tales of the Grotesque and Arabesque."

Poe edited the "Gentleman's" until June, 1840, when it changed hands, and became known as "Graham's Magazine." Griswold states that Mr. Burton, the former proprietor of the publication, found the poet so unreliable, that he "was never sure when he left the city that his business would be cared for," and sometimes had to perform the editorial duties himself. Wonderful to relate, however, Poe was retained in his post until the last moment, when the following scene is alleged to have occurred: (somebody, of course, had taken shorthand notes of the conversation). Mr. Burton is supposed to have been absent for a fortnight, and, on his return, to have learned that his editor has not only not furnished the printers with any copy for the forthcoming number of the Magazine, but has availed himself of the time to prepare the prospectus of a new monthly, to supplant that he is now editing. Burton meets "his associate late in the evening at one of his accustomed haunts," and says, " 'Mr. Poe, I am astonished!—Give me my manuscripts, so that I can attend to the duties you have so shamefully neglected, and when you are sober we will settle.' Poe interrupted him with 'Who are you that presume to address me in this manner? Burton—I am—the editor—of the "Penn Magazine"—and you are—hiccup—a fool.' " Such absurd anecdotes are not worthy refutation, but an almost certain proof of their incredibility is furnished by the fact that not only did Mr. George R. Graham engage Poe to continue the editorial duties of the said magazine, but he was also the first to denounce Griswold's "Memoir" of the poet, as "the fancy sketch of a jaundiced vision," and as "an immortal infamy."

Poe retained the editorship of "Graham's Magazine" for about two years, during which period some of his finest analytical tales were produced. In 1843, not 1848, as stated by his inaccurate biographer, he obtained the one hundred dollar prize for his story of "The Gold Bug"; a story written in connection with his theory that human ingenuity could not construct any cryptograph which human ingenuity could not decipher. Tested by several correspondents with difficult samples of their skill, the poet took the trouble to examine and solve them in triumphant proof of his theory.

In the autumn of 1844, Poe removed to New York, where, in literary circles, his fame had already preceded him. He speedily found employment on the "New York Mirror," and Willis, who was one of the proprietors of that paper, has left us a highly interesting portraiture of the poet at this epoch of his life.

"Apropos of the disparaging portion of Dr. Griswold's sketch, which appeared at Poe's death," he remarks, "let us truthfully say, some four or five years since Mr. Poe was employed by us for several months as critic and sub-editor. He resided with his wife and mother at Fordham, a few miles out of town, but was at his desk in the office from nine in the morning till the evening paper went to press. With the highest admiration for his genius, and a willingness to let it atone for more than ordinary irregularity, we were led by common report to expect a very capricious attention to his duties. Time went on, however, and he was invariably punctual and industrious. With his pale, beautiful, and intellectual face, as a reminder of what genius was in him, it was impossible, of course, not to treat him always with deferential courtesy. . . . With a prospect of taking the lead in another periodical, he, at last, voluntarily gave up his employment with us, and, through all this considerable period, we had seen but one presentment of the man—a quiet, patient, industrious, and most gentlemanly person, commanding the utmost respect and good feeling by his unvarying deportment and ability.

"Residing as he did in the country, we never met Mr. Poe in hours of leisure; but he frequently called on us afterwards at our place of business, and we met him often in the street—invariably the same sad-mannered, winning and refined gentleman, such as we had always known him. It was by rumour only, up to the day of his death, that we knew of any other development of manner or character. . . . Such only he has invariably seemed to us in all we have happened personally to know of him through a friendship of *five or six years*. And so much easier is it to believe what we have seen and known, than what we *hear* of only, that we remember him but with admiration and respect."

Poe left the "Mirror" in order to take part in the "Broadway Journal," and in October, 1845, he was enabled to buy his partner out, and to obtain the entire possession of this periodical. Under his control it became, probably, the best work of the kind ever issued, but, from the very nature of its contents, must have appeared to too small though select a class to make it remunerative. Accordingly the poor poet had to relinquish its publication, and on the 3rd of January, 1846, the last number was issued. What he did for the next few months heaven only knows; but in the May number of the "Lady's Book" he commenced a series of articles on the "The Literati of New York City", in which, "he professed," remarks Griswold, with the wonted sneer, "to give some honest opinions at random respecting their autorial merits, with occasional words of personality." The papers seem to have made the literary quacks of New York shake in their shoes. One unfortunate who came under the lash, unable to bear his castigation quietly, retorted in no measured terms; in fact, instead of waiting, as Griswold did, for Poe's death—when every ass could have its kick at the dead lion—this Dr. Dunn Brown, or Dunn English, for both names are given, in a personal newspaper article, referred to the alleged infirmities of the poet. The communication being inserted in the "Evening Mirror," on the 23rd of June, 1845, Poe instituted a libel suit, and recovered several hundred dollars for defamation of character. Let anyone who has the slightest belief in Griswold's impartiality now turn to his garbled account of this dispute. He never mentions the suit for libel or its results; indeed his *suppressio veri* is as iniquitous as his *suggestio falsi*.

In the autumn of this year Poe was residing in a little cottage at Fordham, near New York. The household comprised the poet, his wife, a confirmed invalid, and her devoted and never-to-be-forgotten mother, Mrs. Clemm, whose name will ever be linked with that of her unfortunate son-in-law. His wife was dying of a long, lingering decline, and the poet himself was ill, and, paralysed by poverty, scarcely able to labour. "Mr. Poe wrote," says Willis, "with fastidious difficulty, and in a style too much above the popular level to be well paid. He was always in pecuniary difficulties, and, with his sick wife, frequently in want of the merest necessaries of life." A most interesting description of the poet's *ménage* at this bitter period of his existence is afforded by a paper which appeared in a London periodical,[5] as "Reminiscences of Edgar Poe." The writer gives us a circumstantial account of the homely abode and its occupants, and [her] description of the family's poverty-stricken condition is heartrending.

> "The autumn came," says the writer, detailing [her] second visit, "and Mrs. Poe sank rapidly in consumption, and I saw her in her bed-chamber. Everything here was so neat, so purely clean, so scant and poverty-stricken, that I saw the sufferer with such a heartache as the poor feel for the poor. There was no clothing on the bed, which was only straw, but a snow white spread and sheets. The weather was cold, and the sick lady had the dreadful chills that accompany the hectic fever of consumption. She lay on the straw bed, wrapped in her husband's great-coat, with a large cat on her bosom. . . . The coat and the cat were the sufferer's only means of warmth, except as her husband held her hands and her mother her feet."

These circumstances being made known by the writer of the above, a paragraph appeared in the "New York Express," to the effect that "Edgar Poe and his wife are both dangerously ill with consumption, and that the hand of misfortune lies heavy upon their temporal affairs. We are sorry to mention the fact that they are so far reduced as to be barely able to obtain the necessaries of life. This is, indeed, a hard lot, and we hope that the friends and admirers of Mr. Poe will come promptly to his assistance in his bitterest hour of need." This appeal was followed by an article by Willis in the "Home Journal," advertising to the dangerous illness of the poet and his wife, and their consequent sufferings for want of the commonest necessaries of life, and evidencing their case as a proof of a hospital being required for educated and refined objects of charity. "Here," he urges, "is one of the finest scholars, one of the most original men of genius, and one of the most industrious of the literary men of our country, whose temporary suspension of labour, from bodily illness, drops him immediately to a level with the common objects of public charity."

The effect of this appeal was to bring instant aid to the poor suffering family; Poe's many friends reading it in a different spirit than that of his biographer, who avers that the article by Willis was only "an ingenious apology for Mr. Poe's infirmities," and that the manly letter to its author from Poe, announcing his own gradual recovery from a long and dangerous illness, but his wife's hopeless condition, "was written for effect. He had not been ill a great while," continued his ruthless assailant, "nor dangerously at all. There was no literary or personal abuse of him in the journals," he adds, alluding to a paragraph in the poet's sad letter to Willis, to the effect that his wife's sufferings had been heightened by the receipt of an anonymous letter containing "those published calumnies of Messrs. ——, for which," says Poe, "I yet hope to find redress in a court of justice."

This letter, which, according to Griswold, "was written for effect," is dated 30th of December, 1846, and was followed in a few weeks by his wife's death. Mrs. Poe's last moments were soothed and her wants administered to, we believe, by the poet's good and noble friend, Mrs. Lewis, in whose hospitable home, when the poet himself died, Mrs. Clemm is said to have found a shelter. It is needless to follow the adventures of the poet through all the labyrinth of errors in which his biographer has enveloped them. On the 9th of February, 1848, he delivered a lecture in New York on the Cosmogony of the Universe. This was the substance of his greatest work, and which was subsequently published under the title of "Eureka, a Prose Poem." It has never been reprinted in England.

From this time to the day of his death Poe steadily worked with his pen and as a lecturer, to obtain a livelihood. And he succeeded. But consumption had long been sapping his system, and enfeebled as it was by long suffering, constant and harassing literary labour, and, more than all, *want*, it was ready to succumb; and on the evening of Sunday, the 7th of October, 1849, he died, if the correct date of his birth is given, in the thirty-eighth year of his age.

The present opportunity does not admit of a complete analysis of the "Memoir" by Griswold—the memoir on which every English life of Edgar Poe has been founded; but it is believed that enough has been said to prove the biographer's animus. Mrs. Whitman, in her clever little brochure of "Poe and his Critics," states that "some of the most injurious of these anecdotes" (i.e. in the "Memoir") "were disproved, during the life of Dr. Griswold, in the New York 'Tribune' and other leading journals, without eliciting from him any public statement or apology." Quite recently we have had, through columns of the "Home Journal," the refutation of another calumnious story, which for ten years has been going the round of the English and American periodicals. "Moreover," adds Mrs. Whitman, "we have authority for stating that many of the disgraceful anecdotes, so industriously collected by Dr. Griswold, are *utterly fabulous*, while others are perversions of the truth, more injurious in their effects than unmitigated fiction."

When Edgar Poe died a long account of his life and writings appeared in the New York "Tribune," signed "Ludwig." Dr. Rufus Griswold was subsequently obliged to acknowledge himself the author of it. It is the well-known paper beginning "Edgar Allan Poe is dead. This announcement will startle many, but *few will be grieved by it . . . he had few or no friends*." In November following the poet's death, a kindly notice of him and his writings was furnished to the "Southern Literary Messenger" by Mr. John R. Thompson, his successor in the editorship of that magazine. It did not contain an unkind or disparaging word. A month or two later appeared a collection of Poe's works in two volumes, and it was most depreciatingly reviewed in the "Tribune" by a writer whose style is easily recognisable, and who signed himself "R."—(Rufus). In March, 1850, appeared an extremely lengthy review of this same collection in the "Literary Messenger;" it is the so-called, by Griswold, "Eulogium," and beginning: "These half-told tales and broken poems are the only records of a wild, hard life. . . . Among all his poems there are only two or three which are not execrably bad." It then proceeds to vilify Willis and Lowell for their tributes to the memory of Poe, the latter of the two, it avers, belonging to that "minute species of literary insect which is plentifully produced by the soil and climate of Boston." The writer then administers a gentle reprimand to Griswold, and forthwith proceeds to detail a life of Edgar Poe. Now comes the strange part of the story. Nearly the whole of this very lengthy life and critique was subsequently embodied in the "Memoir" by Griswold as original matter, without any acknowledgment or inverted commas, save for the paragraph relating to the poet's quarrel with Mr. Allan's second wife; we have, therefore, this conclusion before us: either Dr. Griswold openly plagiarized whole-sale from the recently published but anonymous article, or *he himself was the author of the paper in question.*

Notes

1. *The Train Magazine*, No. 16, vol. iii. pp. 193, &c. [Ingram's note]
2. Rosalie, Edgar Poe's sister and only surviving relative, is stated to be now living at Hicks' Landing, in Virginia, in the most necessitous circumstances. [Ingram's note]
3. In his account of Poe's death, Griswold himself stated Mr. Allan to have been sixty-five.
4. The italics are ours. [Ingram's note]
5. *The Sixpenny Magazine*, No. xx. February 1863. [Ingram's note]

John Henry Ingram, "Edgar Poe," *Temple Bar*, June 1874: 375–380.

"A Mad Man of Letters" (1875)

Francis Gerry Fairfield

In contrast to Ingram, who attempted to present a balanced account of Poe and his writings, Francis Gerry Fairfield's hypothesis, that Poe was epileptic, thus probably mad, stirred controversy among those who had known Poe. Fairfield's article, in *Scribner's Monthly*, is none the less important as an example of the enigma of Poe, that is, what motivated the man and the writer. Like many others, Fairfield thinks that Poe the man shows through Poe's creative writings, not allowing that imagination is more important in creative writing than an author's predilections for food, recreation, or fashions in clothes.

THERE ARE MANY now living who will remember the hero of this story. He was an elegantly molded and rather athletic gentleman, of five feet six, somewhat slender, lithe as a panther, with blue eyes that darkened or lightened as passion or fancy was uppermost, and a head that might have been set on the shoulders of Apollo: a poem in human form, with the exception of his nose, which was abnormally long and lynx-like, and the index of that wondrous keenness of analysis that answered him in place of the deeper philosophical insight generally associated with the critical faculty. He was a poet, too, though poems in human form are not always such, who sang in strange alliterative strains when the passion beset him. But he generally wreaked his soul on the weird prose creations, that, when once the reading was begun, intoxicated the reader like opium, and led him through perplexing mazes of the impossibly beautiful to perplexing conclusions of the impossible; yet, so subtly, and with such rapid and logical progression, that, though the impossibility was apparent from the first, the reader accepted it in the same manner, and for the same reason, that he accepts the disordered fantasies of an opium reverie. On Broadway he was a kind of dandy; in literature, an egotist.

One receives different impressions from the poetry of different men. For Byron, my fancy paints a mocking devil laughing at the world in rhyme.

In reading Shelley, it is as if I saw lightning fall from the clouds, mingled with the incessant rush of rain. His "Lines to an Indian Girl," have, with all this, a tropical luxury of landscape, amid which, here and there, by dark and sluggish streams, I see strange serpents writhing uneasily through the tall, rank grass. With Coleridge, it is as if I stood on the top of a mountain about to break into a volcano. The ear hearkens attentively to the rumble beneath; vapors, seething hot, come up in volumes from long, irregular fissures; here and there spouts up into the dark a tall and lurid jet of flame, mixed with the red-hot bowlders; then there is lull. Reading Tennyson is to me like walking all alone by the side of a broad river of molten gold. Longfellow takes me to walk on hazy moonlit eves, through which trembles the music of far-off lutes. The ear strains to hear, yet cannot hear distinctly; the melody is like something listened to in a dream. These different impressions—and they vary indefinitely, depending upon the associations habitual to the reader—are only so many reflections from the intellectual aura of the poet; and that they exist in the mind of every impressible reader is only another way of saying that every great poet has his prevalent intellectual aura, which constitutes the subtler and more intangible part of his originality—the soul of his poem.

This mad man of letters had his own intellectual aura, and has described its two eras—the one when the June of life was fresh upon him, the other when madness had converted it into a bleak and terrible December—in an allegorical poem of singular power, sobbing with an undercurrent of pathetic despair. Two contrasting stanzas of the poem portray these contrasting eras. In green valleys, tenanted by good angels, once stood a palace;

> "Wanderers in that happy valley
> Through two luminous windows saw
> Spirits moving musically
> To a lute's well-tuned law,
> Roundabout a throne where sitting—
> Porphyrogene!—
> In state his glory well befitting,
> The ruler of the realm was seen."

Unearthly beautiful as this is, preserving the rhythm, and with slight alteration of terms, rather than of imagery, it is converted into something fantastically terrible. The palace is still there;

"And travelers now within that valley
Through the red-litten windows see
Vast forms that move fantastically
To a discordant melody;
While, like a ghastly, rapid, river,
Through the pale door
A hideous throng rush out forever,
And laugh—but smile no more."

Critics have described the aura of this poem as weird. The fancy that comes to my mind as I read it is that of a man who like Anacreon's Cupid, wanders alone under a moonless night, muttering to himself, now with eyes introverted, and scanning his own soul—a dark tarn of Auber in a misty mid-region of Weir; now with lips moving uneasily, as if the recollection of what might have been, but, alas, can never be, passionately haunted him. The lone night-wind, that talks to him in the strange way of night-winds, is full of harrowing voices; ghouls gain from every thicket as he threads the desolate tract through which his journey lies. To him, alas, a life journey! His own face, reflected from the tarn, is ghastly, ashen, haggard, and distorted. Yet, through all run strange refrains of rhythm and rhyme, till the vapors about him thrill and tremble with a music they distort, but cannot wholly suppress. He wanders on, muttering incoherently, till, as in his own ballad of "Ulalume," he has passed to the end of a strange vista, and is stopped by the door of a tomb. Here he enters, and lies down to rest, or to toss uneasily in a kind of disturbed slumber.

Such to me is the impression created by the prevalent aura of the poems and prose tales of Edgar A. Poe, with the exceptions of "Annabel Lee," which has a sweet unearthliness peculiar to itself; of "The Valley of the Many-colored Grass," which is a prose version of the ballad, and of several of the tales dependent upon the analytic faculty for their point and effect, and having, therefore, no special psychical significance. The latter are clever, but—as in the living with M. Dupin in a room forever darkened—betray only glimpses of the psychical traits that rendered Poe what he was, and determined his career, not only in its poetic and literary, but also in its moral aspects.

Was Edgar A. Poe mad? This is the main question that (with occasional critical comments by the way) I propose to discuss in this paper. In other and more exact terms, was he the victim of what Dr. Leblois, of the Asylum of Saint Yon, France, very happily styles *cerebral epilepsy*, and Morel describes as larvated or masked epilepsy? Its main traits consist of sudden attacks of maniacal type, without contemporaneous convulsions such as distinguish the two commoner forms, termed respectively *grand mal* and *petit mal*. Dr. Leblois, in his thesis on the subject, Paris, 1862, uses the phrase *mania périodique* (periodic mania) as synonymous with the larvated form of this very common nervous disorder. It is invariably accompanied by a state of unconscious cerebration—the natural product of a masked or cerebral fit—and, generally, by singular hallucinations, such as seem to form the basis of stories like "The Black Cat," "Ligeia," "Morella," "William Wilson," and the later products of Poe's pen almost without exception. When Mr. Lowell styled the prevalent quality of these productions *fantastic invention*, that eminent writer by no means covered the ground. As instances of fantastic invention, they are too methodical and too distinctly determined by a single idea. There is method in their madness, and method is as inconsistent with fantasy as it is with humor, fantasy's twin-sister. It seems to me that there is also madness in their method, and such madness as accords exactly with the intellectual aura that proverbially accompanies larvated epilepsy, and is one of its distinctive symptoms.

In some cases, for example, the same idea, the same recollection or the same hallucination springs up spontaneously just before the fit. The patient sees flames, fiery circles, red or purple objects, a ghost or a phantom; he hears the sound of bells, or a determined voice always repeating the same word. These ideas and recollections, or these false sensations, variable as they are to individuals, reproduce themselves with singular uniformity, and are the habitual exponents of the malady. They are generally of an alarming and sinister nature. Fantastic figures address the epileptic in words, or mysterious voices of airy origin command him to commit some insane act; so that, says the eminent M. Boisont, "It is probable that many of the misdeeds committed by these unfortunate creatures are but the results of hallucinations of hearing or sight." In cerebral epilepsy the fit is mainly represented by a mental aura of this kind, no paroxysm supervening, and may or may not beget morbid impulses, thus exposing itself in the external form of insanity. To apprehend the nature of the disorder it is only necessary to state the principle long since insisted upon by Marshall Hall, that epileptic paroxysms, like all reflex actions, must always be due to peripheral incitations. This has been demonstrated by physiological experiment. Brain epilepsy is, therefore, a reflex excitability of the brain, kindred to somnambulism, to dreaming, and to the various morbid phenomena now constituting a sort of dreamland to writers of so-called psychological fiction. Its aura, usually involving the sensorial nerves, accounts, no doubt, for many of the morbid phases of imagination that occur in literature. Dr. Maudsley, the eminent English alienist, for example, attributes the visions of Swedenborg—his trances—to periodical attacks of this malady; and several eminent scientific writers regard the trances of Spiritualism and the well-known phenomenon of clairvoyance as kindred to the sensorial impressions of what physicians style artificial epilepsy—that is to say, as epileptic fits induced by artificial means, at the will of the medium.

The same learned gentleman is also very positive in his opinion that the world is indebted for a great part of its originality, and for certain special forms of intellect, to individuals who themselves, directly or indirectly, have sprung from families in which there is some predisposition to epileptic insanity. That which was inspiration to the ancients (even as late as Plato's time) thus appears in medical phraseology as an intellectual aura more or less allied to madness. Aristotle was, perhaps, the first to put the idea (which Maudsley scientifically paraphrases) in the form incipient to modern literature, in the well-known apothegm: "*Nullum magnum ingenium sine mixtura dementiæ*," which Dryden draws out in verse in his famous couplet.

So many times has the maxim of Aristotle reverberated "down the corridors of time," that almost every eminent writer has given it voice in some form or other—Madame de Staël, in her *ébranlement*, to which she refers all that is beautiful in poetry and the arts; Hawthorne, in the remark that the world owes most of its onward impulses to men ill at ease; lastly, Poe, the typical mad man of letters, in the venturesome but acute observation, occurring somewhere in his "Marginalia," that one must look for the most wonderful intellects of the past, not among the traditionally great, but among those who dragged out their lives in madhouses or died at the stake as sorcerers. Moreau de Tours, one of the first alienists in France, elucidates this subject very fully amid the masses of evidence he has collected in reference to epileptic mania, during his long service as an alienist physician at Bicètre. His testimony is coincident with that of Dr. Maudsley, both holding that the mental aura of poetry and of the more original orders of fiction is near akin to that of madness—under which view of the subject the critic must look for the physiological basis of poetic inspiration in a reflex excitability of the brain, distinguished from other forms of periodic excitability by a tendency to rhythmical expression. A poem, then, according to modern psychology, is a cerebral fit of more or less intensity, having little or nothing to distinguish it from masked epilepsy of a mild type, except the single trait or impulse of musical utterance; the outward exponent of a periodical frenzy engendered by constitutional irritability or sensitiveness of nervous organization.

I have crowded these conclusions of modern scientific investigation into a few preliminary paragraphs, by way of showing that there is nothing specially unusual or specially absurd in the propositions to follow, and that the only just test of them is to be sought in the works and life of the unfortunate man to whom they are applied. They are, that Edgar A. Poe was the victim of cerebral epilepsy, and that the majority of his later tales are based upon the hallucinations incident to that malady; furthermore, that he was always aware, in his later years, of impending dementia, and lived and wrote on amid the impenetrable gloom occasioned by his condition; tortured in soul by the imminence of a doom that no medical skill could hope to avert or materially to mitigate, yet exulting at intervals in the strange power thereby imparted to his creations. The events of his singular biography are explainable upon no other hypothesis. The mental aura of all his later productions partakes of the hallucination and delusion of cerebral epilepsy, and has the peculiar cast of morbid sensorial impression medically associated with that disease. In other words, such tales as "The Black Cat," "William Wilson," "Ligeia," and "Morella," not to mention as many more of the same type, appeal to the critic as the frenzied imaginings of a cerebral fit, recollected and wrought out in artistic form at lucid intervals.

The facts of this life, so far as they are accessible, have been thoroughly sifted by his biographers, Mr. Griswold, who knew him well, and Mr. Stoddard, who has tried to find the clue to his irregular perversity in the study of his life and works. So far from having been an habitual drunkard, as is popularly supposed, at the period when he was in the height of his fame a single glass of wine was enough to render him a madman, unconscious of what he did, and hence irresponsible; and it seems to me more than probable that, in many instances, when to the non-medical eye, he appeared to be deliriously intoxicated, he was simply laboring under the effects of a mental aberration incident to such a malady.

The conflicting testimony in his case can only be adjusted in this way. Says a gentleman now resident in Brooklyn, who knew him well, and whose testimony corroborates this view of his delinquencies: "He would often drop in at my house along in the evening, muttering to himself and taking no notice of anybody, and curl himself down on the sofa in the corner of the room, where he would sit for hours sometimes, muttering incoherently. Sometimes he would get up and leave the house without saying a word to me; sometimes, after sitting an hour or two in that way, he would come out of his mood and talk away another hour or two as cozily as possible, then take his leave, like the gentleman he was when the mood wasn't on him." In opposition to this testimony, Willis, who employed him for several months on the "Mirror," soon after his advent in New York, describes him as of habitually quiet and courteous manners and of pleasant and flexible temper. This was during the earlier part of his career. On the other hand, according to Griswold, who knew him later and corroborates the story of his Brooklyn admirer, he was of excitable temper, and in conversation his eloquence was at times superhuman, eye answering to emotion with lurid flashes. Griswold represents him, after the death of Mrs. Poe, as calling at the house of a lady to whom he was engaged to be married, and conducting himself in a manner so gross as to occasion his expulsion from the parlor. The inference is that he was in a state of brutal intoxication. This is possible, but not likely. On the contrary, Mr. C. C. Burr, who was intimate with him at that date, assures me as the result of one of Poe's bursts of confidence, that he accepted the idea of a second wife only for the sake of his mother-in-law and guardian-angel, Mrs. Clemm. The lady in question had some property; and although he could always earn enough with his pen to keep him from want, he was willing and anxious, in order to soften the declining years of one who clung to him through good and evil report, to give another the place of the lamented Virginia, the Annabel Lee of his most beautiful ballad. To this end he visited his affianced on that fatal evening when his malady once more overtook him and pulled down the new castle of life he had erected upon the ruins of the old.

Thus, as the malady made progress, his temper became moodier and moodier, more and more uncertain, until at times it was terrible. In the fall of 1864, William C. Prime, author of "Boat Life in Egypt," and then editor of the "Journal of Commerce," in this city, related to me an incident illustrative of his irascibility during the last years of his life. Soon after the publication of "The Raven," some clever metropolitan critic wrote an article for one of the newspapers of the day, in which he professed to test the poem by the author's own standard—that of the verisimilitude imparted to the supernatural by introducing nothing scientifically improbable. The poem turns, it will be remembered, upon the introduction of a raven through the open window, the bird, after many a flirt and flutter, taking its stand upon the pallid bust of Pallas, just over the door in the poet's room, which is presumed to be on the second or third story, and replying, at proper intervals, to the remarks of the lonesome student, with an ever-repeated "Nevermore,"

> "Caught from some unhappy master, whom unmerciful disaster
> Followed fast and followed faster, till his song one burden bore"—

that burden being the sonorous trisyllable since so familiar with readers and elocutionists. Thus far it was well enough. It was very natural, too, that the raven's solemn repetition of the refrain should finally recall the poet to saddened reminiscences of his lost Lenore, and startle from the nooks and corners they occupy in every human soul a train of superstitious associations. In this mood—half one of fantastic humor, half one of self-torment— the poet begins to question his sable visitor, and ends by requesting it to leave the room, to take its beak from out his heart, also to take its form from off the door; to which multiplied objurgation the raven rejoins, with the same doleful trisyllable, that it will not. The end is that the bird has its way, and continues to occupy the bust of Pallas just above the door;

> "And his eyes have all the seeming of a demon's that is dreaming;
> And the lamplight o'er him streaming throws his shadow on the floor."

Says the perplexed poet in conclusion:

> "And my soul from out that shadow that lies floating on the floor
> Shall be lifted—nevermore."

The question put by the critic was this: How could the raven's shadow be thrown on the floor and lie floating there, when it was sitting on a bust of Pallas above the door? The lamplight in the room would certainly throw it back and upward against the wall, provided the lamp was situated at any point at which, for practical purposes, lamps are ordinarily placed. That this was intended to be the case in the room occupied by lost Lenore's lover is proved by the fact that at the moment the tapping of the raven was heard he was engaged in pondering

"Over many a quaint and curious volume of forgotten lore."

Nor is there any record that the lamp was moved during the interview. It is possible, of course, to suppose a window over the door, and a lamp in the hall at such an angle as to throw the raven's shadow on the floor; but, besides the fact that upper rooms are not usually arranged in that way, if there was light enough in the poet's room to enable him to read, then there was light enough to render the hall-light neutral and the bird shadowless. Again, the poem provides for no such light; and it was part of Poe's theory of criticism that every poem should provide for its own understanding; though poets cannot be expected to furnish the brains to write poems, and the brains to comprehend them also.

"I called on Poe who then had an obscure office in Ann street," said Mr. Prime, after relating the facts, "on the afternoon of the day that the criticism appeared, and never in my life before had I heard such swearing. It was simply appalling—terrible. Such reckless profanity was never listened to outside of a madhouse."

Now it was not pleasant to be caught in his own trap, as Poe really was in this case; but "The Raven" had been received by almost universal consent of the literary world as a signal hit, and the author could amply afford to laugh at the clever squib of his anonymous assailant. Men had acclaimed the poem one of those rare exotics, which, when life presses hard upon him at some sad crisis, are wrung from the poet's soul, rather than written by him. His fame was henceforth a fixed fact, and yet this puny sting had the power to put him in such a very insanity of passion that his oaths were shocking.

Another fact that seems to witness to his epileptic condition is constituted by the habitual lying that marked the later and best-known part of his career. One instance must illustrate the many. I shall take it for granted that the general reader is familiar with that remarkable analytic paper in which he describes the composition of "The Raven," and the plan upon which it was constructed. American literature contains nothing cleverer in its way, and its cleverness is manifold enhanced when it is understood that it is simply and unequivocally fiction, as the actual circumstances under which the poem was written conclusively show.

Poe then occupied a cottage at Fordham—a kind of poet's nook just out of hearing of the busy hum of the city. He had walked all the way from New York that afternoon, and, having taken a cup of tea, went out in the evening and wandered about for an hour or more. His beloved Virginia was sick almost unto death; he was without money to procure the necessary medicines. He was out until about ten o'clock. When he went in, he sat down at his writing table and dashed off "The Raven." He submitted it to Mrs. Clemm for her consideration on the same night, and it was printed substantially as it was written.

This account of the origin of the poem was communicated to me in the fall of 1865 by a gentleman who professed to be indebted to Mrs. Clemm for the facts as he stated them; and in the course of a saunter in the South in the summer of 1867, I took occasion to verify his story by an interview with that aged lady. Let me now drop Mrs. Clemm's version for a paragraph to consider another, resting upon the testimony of Colonel du Solle, who was intimate with Poe at this period, and concurred in by other literary contemporaries who used to meet him of a midday for a budget of gossip and a glass of ale at Sandy Welsh's cellar in Ann street.

Du Solle says that the poem was produced stanza by stanza at small intervals, and submitted by Poe piecemeal to the criticism and emendation of his intimates, who suggested various alterations and substitutions. Poe adopted many of them. Du Solle quotes particular instances of phrase that were incorporated at his suggestion, and thus "The Raven" was a kind of joint-stock affair in which many minds held small shares of intellectual capital. At length, when the last stone had been placed in position and passed upon, the structure was voted complete.

The reconciliation of these conflicting versions lies, possibly, in the hypothesis that he wrote the poem substantially as stated by Mrs. Clemm, and afterward, with the shrewd idea of stimulating expectation a little, or by way of subtle and delicate flattery, submitted it to his friends stanza by stanza, adopting such emendations and substitutions of phrase as tickled his ear or suited his fancy. Such alterations would scarcely affect the general tenor of the text, as Mrs. Clemm first heard it, and, considering the length of the poem, appear to have been very few and of small importance, granting all that Colonel du Solle claims. Besides, it was like him to amuse himself in this way, hoaxing his friends, and then laughing in his sleeve at them.

But, leaving both versions to the reader for what they are respectively worth, there are other considerations fatally destructive to Poe's analytic account of how "The Raven" came to be written; and they are the facts of its intellectual history, happily not dependent on his own testimony. That, either consciously or unconsciously, he was indebted for the thesis of the poem to the raven in "Barnaby Rudge," the publication of which was then recent, is evident from a single passage in his review of that strange novel, in which he suggests that between the raven and the fantastic Barnaby, its master, might have been wrought out an analogical resemblance that would have vastly heightened the effect intended by Mr. Dickens. This analogical resemblance, which he denies to exist in the novel, but which exists there, nevertheless, constitutes the thesis of Poe's great literary hit.

Thus far the thesis of "The Raven." It will be remembered that perhaps "Lenore," which precedes it in his collected works, was written in his youth. "The Raven" appears, then, as its sequel. It was, therefore, the sonorous flow of the dissyllabic "Lenore" that suggested the refrain of "Nevermore," if the ordinary laws of association are to be regarded as of any avail in determining the structure and evolution of a poem. What then becomes of the long train of ratiocination by which he represents himself as fixing upon the word nevermore for the basis of his refrain, and finally upon the raven as the vehicle of its repetition?

To associate any special moral turpitude with acts such as the foregoing would be, if he was epileptic, quite unjust to the memory of one of the most unfortunate beings that ever figured in American literature; for, as any alienist will bear witness, habitual lying is almost invariably a marked symptom of mental aberration, and follows naturally in the train of hallucinations and delusions constituting the intellectual aura of epileptic madness, being sometimes but the direct result of the morbid phenomena that generally accompany the fit, and sometimes the exponent of a morbid impulse, which the epileptic distinguishes as such, but is unable to deny or repress.

His audacious plagiarisms deserve a separate paper as so many examples of his mental habit. His "Colloquy of Monos and Una" was taken almost word for word from an obscure German mystic. His "Dreamland," commencing

> "By a route obscure and lonely,
>   Haunted by ill angels only,
>   Where an Eidolon named Night,"

[276]

palpably paraphrases Lucian's "Island of Sleep." Mr. Prime tells me that for the rhythmical form of "The Raven," which he professes to have evolved by an elaborate process of ratiocination, he was indebted to a medieval ballad. Aside from the mental aura that colors them, the reader has only to make a study of the literature of Mesmerism to identify the thesis and anatomical structure of many a strange, hallucinative tale. His "Eureka"—regarded by Willis as a masterly philosophical creation—contains scarcely an original thought from egotistic exordium to pantheistic finis. He did not think. He was merely a dreamer, having a singular faculty for the coherent organization of his dreams.

An egotist to the core, his fatalism was (as generally occurs in such cases) the moral exponent of his egotism—that is to say, of the deficiency in ethical emotion that egotism always implies. Again, the æsthetic deficiency noticed by Mr. Lowell in his brief but admirable article on Poe, was but the psychical exponent of the same unfortunate deficiency. By an intimate law of our organization (it would require a volume to show how and why) the moral faculty is the realizing faculty, and perversion of the moral natural fatally perverts our perception of reality. Hence it came to pass that to him beauty was synonymous with a kind of sensuous insincerity, and poetry a wild word-music to lull the ear with—a farrago of sweet sounds to tickle the auditory nerve.

Judging from these phenomena, as exhibited in his life and works, he habitually lived in a state bordering upon somnambulism—a disorder that cerebral epilepsy closely resembles. He was a denizen of two worlds and the remark of Mr. Maudsley, that the hereditary madman often gives the idea of a double being, rational and underanged when his consciousness is appealed to, and mastered by his unconscious life when left to his own devices, might have been written after a study of him. He lived and died a riddle to his friends. Those who had never seen him in a paroxysm (among them Mrs. Frances Sargent Osgood) could not believe that he was the perverse and vicious person painted in the circulated tales of his erratic doings. To those who had, he was two men—the one an abnormally wicked and profane reprobate, the other a quiet and dignified gentleman. The special, moral, and mental condition incident to cerebral epilepsy explains these apparent contradictions as felicitously as it elucidates the intellectual and psychical traits of his literature. Its mental phenomena supervene after a stage of incubation more or less prolonged, and the fit generally lasts two or three days. Its supervision is evinced by extreme susceptibility and impulsiveness. Tendency to repeat the same phrase over and over witnesses to the perversion of the will. Distressing delusions and hallucinations prompt to eccentric and impulsive acts. The face is livid, and the eyes have the expression of drunkenness. Monomania may supervene, or dipsomania, or erotomania—as when Poe was expelled from the house of Mr. Allan, his friend and benefactor. Finally, the sufferer falls into a prolonged sleep, easily mistaken for that of drunkenness, and wakes up with re-established sanity.

The victim, after coming to himself, remembers those morbid sensorial phenomena as things that happened in a dream, but seldom talks of them; and thus, as (when its symptoms are not strongly marked) only an experienced observer can detect the inception of the fit, and as it always passes off in sleep, a man may be subject to cerebral epilepsy perhaps for years, and impress his friends as merely capricious and eccentric. Edgar A. Poe was just the man to conceal the malady, and convert its mental phenomena to the purposes of fiction. His sleepless and almost abnormal analytic activity took note, even in the exacerbations of his madness, of each distorted fancy and each morbid impulse as it occurred, instinctively tracing out its relations and linking it to its proper and attendant physical and nervous *secousses*. Not a fluctuating shade of his mania eluded him. He studied the writhing of his lips, flecked with foam, and dissected with critical exactness the disordered associations that flitted through his disturbed brain. With apparent deliberation, and with microscopic fidelity, he transferred the morbid delusions of his fit to his store of recollections, and thus established a tremendous warehouse of weird imaginings and fantastic sensations, to be worked in his serener moods into literary form. In almost any organization, except his, these maniac sensorial impressions would have overwhelmed and swamped the analytic faculty; but, in his case, so abnormally was it developed, and so fixed the habit of analyzing, that it could not be unseated. Thus it constituted the only part of him that was never mad, and rendered him in the throes of the cerebral attack, not only a double being when his consciousness was appealed to, but a double being to himself—conscious analytically of the unconscious life that had mastered his brain and nervous system. Hence results the fact that at first reading, and until subjected to critical tests his creations impress the reader like those of a person addicted to the opium habit, and have an affinity with those of Baudelaire and

[278]

De Quincey. That is to say, he writes like a dreamer rational in his dreams. With this superficial trait, however, the resemblance ceases.

From this source seems to have arisen the wonderful power in painting a monomania that distinguishes his later reveries, and is particularly illustrated by such productions as "The Imp of the Perverse" and "The Masque of the Red Death," and in that singular narrative in which he kills an old man because the old man's eye vexes him. It was the ground of his marvelous minuteness of psychological analysis, of the peculiar facility with which he traced a morbid impulse to its root, and of the terrible felicity of imagination that enabled him to follow out, step by step, link by link, the hideous trains of associations set in motion by madness. In fiction spun from his own consciousness, as Poe spun his, no man can outpass the limits of his own subjective experiences. They bind him to himself on every hand; he can only project what he finds within him. In observational fiction, on the contrary, the case is different; a man may study madness for the purpose of painting it, as the greatest actress of this age studied death agonies in the hospitals of Paris, that her stage throes might be true to nature. There exists no evidence, save the absurd story of "Dr. Tarr and Professor Fether," that Poe ever observed madness from life with a view to artistic perfection of detail. He seems, on the other hand, to have found it in him and to have pursued it through all its hideous windings, as an element of his own consciousness.

His most powerful tale, "The Fall of the House of Usher," in which he traces the subjective and objective phenomena of epilepsy from origin to final catastrophe, symptom by symptom, sensation by sensation, delusion by delusion, introduces the psychological series; and is such as could have been written by no man with whom the physiological and psychological traits of the malady had not become personal matters of fact—not even by an alienist who had made them subjects of life-study; certainly, by no *littérateur* who had not observed and traced them, day by day, in his own person. There existed at that date no ponderous tomes of the literature of epilepsy, such as have been developed during the last thirty years by Delasiauve, Boileau de Castelnau, Falret, Morel, Legrand du Saulle, Trousseau, Leblois, Dumesnil, Marshall Hall, Van Swieten, Moreau de Tours, Dr. Maudsley, and many others. What is now styled medical psychology then consisted of crude metaphysical speculations, while madness was a metaphysical dreamland, and the unconscious cerebration of epilepsy—

with its trances—was dimly supposed to have a supernatural origin. The conclusion from these premises is obvious. With all the materials at hand, which thirty years of careful observation have supplied, no man living, not subject to the malady it paints, could write a "Fall of the House of Usher;" and if critics are to suppose that Poe elaborated his story without facts upon which to proceed, then they must accept the miracle, that by a simple process of analytic ratiocination, he anticipated all the discoveries and observations of the last quarter of a century. If, on the other hand, he was subject to the malady, the story explains itself and furnishes the clue to the fantastic invention incident to all his tales of monomania, through every one of which, thinly draped and enveloped in impenetrable gloom, stalks his own personality—a madman muttering to himself of his own morbid imaginings. This haunting consciousness becomes, with the progress of the malady, an awful *doppelgänger*, as in "William Wilson;" an imp of the perverse, as in the story of that name; a second soul after the loss of his true poetic soul, Ligeia, as in the story of "Ligeia," yet a second soul from when at fitful intervals rises the image of the first; or a second Morella, as in the tale of that title, drawing her nutrition from the dead corpse of the first, and developing into womanhood with strange suddenness—living, yet the image of the dead—dead, yet identical with the living. Or, again, as in the "Valley of the Many-colored Grass," he lives in happy solitude with his true soul, Eleonora, upon whose bosom is written ephemera. She dies and is buried from sight in the valley; and the scene shifts, and he finds himself in a new world of bustle and tumult, with the haunting memory of the dead pursuing him amid mazes of the living. It is the black cat he cannot kill—the raven that croaks a Nevermore in answer to all his yearnings for the beautiful that once might have been, but is now a lost opportunity.

Were it possible to ascertain the exact order of their production, it would, I think, be no very difficult task to construct from Poe's tales a kind of psychological biography illustrating the progress of the mental alienation, beginning with the formation of that morbid habit of introspective analysis which grew upon him with years, and finally ended in cerebral disease. A map of the general order present three well-marked eras of literary production, having distinctive traits, but merging gradually the one into the other:

First. A period during which he seems to depend for artistic effect upon minuteness of detail. To this type belong "A Descent into the Maelstrom,"

"The Gold Bug," "The Adventures of one Hans Pfaall" (imitated from the "Moon Hoax"), the "Narrative of A. Gordon Pym," "The Facts in the Case of M. Valdemar," and some others of less importance. The prevalent motive running through them is that incident to the literary hoax. The egotist glories in his capacity for deception.

Secondly. A period during which minute analysis takes the place of mere minuteness of detail. "Marie Roget" and kindred productions appertain to this period, which gradually merges into the third and last. The egotist now exults in his capacity for the intellectual prestidigitation.

Thirdly. A period marked by tales of morbid introspection, which commences with "The Fall of the House of Usher," in which "The Haunted Palace" occurs as a ballad sung by the epileptic hero, and proceeds with the series I have elsewhere named. They are distinguished from the rest by the use of the *first person singular* and by the prevalence of a mental aura of the type so familiar to physicians with whom madness is a specialty. True to himself to the end, he now takes pleasure in startling the world with his own hallucinations.

His last poem, the ballad of "Ulalume," first printed in 1846, and shorn of its final stanza in the existing edition of his poems, appears to embody in an allegorical form the terrible truth that rendered his later years years of secret and gnawing sorrow. It commences:

> "The skies, they were ashen and sober,
> The leaves they were crispèd and sere—
> The leaves they were withering and sere;
> It was night in the lonesome October
> Of my most immemorial year;
> It was down by the dim lake of Auber,
> In the misty mid-region of Weir—
> It was down by the dark tarn of Auber
> In the ghoul-haunted woodland of Weir."

It is here through a Titanic valley that the poet wanders all night with Psyche (his soul), amid silent and moody trees, himself silent and moody. The moon rises with liquescent and nebulous luster. The poet and his Psyche—the latter stricken with a strange tremor and imploring him not to linger—toil on by moonlight, he pacifying her by expatiating upon the beauty of Astarte's bediamonded crescent, she alternately listening and sobbing with an agony of dread. It is near morning—that is to say, the night is senescent, and the star-dials point to the morn—when the two find themselves at the end of the vista of the valley, adown which gloats the low-hanging and duplicate-horned moon, and are stopped by the door of a tomb. He asks: "What is written, sweet sister, on the door of the legended tomb?" Psyche answers: "Ulalume, Ulalume; 'tis the vault of thy lost Ulalume." Then he remembers that it is the anniversary of her burial, and the poem leaves him at her grave.

Muffled in an unusual number of thicknesses of elaborate rigmarole in rhyme, this is the pith of a ballad, which borrows interest from its position as the last exponent of the perpetual despair that enshrouded Poe's manhood, and the last visit of his tortured soul to the tomb of his lost beautiful, typified by the dead Ulalume. The *geist* of the ballad—that which transfuses it with meaning, and redeems it from the criticism so often passed upon it, that it is mere words—lies solely in the fact of its interpretation with a kind of psychological significance. Thus sang he, then died. It is also the exponent of that passion for refrain and repetition, which itself symptomatic of madness, grew upon him with the progress of his malady, and thus appears as one of its morbid results. The same passion infects his later prose, and renders it in many instances a wearisome series of dashes.

"Had Poe but lived," say many. Believing that intellectual decay had already laid its hand on him when he died, and that he was despairingly aware of it, I am not sorry he went so early. This last poem—a vagary of mere words—seems to me, in its elaborate emptiness, very lucidly to evince growing mental decrepitude.

The causes that led to his madness demand a brief consideration. Did he inherit an epileptic predisposition? This question naturally occurs first. His father was a man of irregular habits, who married an obscure actress and dropped into his grave, leaving to the tender mercies of the world at large a bright, sensitive boy. Of what malady he died it is now impossible to ascertain; but that the habitual use of alcoholic stimulants prevailed with the elder Poe or his actress wife, is evident from the fact that the son was a dipsomaniac of the type having paroxysms of drunkenness, though not habitual drinkers. Now, according to Dr. Anstie ("Hereditary Connections between Nervous Diseases"), "Of all depressing agencies alcohol has the most decided power to impress the nervous centers of a progenitor with a neurotic type, which will necessarily be transmitted under various forms, and with increasing fatality, to his descendants." This learned master in psychological medicine utters the foregoing as the result of personal observation, expressing the opinion that alcohol is capable, in a generation or two of fatally perverting the organization of the nervous system.

Under such auspices Edgar A. Poe was ushered into the world. Inheriting an impulsive and undisciplined nature, his brain life as a boy constantly exposes a preponderance of emotion over steady intellectual work. His first volume of poems, written how early it is impossible to know except from his own witness, evinces this fact very conclusively. With a passion for the beautiful in its sensuous forms, they are the exponents of a vague, mystic, and oppressive unrest; of matured passions with immature intellect; of an emotional activity seizing with mad hand upon the problems of life, while yet the mind was incapable of apprehending, still less of comprehending, them. He dreams well, beautifully, though his numbers halt a little now and then; but his work is only dream work. Great room for impulses to grow and wax ungovernable in a boyhood such as this.

As he grew older, this want of intellectual training seems to have forced itself upon his attention. Sent to college, he had found his work interfering with his dreams. Hence he ran away. Once matriculated in the great college of life, he tried to atone with cunning devices for lack of mental culture. His dreams now interfered with his work; rather, he had dreamed so long that he was incapable of honest work. Hence mentally he never grew up. For the altitude and sincerity of intellectual manhood were, on the other hand, substituted puppet-show cleverness and analytic feats of the solve-a-puzzle kind. Thus equipped he came upon the stage, scarcely caring what his words mean, so that they sounded well: not as a man, but as an extremely clever actor of manhood. Without insight, to him the only thing real in life was the stage scenery. Years of vagabond life and privation followed: of alternate work and wassail. The inherited devil of dipsomania, dormant only for a little while, asserted itself. Now and then in a tussle he threw it; generally it threw him. But, with whatsoever result the wrestle ended, it contributed its quantum to the fatal perversion of a nervous system hereditarily determined in the direction of epilepsy. The late J. R. Thompson, among his reminiscences of Poe, witnesses to the fact that at this period he could take an extraordinary dose of brandy without being at all affected by it; but as the nervous degeneration went on, and the epileptic tendency developed, he became (as is generally the case) so sensitive to alcoholic stimulants that a thimbleful of sherry transformed him into a madman, with the unconscious cerebration and the morbidly vicious impulses, the sullenness alternating with fury, associated with epileptic insanity. This was about the date of "The Fall of the House of Usher," and of that singular allegory of madness, "The Haunted Palace." He now abstained, except at fitful intervals. But the malady, accelerated by the habit of morbid introspection which was its exponent, and gathering force from somewhat at least of hereditary predisposition, went on eating into his brain until sanity was only a recollection, and in the gutter he fell and died.

Francis Gerry Fairfield, "A Mad Man of Letters," *Scribner's Monthly*, October 1875: 690–699.

From "The Poet Not an Epileptic" (1875)

F. R. M.

Another respondent challenges Fairfield.

CONTRARY TO FAIRFIELD, epilepsy is not insanity, and his ideas regarding poems are also incorrect.

From F. R. M., "The Poet Not an Epileptic," *New York Tribune*, 18 October 1875 (Supplement): 2.

From "Poe, Critic, and Hobby. A Reply to Mr. Fairfield . . ." (1875)

SARAH HELEN WHITMAN

Sarah Helen Whitman, whom Poe had been nearly ready to marry some time after Virginia's death and who was author of *Edgar Poe and His Critics* (1860), proved helpful in correcting the image of Poe initiated by Griswold and picked up by others, many among whom knew actually little about Poe. She provides a good antidote to Fairfield's misapprehensions concerning Poe. Mrs. Whitman probably had better firsthand knowledge than Fairfield concerning Poe's writings. The *Tribune* Editor reinforced Mrs. Whitman's opinions concerning Fairfield and Poe.

SIR: Mr. F. G. Fairfield, a gentleman who has had the temerity to pass "ten years among spiritual mediums" in the cause of science, having demonstrated that they are all more or less afflicted with epileptic mania, has recently turned his attention to poets and men of inspirational genius, and finds that they, too, from Ezekiel to Æschylus, from Æschylus to Coleridge, are all as mad as March hares. If there is method in their madness, there is also madness in their method. He frankly confesses in his book of mediums that he has himself had personal experience of the malady. He has studied it in all its phases. He intimates that "habitual lying" is one of its most trustworthy exponents. I by no means wish to undervalue Mr. Fairfield's researches in the nebulous atmosphere of peripheral nerve-auras. They are valuable and interesting, but does not his theory threaten to cover too much ground?

In the October number of *Scribner's* this gentleman has an article entitled "A Mad Man of Letters," in which he selects the author of "The Raven" as a favorable specimen of the epileptic type. Assuming chronic lying as symptomatic of the disease, he gravely quotes the following story in evidence of Poe's habitual mendacity. A single instance, he says, may suffice to prove the many. Here is the instance: A gentleman who professed to have received the "facts" from Mrs. Clemm told him that Poe, once on a time, after walking all the way from New-York to Fordham, swallowed up a cup of tea, sat down to his writing-desk, and dashed off "The Raven" substantially as it is now printed, and submitted it to Mrs. Clemm as the result of his evening's incubation! Unmindful of the fact that Poe did not reside in Fordham until long after "The Raven" was printed and published, Mr. Fairfield naively accepts this story as a choice bit of veritable history, illustrative of Poe's epileptic tendency to habitual lying. For how could "The Raven" have been composed at a single sitting, when Mr. Fairfield assures us that he has the evidence of Poe's literary contemporaries on this matter—gentlemen who were in the habit of meeting him at midday for a cozy chat in Sandy Welch's cellar. And did not these gentlemen assure him that the poem was produced line by line, stanza by stanza, and submitted by Poe, piecemeal, to the criticism and emendation of the Ann-st. clique?—gentlemen who doubtless "know a hawk from a handsaw when the wind was southerly," and who suggested many valuable alterations and substitutions. One of these gentlemen, says Mr. Fairfield, has even pointed out to me particular instances of phrases that were incorporated at his own suggestion, "showing that 'The Raven' was a kind of joint-stock operation in which many minds held small shares of intellectual property." After this we may not hope that the gentlemen who assisted at the incubation of this remarkable fowl in Sandy Welch's cellar will come forward in a body to claim their respective shares in this piece of joint-stock property, thus setting at rest forever all questions as to "Who wrote 'The Raven?'" "Was 'The Raven' a Persian fowl?" "Whence came the manuscript found in Mr. Shaver's barn?" and other interrogations of like import which have from time to time agitated the purlieus of Parnassus.

Having disposed of "The Raven," Mr. Fairfield applies his scalpel to Poe's wonderful poem of "Ulalume," calling it, in his haphazard way, "his last poem—a mere rigmarole in rhyme, exhibiting in its elaborate emptiness the last stages of mental decrepitude and decay." "Thus sang he, then died," exclaims this careful and conscientious commentator. On the contrary, "thus sang he," then wrote "Eureka," "The Bells," "Annabel Lee," and other of his most memorable poems. But when an "alienist"—I believe that is the correct word—mounts his hobby and rides rough-shod in pursuit of an epileptic subject to illustrate a favorite theory, he cannot be expected to pay much attention to such hard facts as happen to lie in his way.

The critic does not, in this instance, accuse the unhappy author of plagiarism; does not even remotely insinuate that the poem has been slicked up in Sandy Welch's cellar. It was altogether too rough a specimen for the contemporaries to have taken stock in. If Mr. Fairfield, who is not without poetic insight, had thought less of his theory and more of his subject, he might have better apprehended what he is pleased to call the *geist* of the poem; might have seen that it was not the "low-hanging moon," but Venus "Astarte"—the crescent star of hope and love, that, after a night of horror, was seen in the Constellation Leo:

> "Coming through the lair of the Lion
> As the star-dials hinted of morn."

He might have seen the forlorn heart hailing it as a harbinger of happiness yet to be, hoping against hope, until, when the planet was seen to be rising over the tomb of a lost love, hope itself was rejected as a cruel mockery, and the dark angel conquered. He might have also discerned in this "empty rigmarole of rhyme" something of that ethical quality which an eloquent interpreter of Poe's genius, in the July number of *The British Quarterly*, finds in this strange and splendid phantasy. Like the Episychidian of Shelley, it is a poem for poets, and will not readily give up "the heart of the mystery" to aliens and "alienists."

When I compare the disparaging tone of this article with a paragraph from the same writer which appeared in *The Boston Radical* for April, 1871, I am perplexed to account for the discrepancy. "'The Raven,' 'The Ancient Mariner,' and 'Queen Mab,' in their ghostly energy and magnificence of beauty, in their subtle etheriality of imagery, in the weird burst of moaning minor of their cadences, are among the most powerful creations of the imagination, and are, in ratio to their power, remarkable for a certain sublimation of the subjective, and dependent upon it for their effect." And again: "In the fiction of Brontë, Hugo, Poe, Hawthorne, Dickens, and other masters of the century, we find an intense subjectivity." How happens it that one of the masters of the century is now labeled, "A Mad Man of Letters." His "sublimation of the subjective" is now "epileptic egotism." "He was an egotist to the core." "In his 'Eureka' there is scarcely an original thought. Poe did not think, he was simply a dreamer." "Sent to college, he found his work interfering with his dreams. Hence he ran away (!) and afterward tried to atone for his lack of mental culture by cunning devices and feats of the solve-a-puzzle kind. He was incapable of honest work."

If this piece of amateur surgery is a specimen of "honest work," one must needs borrow Æsop's lantern to find out its honesty.

From Sarah Helen Whitman, "Poe, Critic, and Hobby. A Reply to Mr. Fairfield. Certain Hard Facts Which Have Been Overlooked in the Search for an Epileptic Subject." 29 September 1875, *New York Daily Tribune*, 13 October 1875: 2.

From [Editorial Notice of Reply to Fairfield] (1875)

[ANONYMOUS]

> This editorial note argues that Mrs. Whitman's response to Fairfield seems authoritative.

MR. FRANCIS GERRY FAIRFIELD could scarcely have expected that on the eve of the dedication of the Poe monument in Baltimore, his theory that the poet was the victim of cerebral epilepsy would pass unchallenged. We print in another column a caustic reply to his essay, in which he is represented as mounting his hobby and riding roughshod over the facts of the case. Whether there was method in the madness or madness in the method, one thing is certain: in regard to the "hard facts" of that mysterious career, Mr. Fairfield's critic knows whereof she [Mrs. Whitman] speaks.

From [Editorial Notice of Reply to Fairfield] *New York Daily Tribune*, 13 October 1875: 4.

From *"Edgar Allan Poe.* A Letter . . ." (1875)

FRANCIS GERRY FAIRFIELD

> Undaunted by negative responses to his article, "A Mad Man of Letters,"
> Fairfield attempts to correct Mrs. Whitman's chronology of Poe's poems,
> and to offer his own ideas about the art, or lack thereof, in some of Poe's
> works, most notably, perhaps, in his dismissal of "Ulalume" as all sound but
> no sense. Many other readers of Poe would strongly disagree with Fairfield's
> assessment of that poem. Fairfield's dating of "Annabel Lee" and "The Bells"
> is also inaccurate. Such inaccuracies place Fairfield in ranks with others who
> misunderstood the chronology of Poe's writings.

To the editor of the *Tribune.*

Sir: While no one can more thoroughly appreciate the delicacy with which
controversy with a lady should be conducted, I must, nevertheless, solicit
the opportunity of a brief rejoinder to the communication from "S.H.W.,"
printed in to-day's TRIBUNE concerning the article on Poe. Passing personal matters, it seems clear to me, from my own memoranda, that your
correspondent is in error as to the order of Poe's poems and other literary
products. Let me give you a synopsis: "Al Aaraaf, Tamerlane, and Minor
Poems, Baltimore, 1829;" "MS. found in a Bottle" took premium in 1833;
connected with *Southern Literary Messenger* from 1835 to 1837; "Narrative
of Arthur Gordon Pym of Nantucket," Harper & Brothers, 1838; "Tales of
the Grotesque and Arabesque," a collection of scattered magazine stories,
Philadelphia, 1840; became editor of *Graham's Magazine,* and wrote the
"Gold Bug," the "Murders of the Rue Morgue," and other singular analytic
tales, besides completing a development of the plot of Dickens's "Barnaby
Rudge" for that periodical; removed to New-York in 1844, and was employed by Morris & Willis on *The Mirror*; "Raven" published in *Colton's
Whig Review* in February, 1845.

"Annabel Lee" and "The Bells" appear to have been written previous to
1847. The "Fall of the House of Usher" had appeared already, and "Ligeia,"

"Morella," and other psychological tales had been printed. His "Eureka" was delivered as a lecture in 1848. It is words, words, words. Any person who will compare it with the various mesmeric speculations of that day, the prototypes of the literature of modern Spiritualism, will find that it contained scarcely an original thought, although abundant in original expressions. The habit of repetition is one of its peculiar features. The first vestige of Poe's "Ulalume" I am able to find occurs in *The Home Journal*, Saturday, Jan. 1, 1848—the year before his tragic death—under the Willisesque caption of "Epicureanism of Language." A brief paragraph in the manner of Willis prefaces the ballad, states that it is copied from *The American Review*, describes it as a poem full of beauty and oddity in sentiment and versification, and inquires, "Who is the author?" The final stanza, elided in the Griswold edition of his poems, is unchanged, and illustrates the vague and empty nature of the poem, and my view of the case more felicitously than all the rest. It runs as follows:

> Said we then—the two, then—"Ah, can it
> Have been that the woodlandish ghouls—
> The pitiful, the merciful ghouls—
> To bar up our way and to ban it
> From the secret that lies in these wolds—
> From the thing that lies hidden in these wolds—
> Has drawn up the specter of a planet
> From the limbo of lunary souls—
> This sinfully scintillant planet
> From the Hell of the planetary souls?"

It would require all the poetic insight of a confirmed Spiritualist to find any meaning in this absurd synthesis of sonorous syllables. If your correspondent has such an insight, there is ample verge for exercising it here. As to my own inconsistencies, I shall frankly confess them. Those who know me are well aware that there was a date when my admiration of Poe was rather excessive. But one outgrows some things, and I find myself at 35 denying the jurisdiction of my former gods. The conductor of *Scribner's Monthly*, years since, when connected with *The Springfield Republican*, once returned certain crudities of mine with the remark that "only one man ever wrote in that way, and he was mad." And having had my attack of Poe fever—and a long one it was—I hope I may be permitted to say that I have recovered, without leaving the delirious ravings of the attack quoted as against my mature and sober opinions.

Francis Gerry Fairfield, *"Edgar Allan Poe*. A Letter from Francis Gerry Fairfield. The Order of His Writings—A Change of View," *New York Daily Tribune*, 18 October 1875 (Supplement): 2.

From "The Personality of Poe" (1877)

CHARLES FREDERICK BRIGGS

Charles F. Briggs, perhaps better known by his nickname "Harry Franco" (derived from his novel by that title), got to know Poe during the latter's last years in the New York City area. He initially admired Poe, but after working with him on the *Broadway Journal* he displayed an antagonistic attitude toward Poe. This reminiscence, published long afterward, is interesting both because of its negative portrayal of its subject and because it nevertheless supplies some important biographical information. Fittingly, Briggs's portrait concludes this book because of the multiple perspectives it accords to Poe's personality. Briggs also reiterates what Poe himself would have relished, possibly moreso if it were not accompanied by stinging criticism of Poe the man—that Poe was, first and foremost, remembered as a poet, precisely what he wished to be, a poet. Circumstances in Poe's economic life often diverted his pathways toward that status, and Briggs does not let readers forget that Poe was also well known as a critic and fiction writer. In the true spirit of American literary nationalism that prevailed during Poe's literary career, and which lasted in some quarters long after that life had ended, Briggs singles out "The Gold-Bug" as the only specific title from Poe's fiction as if it were the chief work among his fictions for which he was remembered.

THACKERAY SAID, in his lecture on Dean Swift, that he would have been willing to be the boot-black of Shakespeare for the privilege of looking in his face; or to have been the pot-boy of Harry Fielding merely to have been spoken to by the great novelist as he came out of his room. A similar feeling has been expressed by every one capable of understanding the productions of a man of genius . . . That there are a good many people who think it would have been a happiness to see the face of that mad genius who wrote "Annabel Lee," and "Lenore," and "The Raven," and "The Gold Bug" [this writer] has abundant reasons for believing.

But the author of "The Raven" was not a pleasant person to know well. Those who knew him only by his fascinating poems and his strange, mysterious stories can form no idea of his triple character. There is hardly a difference of opinion in relation to the place he is entitled to occupy as an author; no one questions his power as a poet, his originality and skill as a romancer, or his capacity as a critic. All concede that as a literary artist he is entitled to rank among the greatest of American writers, if not of contemporary writers in the English language. He stands in no need of defense or apology as an author, and he cared for nothing else than a literary reputation. If he were alive, to read the angry discussions that have been going on ever since his melancholy death respecting his morals and manners, he would laugh scornfully to think that anybody should deem it worth while to waste a word on a point which to him was a matter of perfect indifference. But, it has been a point of honor with the onetime admirers of Poe's genius to defend his character against what they choose to consider the malignant slanders of Dr. Griswold . . . The people who attempt those angry refutations of undeniable facts really know nothing about Poe beyond what they find in his published writings, and there is nothing in them that affords the slightest clew to the peculiarities of his character. He took good care that no one should ever learn anything about him from what he chose to give the world, and he was never so fanciful and so inventive as when he pretended to give little scraps of his personal experiences and surroundings. His "Annabel Lees," his "Leonores" [*sic*] were, like his "Ravens," purely creations of his imagination. He loved no one, though the objects of his hatred were many; and, if Dr. Griswold had not been restrained by a foolish delicacy, he might have given some startling evidences of the utter contempt which the poet entertained for persons who trustingly believed they were passionately beloved by him. He could write the tenderest and touching letters, which he would bedabble with real tears, as he folded the paper, to women upon whom he had no other designs than an intention of sending his wife or her mother to them to solicit a loan of $50. Some of these women fondly believed in his passionate infatuation for them; but some others were cruelly undeceived before he died.

There are but few persons living who knew Poe sufficiently well to have seen him in both sides of his personality, and they are disinclined to tell what they know. There were some, who knew him only on one side; who were utterly incredulous to his appearance on the other, and who preferred not to know him in any other character than that of the decorous, genial, respectful, and accomplished gentleman in which he was presented to them. The late N. P. Willis, who had seen him frequently, who enjoyed his conversation, and had found him always exact in his appointments, strictly honorable in the fulfillment of his engagements, scrupulously neat in his attire, and deferential in his manners, could not believe that he was ever any different. Some of the ladies who have volunteered their testimony to the gentleness and sweetness of his manners, to the tender devotion which he manifested for his delicate wife, and the fondness he exhibited for his mother-in-law, honestly believed all they wrote, no doubt, and looked upon the wicked Dr. Griswold as a dreadful ogre, who wanted to represent their angel poet as a demon.

Of all the biographies that have been published of "The Raven" that by Mr. Stoddard is probably the best; and, as he seems to have been influenced by no other than a sincere disposition to discover and narrate the truth, it is greatly to be regretted that he could not have had access to the materials which were left by Dr. Griswold, and which, it is understood, are now in the possession of that much abused gentleman's last wife, or of her brother. When Poe died, all of his literary remains were placed, by his aunt, Mrs. Clemm, the mother of his wife, in the hands of Dr. Griswold, with full permission for him to make such use of them as he saw fit. She knew the relations which had existed between the Doctor and her "darling Eddie," and thought him the most fitting person to be intrusted with the delicate duty of selecting from them such portions as might be of interest to the public. How the Doctor performed his duty, and how he had been abused for it, need not be considered here. But the great pity is that illness prevented Dr. Griswold from fulfilling the duty that he owed to himself, as well as to Poe, of giving the world a fuller and more comprehensive biography, which would have been a complete justification of what he had already done, and might, perhaps, have satisfied the admirers of the poet, who find it hard to believe that he was possessed of two such contradictory characters as he seems to have borne.

But why, it may be asked, exhibit any one except in the best phases of his character? When Queen Elizabeth sat for her portrait, she ordered the Italian artist who had undertaken to put her unlovely features upon canvas to paint her face without any shadows. Shadows, she knew, would reveal her wrinkles, of which she was not in the least vain. But when honest old Oliver Cromwell sat for his picture, he ordered the artist to paint him just as he was, "warts and all." There are many people, however, who do not like to have the whole truth told about themselves, or about other people, if the whole contains any unpleasant facts. . . . In the case of Poe a different course has been followed, and consequently no biography of him has any pretentions to completeness and his character has been strangely misunderstood. Such a shower of abuse upon the head of Dr. Griswold, for his moderate revelations to the author of "The Raven," that no one has since had the courage to do for him what Oliver Cromwell wanted, and painted him as he was, warts and all. The warts have been omitted, and the world has had one of the most remarkable portraits that it was likely ever to possess.

In personal appearance Poe was extremely interesting, and it was hardly possible to meet him in his sober moments and converse with him without being strongly impressed in his favor. His remarkably shaped head, high and broad forehead, his pale complexion, large grey eyes, which always had a sad and tearful look, and his finely-formed mouth—all indicated delicacy and refinement, of thought and tenderness of feeling. He never laughed and rarely smiled; but when he did smile there was always a partially-suppressed expression of sadness, which might be easily interpreted as a sardonic reproach for his levity. He spoke with great precision, as though he was dictating to an amanuensis, and never for a moment gave utterance to what might be thought a spontaneous or unconsidered idea. His dress was always scrupulously neat and free from anything bizarre or eccentric. He never wore an ornament of any description and wholly avoided colors. His manners were free from affectation, and although they were graceful and unrestrained, yet he was perfectly respectful and deferential, and made every one feel as if he had considered himself under a personal obligation to those who had the patience to listen to him. Such was his appearance when he was free from the excitement of a controversy and when he had not been disturbed by any intoxicating drink.

Those who had seen him only in his serene moments were amazed and overwhelmed with disgust when he presented himself before them either during the wild excitement of a debauch or in the dreary moments when he was shattered in strength, feeble, and nervously striving to get the better of his conscious degradation. After drinking much less liquor than an ordinary man could have easily carried off without showing any ill effects from it, he was wild in his looks, insolent and aggressive in his language, reckless as to his personal appearance, filthy to an offensive degree in his talk, and in every respect intolerably indecent. In such a condition he would have been a terror to his wife and aunt; and she had on several occasions been compelled to call for help to prevent his committing violence upon the unresisting and helpless creature whom he represented as loving so tenderly. When he was recovering from these fits of intemperance he was one of the most pitiful objects conceivable—ghastly in his countenance, filthy in dress, weak, trembling, and piteous in valor—a disgusting and distressing object to look upon and a person to be shunned and avoided. No one who had ever seen him in this degraded condition could ever forget it or have any desire to see him again; and there was no difficulty for those who had been so unlucky as to be the witnesses of his degradation to believe the stories of his wretched state when he was found on that dismal, wintry night, in Baltimore, on which he died.

But his dissipations—which were not intentional, for he was extremely temperate both in his diet and drink, unless he was subjected to strong temptations—were not the repulsive traits of his character. What rendered him so obnoxious to those who knew him intimately were his treachery to his friends, his insincerity, his utter disregard of his moral obligations, and his total lack of loyalty and nobleness of purpose. He aimed at nothing, thought of nothing, and hoped for nothing but literary reputation; and in this respect he gained all that he aspired to, and his friends should be satisfied to know that he accomplished all he labored for, and not endeavor to compel the world to award him a character which he never coveted and held in supreme contempt.

He was an artist, pure and simple. He aimed at nothing beyond artistic expression, and he regarded all didactic poetry as absurd in the extreme. To appear, and not to be, was what he aimed at. When he made his first entrance into a literary circle in New York he created at once a most favorable impression. It was at a reception at the house of Mrs. Kirkland, where there were a good many of the New York literati, not one of whom had ever before seen him, and only a few had ever read anything of his writings except "The Raven," which had just been published in Colton's *Whig Review*. He had not been long in New York, and there was great curiosity to see the writer of that wonderful poem. He conducted himself with as much propriety on the occasion as a young lady at her first party, and astonished everybody by his perfect good manners, gentleness, and ready replies to all questions.

But, notwithstanding the popularity of "The Raven" and the brilliant review of Mrs. Browning's poems which he published soon after, he could not succeed in attracting an audience when he delivered a lecture on American poets, and he was greatly exasperated at his failure. His popularity increased; but evil times fell upon him, indiscreet friends led him into rash undertakings, he lost his wife, and at last the end came on that dismal wintry night in Baltimore, when he died at the zenith of his fame, and when a prospect of better days than he had ever known was opening to him. But it is unnecessary to repeat here the melancholy story of his last days, for it is already too familiar to the readers of his productions.

From Charles Frederick Briggs, "The Personality of Poe," *Independent*, 13 December 1877: 1–2.

Bibliography

Allen, Hervey. *Israfel: The Life and Times of Edgar Allan Poe*, 2 vols. New York: George H. Doran, 1926. Revised edition New York: Farrar and Rinehart, 1934.

Allen, Hervey, and Thomas Ollive Mabbott. *Poe's Brother*. New York: George H. Doran, 1926.

Eddings, Dennis W. "Theme and Parody in 'The Raven.'" In *Poe and His Times: The Artist and His Milieu*, edited by Benjamin F. Fisher. Baltimore: Edgar Allan Poe Society, 1990. 209–217.

Ellmann, Richard, ed. *The Artist as Critic: Critical Writings of Oscar Wilde*. New York: Random House, 1968.

Fields, M. B. *Memories of Many Men and of Some Women*. New York: Harper's, 1875.

Fisher, Benjamin F. *The Cambridge Introduction to Edgar Allan Poe*. Cambridge, NY: Cambridge University Press, 2008.

———. "Edgar Allan Poe." In *Research Guide to Biography and Criticism*, 2 vols., edited by Walton Beacham. Washington, DC: Research Publishing Company, 1985. 1: 922–926.

Gill, William Fearing. *The Life of Edgar Allan Poe*. New York: Dillingham, 1877.

Griswold, Rufus W., ed. *The Poets and Poetry of America*. Philadelphia: Carey and Hart, 1842.

———. *The Works of the Late Edgar Allan Poe*, 4 vols. New York: J. S. Redfield, 1850–1856.

Hammond, Alexander. "On Poe Biography: A Review Essay." *ESQ: A Journal of the American Renaissance* 38 (1982): 197–211.

Harrison, James A., ed. *The Complete Works of Edgar Allan Poe*, 17 vols. New York: Thomas Y. Crowell, 1902. Reprint New York: AMS Press, 1965; reprint, with "Introduction" by Floyd Stovall, New York: AMS Press, 1979.

Hart-Davis, Rupert. *The Letters of Oscar Wilde*. New York: Harcourt, Brace & World, 1962.

Ingram, John Henry. *Edgar Allan Poe: His Life, Letters, and Opinions*, 2 vols.

London: John Hogg, 1880. Revised edition London, New York, and Melbourne: Ward Lock, Bowden, 1891.

Ljungquist, Kent, and Cameron Nickels. "Elizabeth Oakes Smith on Poe: A Chapter in the Recovery of His Nineteenth-Century Reputation." In *Poe and His Times: The Artist in His Milieu*, edited by Benjamin F. Fisher. Baltimore: Edgar Allan Poe Society, 1990. 235–246.

Lowell, James Russell. "Edgar Allan Poe." *Graham's Magazine* 27 (February 1845): 49–53.

Mabbott, Thomas Ollive, ed. *Collected Works of Edgar Allan Poe*, 3 vols. Cambridge, MS, and London: Belknap Press of Harvard University Press, 1968–1978.

Miller, John Carl. *Building Poe Biography*. Baton Rouge and London: Louisiana State University Press, 1977.

———. *Poe's Helen Remembers*. Charlottesville: University Press of Virginia, 1979.

Moss, Sidney P. *Poe's Literary Battles*. Durham, NC: Duke University Press, 1963.

Pollin, Burton R. "Maria Clemm, Poe's Aunt: His Boon or His Bane?" *Mississippi Quarterly* 48 (1995): 218–224.

Quinn, Arthur Hobson. *American Fiction: An Historical and Critical Survey*. New York and London: D. Appleton-Century, 1936.

———. *Edgar Allan Poe: A Critical Biography*. New York: Appleton-Century-Croft, 1941. Reprint 1969 and 1985.

Reiman, Donald H. "Introduction." In *Poems* by Thomas Dermody. New York and London: Garland, 1978. iv–xii.

Silverman, Kenneth. *Edgar A. Poe: Mournful and Never Ending Remembrance*. New York: HarperCollins, 1991.

Stoddard, Richard Henry. *Recollections: Personal and Literary*. New York: A. S. Barnes, 1903.

Stovall, Floyd, ed. *Eight American Authors: A Review of Research and Criticism*. New York: Modern Language Association of America, 1956. Paperback version New York: W. W. Norton, 1963. Revised edition edited by James Woodress, New York, W. W. Norton, 1971.

Tracy, Clarence. *The Artificial Bastard: A Biography of Richard Savage*. Cambridge, MS: Harvard University Press, 1953.

Whitman, Sarah Helen. *Edgar Poe and His Critics*. [1860]. Reprint edited by Oral Sumner Coad, New Brunswick, NJ: Rutgers University Press, 1949; reprint New York: Gordian Press, 1981.

Wilmer, Lambert A. *Merlin; Baltimore, 1927; Together with Recollections of*

Edgar A. Poe, edited by Thomas Ollive Mabbott. New York: Scholars' Facsimiles and Reprints, 1941. Reprint Folcroft, PA: Folcroft Library Editions, 1973.

Wilson, James Southall. "Poe and the Biographers." *Virginia Quarterly Review* 3 (April 1927): 313–320.

Woodberry, George E. *Edgar Allan Poe*. Boston: Houghton Mifflin, 1885. Reprint New York: AMS Press, 1968.

———. *The Life of Edgar Allan Poe, Personal and Literary*, 2 vols. Boston and New York: Houghton Mifflin, 1909.

Index